The IMF and Economic Development

Why do governments turn to the International Monetary Fund (IMF) and with what effects? In this book, James Raymond Vreeland examines this question by analyzing cross-national time-series data from throughout the world. Vreeland argues that governments enter into IMF programs for economic and political reasons, and he finds that the programs hurt economic growth and redistribute income upward. By bringing in the IMF, governments gain political leverage – via conditionality – to push through unpopular policies. For certain constituencies, these policies dampen the effects of bad economic performance by redistributing income. But IMF programs hurt doubly the least well-off in society: They lower growth and exacerbate income inequality.

James Raymond Vreeland, Ph.D., New York University, 1999, is Assistant Professor of Political Science at Yale University and Director of Undergraduate Studies for the International Studies Program. His research has appeared in the *Journal of Development Economics, Political Analysis*, and *World Development*. He teaches courses on political economy, quantitative methods, and the IMF.

To Mom, Dad, and Kristen

The IMF and Economic Development

JAMES RAYMOND VREELAND
Yale University

CAMBRIDGE UNIVERSITY PRESS
Cambridge, New York, Melbourne, Madrid, Cape Town, Singapore,
São Paulo, Delhi, Dubai, Tokyo

Cambridge University Press
32 Avenue of the Americas, New York, NY 10013-2473, USA

www.cambridge.org
Information on this title: www.cambridge.org/9780521016957

First published 2003
Reprinted 2005

A catalog record for this publication is available from the British Library

Library of Congress Cataloging in Publication data

Vreeland, James Raymond, 1971–
The IMF and economic development / James Raymond Vreeland.
  p. cm.
Includes bibliographical references and index.
ISBN 0-521-81675-0 – ISBN 0-521-01695-9 (pb.)
1. International Monetary Fund.   2. Economic assistance.   3. Economic policy.   I. Title.
HG3881.5.158 V74   2003
332.1′52 – dc21   2002071482

ISBN 978-0-521-81675-5 Hardback
ISBN 978-0-521-01695-7 Paperback

Transferred to digital printing 2010

Contents

v

Tables and Figures

FIGURES

Acknowledgments

This study would not have been possible without the guidance and support of many colleagues and friends. Special thanks go to Adam Przeworski, who has been there every step of the way. Rare is the professor who takes on an apprentice and teaches his craft as Adam does. This book was born out of collaborative work with him, and I am fortunate to have him as both a teacher and a friend.

I began this project as a graduate student in the Department of Politics at New York University where I benefited from close personal interaction and great collegiality with my professors and fellow students. For specific suggestions in the early stages of this project I am grateful to Bill Clark, George Downs, Mike Gilligan, Stathis Kalyvas, Marek Kaminski, Carmela Lutmar, Bill Pink, and Sebastian Saiegh. I am especially grateful to Youssef Cohen, David Denoon, Jennifer Gandhi, Covadonga Meseguer, and Elisabeth Wood, who read a first draft of the manuscript, offering many detailed comments and much helpful advice.

Leaving NYU, I was fortunate to join the Department of Political Science at Yale University where I have been surrounded by a wonderful group of colleagues who make coming to the office a real pleasure for me. For reading drafts of chapters and offering helpful comments, I am grateful to José Cheibub, Keith Darden, Geoff Garrett, Bill Foltz, Tasos Kalandrakis, Fiona McGillivray, John Roemer, Susan Rose-Ackerman, Frances Rosenbluth, Bruce Russett, Nicholas Sambanis, Ian Shapiro, Alastair Smith, and Allan Stam. I would especially like to thank Greg Huber, who read a close-to-final draft of the entire manuscript and whose suggestions greatly improved the substance and style of the book. I have also benefited from fantastic students at Yale who took my seminar on the IMF while I was working on this project. They were a special group who offered helpful suggestions on various aspects of the study.

I received helpful comments from many colleagues outside of Yale and NYU. In particular, I thank Bob Albritton, Neal Beck, Sarah Brooks,

Tom Callaghy, Jon Elster, Barbara Geddes, Miriam Golden, Ira Katznelson, David Lake, Martin Edwards, Louis Pauly, Beth Simmons, George Tsebelis, and Tom Willett. Research for this project was presented at the Claremont-Fletcher Workshop on the Political Economy of the IMF, the Rockefeller Center at Dartmouth College, the International Relations Colloquium at the Institute of International Studies at the University of California at Berkeley, the Department of Political Science at Ohio State University, the Department of Political Science at Columbia University, the Department of Political Science at the University of California at San Diego, the Duke University Conference on International Institutions, and meetings of the American Political Science Association, the International Studies Association, the Midwest Political Science Association, the Latin American Studies Association, and the Public Choice Society. Numerous participants in these various forums have offered useful comments and suggestions for which I am grateful.

I also thank the anonymous reviewers of the manuscript for their excellent suggestions, and my editor at Cambridge, Lewis Bateman, for his interest in the project and his help throughout. For financial support, I thank Carnegie Corporation of New York and the Bradley Foundation.

On a personal note, I would like to acknowledge people whose influence much earlier in my life led me to this project. For first introducing me to the study of politics, I thank Donn Avallone, and for first introducing me to the study of the IMF, I thank Winsome Downie. Beyond academia, I am grateful to all of my friends and family who have taken an interest in my work.

Finally, I am grateful to my mother, father, and sister, who not only have provided loving support but also have contributed to the book by reading and commenting on several drafts. In addition, my sister Kristen generally took care of me while I was a graduate student, buying me clothes and providing me a place to stay when I needed it. My mother, an avid reader of *The New York Times*, scoured the newspaper on a daily basis, clipping articles for me to make sure that no news about the IMF would ever slip past her son. I thank my father for his undivided attention to my manuscript, his many suggestions, and his countless hours of meticulous editing. He is a great teacher, both as a father and as an academic, and my decision to enter into academia has been due to his influence. It is to my family that this book is dedicated.

1

Introduction

The International Monetary Fund is at a crossroads. Its apparent power to dictate broad programs to sovereign nations has never before been greater. In the year 2000 alone, sixty countries participated in IMF programs intended to promote international financial stability and national prosperity. Yet, in the aftermath of the East Asian financial crisis (1997–8), where financial instability in Thailand, Indonesia, Korea, and Japan, followed by Russia and Brazil affected the lives of hundreds of millions of people and threatened economic turmoil in the rest of the world, the IMF has come under close scrutiny. Calls for its reform or even dissolution have come from across the political spectrum.

The recent debate has largely focused on the question of whether the IMF should be in the "development business." That is, when providing loans to developing countries, should the Fund impose specific policy prescriptions (a practice called conditionality) to promote economic growth? At one extreme is the International Financial Institutions Advisory Committee (the Meltzer Commission), commissioned by the U.S. Congress in the aftermath of the East Asian crisis. It recommends that the IMF focus entirely on crisis prevention and cease the practice of providing loans with policy conditions after a country has already entered into a crisis. A more moderate view is taken by the Council on Foreign Relations, commissioned by President Clinton, which does not advocate doing away entirely with *ex post* policy conditions, but recommends that the IMF avoid long-term reform programs and focus rather on short-term crisis management.[1] Both these commissions – one put together by Republicans, the other by Democrats – conclude that the IMF should not focus on promoting economic growth.

---

[1] For a review of these recommendations, see Willett (2001a) and Mosley (2001). Also see Jager (2001). For a broader look at reform of the international financial system, see Eichengreen (1999).

But the promotion of "national prosperity" (*IMF Articles of Agreement*) has long been a goal of the Fund. According to the former Managing Director of the Fund, Michel Camdessus,

Our primary objective is growth. In my view, there is no longer any ambiguity about this. It is toward growth that our programs and their conditionality are aimed. It is with a view toward growth that we carry out our special responsibility of helping to correct balance of payments disequilibria and, more generally, to eliminate obstructive macroeconomic imbalances. When I refer to growth, I mean high-quality growth, not . . . growth for the privileged few, leaving the poor with nothing but empty promises. (*IMF Survey 1990*: 235)

After the East Asian crisis, a new Managing Director, Horst Köhler, took the helm at the IMF. Although Köhler has emphasized the importance of promoting world financial stability, he continues to echo the views of his predecessor, contending that "the IMF should strive to promote non-inflationary economic growth that benefits all people of the world" (Köhler 2000). The IMF is experimenting with some new lending programs in line with alternative views, focusing on *ex ante* rather than *ex post* policy conditions.[2] Still, the old lending windows, where loans are provided in exchange for policy changes designed ultimately to promote growth, remain open.

Do these economic programs sponsored by the IMF succeed in promoting economic growth? This question has been posed since the inception of the IMF after World War II. Throughout its history, the Fund has faced what economist Manuel Pastor (1987a, 1987b) calls the *growth critique*. In the 1950s, for example, opponents of tight monetary controls, designed by the IMF to stabilize exchange rates and limit inflation, argued that these policies stifled economic growth. As the Fund became more involved in the policies of developing countries, scrutiny of its policies increased.

In the 1960s, and particularly in the 1970s when the United States went off the gold standard and the fixed exchange system collapsed,[3] the IMF changed its focus from regulating currency to managing balance of payments crises and assisting countries with market-oriented growth strategies. These programs involved stabilization packages designed to address balance of payments disequilibria. The strategy of the IMF was to lower demand by cutting government budget deficits and raising interest rates. Many charged that these programs were contractionary, but the IMF contended that its policies favored growth in the long run.

With the onset of the Latin American debt crisis in 1982, the IMF faced new criticism. Fixing the economic problems of the Third World was no longer viewed as merely a question of stabilization. Rather, the fundamental

---

[2] Such as the "Contingent Credit Lines."

[3] See Gowa (1983). Note that surveillance of exchange rates remains an important function of the IMF. See Simmons (2000).

structure and management of the economy was now seen to be at fault. In the long run, stabilization was a futile task as long as the underlying problems in the economy remained. Hence, the IMF began to require that countries receiving foreign exchange assistance implement structural adjustment. In the 1990s, the IMF stepped up the number of specific conditions it required countries to meet. IMF opponents nevertheless continued to believe that the policies of the IMF hurt growth, whereas the Fund argued the opposite.

The early empirical evidence seemed to slightly favor the Fund. Obviously countries selected to participate in IMF programs had low growth, but this appeared to be because these countries had problems to begin with. In study after study, after one accounted for observable factors that led to participation in Fund programs, the IMF seemed to have no negative consequences for economic growth (Reichmann and Stillson 1978; Connors 1979; Pastor 1987a, 1987b; Gylfason 1987; Killick 1995). The "growth critique" of the IMF was pronounced dead (Pastor 1987a). Later, additional studies showed that although the immediate impact of IMF programs might be negative, improved growth resulted within three years (Conway 1994; Khan 1990). But when the contagion of the East Asian financial crisis spread from Thailand to Indonesia, Korea and Japan, then on to Russia and Brazil – even shaking U.S. capital markets – the growth question resurfaced.

The importance of this question is clear. How well IMF programs have performed indicates whether the Fund should be in the business of promoting economic development. The purpose of this study is to apply a new methodology to the question of IMF performance. How does one assess the effectiveness of IMF programs? The answer eludes straightforward observation. Significantly, what one observes in the world is not a random experiment. Governments enter into agreements with the IMF only under certain conditions. Economically, they may have shortfalls in foreign reserves and high levels of debt. Politically, they may have the will to change these situations. As a result, observed outcomes are due in part to the effects of IMF policy prescriptions and in part to the characteristics of countries entering into IMF programs. To answer the important policy questions surrounding the IMF, one must be able to identify what part of the outcome should be attributed to circumstances under which countries find themselves and what part to the effect of IMF policies under these circumstances.

Hence this study entails two related questions: Why do governments and the IMF enter into agreements, that is, what is the mechanism of *selection*? And what are the consequences for economic growth? To underscore the importance of these questions consider the following. According to my "full model" sample of observations (described at the end of this chapter), sixty-seven out of seventy-nine countries participated in IMF programs during 465 of a possible 1,024 country-years from 1970 to 1990. While participating in Fund programs, growth was observed to be lower by 2.35 percent per year compared to observations of countries not participating. Cumulatively, this amounts to hundreds of billions of dollars of output. Was this outcome entirely due to nonrandom selection or is some of the difference due to the inherent effect of IMF programs?

A NEW APPROACH AND NEW FINDINGS

Because countries often turn to the IMF under bad economic conditions, it is not surprising that countries participating in IMF programs experience lower growth rates than countries not participating. To conclude from this observation that IMF programs hurt economic growth, however, is akin to concluding that aspirin causes headaches or that doctors hurt their patients. People do not go to the doctor randomly. They often go because they are ill. If one fails to account for the initial health of a patient, one may understate the effectiveness of the doctor's treatment and conclude that the treatment hurts the patients.

Similarly, one must account for the fact that countries participating in IMF programs have economic problems to begin with. That is why they turn to the Fund. It turns out that if one compares countries participating with countries not participating in IMF programs – under the same *observed* conditions – the programs appear to have no negative effect on economic growth. Study after study replicates this result.

These previous statistical evaluations of the effects of IMF programs have all paid attention to the *selection* question, from early before-after studies (Reichmann and Stillson 1978; Connors 1979; Pastor 1987a, 1987b) and with-without studies (Gylfason 1987; Edwards and Santaella 1993), to more recent work which corrects for observable determinants of nonrandom selection of program countries (Khan 1990; Conway 1994). Each of these approaches makes implicit assumptions about what drives selection into IMF programs. For instance, the before-after approach evaluates IMF program effects by looking at the performance of countries before entering the program and after the program ends. One problem with this method is that other factors outside of the program may also change over the course of the program. The with-without approach attempts to control for this possibility by comparing the performance of countries with programs to the performance of countries without programs. A problem with this method, however, is that countries entering into programs may be systematically different from countries that do not participate in programs. Methods that correct for the observable determinants of selection begin to address this problem by separately estimating the probability that countries participate in programs and then including the probability of participation in the subsequent analysis.[4]

---

[4] For an excellent formal presentation of what can go wrong with each of these methods when evaluating IMF programs, as well as some empirical results, see Goldstein and Montiel (1986). I return to these methods with greater detail in Chapter 5.

None of these studies, however, accounts for the possibility that *unobserved* factors may also play a role in selection and performance.[5] How can unobserved factors influence the apparent effect of IMF programs on growth? Consider once again the analogy of doctors and their patients. Not all people go to the doctor when they are sick. People who are highly motivated to stay healthy may go to the doctor with more frequency, whereas people with low motivation may ignore health problems. One may not be able to observe "motivation," but it may play a role, not only in determining who goes to the doctor, but also in who fares the best. Suppose highly motivated people get well faster than people with low motivation, independent of treatment. If one fails to account for unobserved motivation, one will mistakenly attribute the effects of motivation to the doctor's treatment, *overstating* its effectiveness.

Unobserved factors may play a role in determining which countries participate in IMF programs and which do not. Consider "political will" as an example. When a country fails to persevere in a program, the Fund often claims that the government lacks the "political will" to continue. Graham Bird, a prominent scholar of the IMF, observes, "The IMF has frequently blamed the poor record of the programs that it supports on a lack of 'political will' to carry them through" (1998: 90). As an example, consider Norman Humphreys' (author of *The Historical Dictionary of the International Monetary Fund*) assertion,

Fund-supported adjustment programs have had mixed success, with failures coming mainly as the result of internal political will ... in the last analysis the elements of the program and the timing of their implementation must rest with the national authorities of the country in question. (1999: 17–18)

Note that by blaming a *lack* of political will when programs fall apart, one implies that countries persevering throughout a program do have political will.[6]

Despite constant references to a failure of political will, however, the IMF is notoriously bad at defining exactly what the term means (see Bird 1998 for a discussion; also see Nelson 1990). Humphreys seems to indicate that it has something to do with a government's timing in following prescribed policies. Bird (1998) conjectures that it may have something to do with the government's commitment to the program. Perhaps Fund officials are referring to the competence of the government and its advisors, or to the government's

---

[5] Goldstein and Montiel note that unobserved variables can play a role, but they do not attempt "a vigorous implementation" of the method (1986: 338). They refer readers to Heckman (1979) "for a description of the appropriate procedure" (1986: 325–6). The Heckman approach is precisely the methodology employed in this study.

[6] Stokes (1996: 6) cites examples of countries who implemented reform packages which "actually went well beyond the advice of international economists." She claims the program itself sends a signal to private lenders of the government's "political will" to economic reform.

reputation or its publicly unobserved negotiation posture with international creditors. Alternatively, it may refer to other, as yet unnamed, factors. The bottom line is that there is some factor that observers close to IMF programs – the Fund officials themselves – claim systematically determines both selection into IMF programs (perseverance) and their outcomes (program failures).

This has important implications for the evaluation of the effects of IMF programs. Suppose the Fund continues signing agreements only with countries that have high levels of political will. If political will also affects economic growth, then one will overstate the effectiveness of IMF programs if one fails to control for this unobserved determinant of participation and performance. The Fund may not be involved just with the "basket cases," but, in particular, with the basket cases that want to do better.

Other unobserved factors may also affect the decision of a government to participate in an IMF program. "Trust," for example, can play an important role in selection and performance. IMF riots in the Dominican Republic, Egypt, Ghana, Indonesia, Jamaica, and elsewhere underscore the importance of trust in being able to persevere through an IMF program. Governments that do not enjoy a certain level of societal support may be less likely to continue participation.

At the same time, trust is a form of social capital that may also independently influence rates of economic growth (see Fukuyama 1995; Levi 1998). As Putnam suggests, trust "can improve the efficiency of society by facilitating coordinated action" (1993: 167; cited in Levi 1998: 83).[7] But if a labor force feels that it is paying unduly for the costs of an IMF adjustment program, or that the program is imposing unnecessary hardships, efficiency may suffer. Mistrust of this sort manifests itself violently in riots and ransacking of supermarkets, but there are many less obvious ways in which it may have effects under IMF programs, such as worker slowdowns.[8] Anticipation of this may make a mistrusted government less likely to bring in the IMF. The governments that actually do turn to the IMF may systematically enjoy higher levels of trust, which may in turn facilitate the success of a program. Thus, trust in government may affect selection into and performance of IMF programs. Although there are many possible ways one might attempt to measure such a variable, there may always be some systematic component that remains unobserved.[9]

[7] Also see Coleman (1988, 1990), Dasgupta (1988), and Hardin (1993).
[8] See, for example, Scott (1985).
[9] Whereas Solow (1995) argues that measurement of social trust "seems very far away," Knack and Keefer (1997) use survey data from 29 countries to develop indexes of trust and trustworthiness in societies. They find that these "social capital variables exhibit a strong and significant relationship to growth." Their data, however, cover just a few countries that have participated in IMF programs for limited years.

Overall, just because we do not observe all factors that affect selection and performance does not imply that we should ignore them. As we will see, it is possible and important to account for unobserved factors when addressing an empirical question. It is particularly important in this setting, where one can identify such factors a priori.

Given that participation in programs is not a series of random experiments, how can one evaluate the effects of IMF programs? To tell a story about the consequences of IMF programs, one must first tell a story about the determinants of IMF program participation. Only after such determinants have been identified can one distinguish between the conditions that lead countries to participate in IMF programs and their inherent effects.

Yet, the selection problem has been largely ignored and misunderstood in the literature on IMF programs. Consider what was said in a review of the statistical findings on IMF programs:

From the research available it is probably legitimate to claim that we now have a reasonable understanding of the overall effects of Fund-backed programs. But is there a similar degree of consensus about the characteristics of user countries? (Bird 1996b: 1753)

These statements exemplify how the literature on IMF programs has put the cart before the horse. One should ask questions about selection into IMF programs before evaluating their overall effects. If one does not know "about the characteristics of user countries," that is, if one does not know what drives program participation, then one cannot claim to have an understanding of the effects of programs. Assessing performance entails understanding selection. Thus, although the ultimate goal of this book is a narrow one – to determine empirically the effect of IMF programs on economic growth – I first address the question of selection: Why do governments and the IMF enter into agreements?

The research strategy employed in this study to address the selection question is triangular. I begin in Chapter 2 by selecting analytically significant cases to explore potentially important features of selection into IMF programs. Chapter 3 develops these features into a coherent argument about selection using formal models of why governments enter into IMF programs. Finally, Chapter 4 presents statistical tests of the story to determine whether a typical pattern of selection can be identified.

Telling a statistical story of selection into IMF programs is of central importance to this study. A statistical story involves predicting different outcomes from observed variables. Predictions are then compared to actual observed outcomes. The difference between the prediction and the outcome is the "error term." This error term is the part of the story that is "unexplained" or "unobserved" or perhaps random. Importantly, it is also a proxy for the unobserved factors discussed earlier that may influence IMF program participation.

Chapter 4 tells a statistical story of selection into IMF programs, and Chapter 5 tells a statistical story of economic growth performance. Each story has its own error term or unobserved factors. These unobserved factors may be "trust" or "political will." If these factors are randomly distributed across countries that participate and countries that do not participate in IMF programs, then there will be no correlation between the error terms from the selection and performance statistical stories. If the error terms are correlated, however, then the unobserved factors are not randomly distributed across the population of countries. A significant correlation indicates that the same unobserved factors that drive selection into IMF programs also drive the performance of economic growth. Once such a correlation is detected, one can derive selection-corrected estimates of the effects of IMF programs. (A more detailed description of the method is found in Chapter 5. The appendix to that chapter provides the technical details.)

The results of this study are striking: after one controls for selection – caused by observed and unobserved factors – *IMF programs have a negative effect on economic growth*. The finding is robust to different specifications and time periods. Ironically, this finding leads back to the question of selection: If IMF programs hurt economic growth, why do governments and the IMF enter into these arrangements? The answer may have to do with the way the negative effects are distributed. Thus, I consider the distributional consequences of IMF programs in Chapter 6. It turns out that not everyone is hurt in the short run by the adverse effects of IMF programs on economic growth. Those persons who are worst off in a country, however, are doubly hurt: Total growth slows and their share of income decreases. The conclusion is clear: The IMF has failed to promote what Camdessus called "high-quality growth" (*IMF Survey* A90: 235).

WHERE DO IMF PROGRAMS COME FROM?

In 1944, forty-four countries signed the Bretton Woods agreement establishing the International Monetary Fund for the purpose of maintaining exchange rates for international free trade.[10] When the world shifted away from the gold standard in the 1970s, the old exchange system collapsed. The new system did not need the IMF, and the organization faced a crisis of purpose. The original purposes of the Fund, however, also included "providing [members] with opportunity to correct maladjustments in their balance of payments without resorting to measures destructive of national or international prosperity" (de Vries 1986: 14).[11] Thus, the IMF changed its

---

[10] This summary follows de Vries 1986, Pastor 1987a, and Bird 1995. For a discussion of the original purposes of the IMF, see Eichengreen (1996).

[11] The IMF defines a country's overall balance of payments as the sum of the current account, the capital account, and the financial account plus net errors and omissions. The

major operation from regulating currency to managing balance of payments difficulties, becoming more involved in the national policies of much of the developing world.

The primary way in which the Fund intervenes in a country's balance of payments problem is by entering into an agreement with the government whereby the Fund promises to provide a loan of foreign currency and the government promises to make specific policy changes. Where does the IMF obtain the resources required to provide these loans? Each country that is a member of the Fund – there are currently 183 – contributes a deposit held by the IMF. This "contribution," which earns interest for the member, is called a quota, and the size depends on the size of the member's economy. The bigger a country's economy, the larger is the quota. The quota determines each member's share of votes. (Most Fund decisions require a 50 percent majority, although some major decisions, such as adjusting a country's quota, require an 85 percent majority.) Thus, the larger the economic size of a country, the greater the voting power, although officials claim that actual voting at the IMF is rare, with most decisions being made by consensus.

The Fund uses the currency provided by quotas to lend to member-countries facing balance of payments shortfalls or shortages of foreign reserves. In this respect, "the financial structure [of the IMF] is close to that of a credit union [with] access to a pool of resources, which it can onlend [sic] to member countries" (Fischer 1999). By providing countries with loans during financial crises, the IMF plays the role of an international lender of last resort. Such an option is designed to lower the risks of international trade and thus encourage countries not to engage in beggar-thy-neighbor trade policies and competitive devaluations of currency.

The existence of this lender of last resort, however, introduces moral hazard concerns (see Bird 1995 and Fischer 1999). Moral hazard can occur whenever there is insurance against bad outcomes and thus risky behavior is encouraged (Spence and Zeckhauser 1971). In this case, shortfalls in foreign reserves may arise from normal trading, but they may also arise from bad policy. If a government knows it has access to an IMF loan (a form of insurance), it will have a weaker incentive to adjust its policies to avoid bad outcomes. The loan simply ends up subsidizing the balance of payments deficit.

current account of the balance of payments is the credits minus the debits of goods, services, income, and current transfers. The capital account refers "mainly" to transfers of fixed assets and nonproduced, nonfinancial assets. The financial account is the net sum of the balance of direct investment, portfolio investment, and other investment transactions. Net errors and omissions reflect statistical inconsistencies in the recording of entries and are included so that all debit and credit entries in the balance of payments statement sum to zero. By construction (of net errors and omissions), the overall balance of payments is equal to minus "reserves and related items," the sum of transactions in reserve assets, exceptional financing, and use of Fund credit and loans. For more, see *International Financial Statistics*, published monthly by the IMF.

How does one distinguish between a balance of payments problem due to normal trading and one due to bad policy? The general view of the Fund is that the ebbs and flows of reserves due to trading-as-usual may lead to small balance of payments deficits, causing a government to draw on no more than 25 percent of its quota. Thus, a member can freely draw on other countries' currency up to an amount equivalent to 25 percent of its quota whenever it faces a balance of payments shortfall (Stiles 1991: 2). If a government needs to draw on more than 25 percent, it is assumed that the balance of payments deficit is due to bad policy. Consequently, in these cases the IMF calls for policy changes as a condition of the loan.

The Fund has instituted four main types of arrangements that involve policy conditions (or "conditionality"): the Stand-By Arrangement (SBA), the Extended Fund Facility (EFF), the Structural Adjustment Facility (SAF), and the Enhanced Structural Adjustment Facility (ESAF).

In 1952, the Fund designed the SBA to address temporary balance of payments deficits.[12] On October 1, 1952, the Executive Board adopted a general policy on SBAs: "[The Fund will consider requests for stand-by credit arrangements] designed to give assurance that, during a fixed period of time, transactions up to a specified amount would be made whenever a member requested and without further consideration of its position" (*Annual Report 1953*: 50).[13] The current definition found in the IMF *Articles of Agreement*, which applies to all four types of arrangements, states that they are "a decision of the Fund by which a member is assured that it will be able to make purchases from the General Resources Account in accordance with the terms of the decision during a specified period and up to a specified amount" (*Articles of Agreement*: Article XXX b). When a government enters into an arrangement, a certain amount of foreign exchange is set aside for the duration of the agreement, hence the name, "Stand-by." Provided the country lives up to the agreed conditions, the government can draw on these funds at scheduled intervals, purchasing hard currency with its own domestic currency. The latter, held by the IMF, is subject to "repurchase" with interest. The arrangement is thus thought of as a "loan" from the IMF, even though the government is under no obligation to actually draw down any of the foreign exchange provided.

---

[12] This summary is based on Polak (1991). Jacques J. Polak was a member of the Bretton Woods negotiations team (1944), is a former IMF economic counselor (1966–79), and a former IMF Executive Director (1981–6) (Bradley 1991: 46–8).

[13] The first transaction under this policy was announced May 12, 1952: "Finland might purchase up to $5 million from the Fund at any time during the next six months" (*Annual Report 1953*: 50). In fact, this agreement was not actually signed until January 1953, and in the interim the first agreement with Belgium was signed on June 19, 1952. Under this agreement, Belgium could purchase with Belgian francs the equivalent of up to US$ 50 million in currencies held by the Fund. The agreement was renewable for additional periods of 6 months for the next 5 years (*Annual Report 1953*: 50).

The SBAs – by far the most common type of program – are supposed to last twelve to eighteen months. Even in the early years, however, countries often signed consecutive agreements. From 1952 to 1962, countries entering into agreements participated for nearly three years on average. And Belgium, Colombia, Honduras, Nicaragua, and Paraguay were under SBAs for six years straight, Bolivia for seven years, and Peru nine.

Recognizing that some balance of payments disequilibria required longer programs, the Fund founded the EFF in 1963 to address medium-term problems. In 1986, the Fund made concessional loans available to low-income members through the SAF. Smaller concessional loans for high-risk countries were made available in 1987 through the ESAF.[14] Following the East Asian crisis, the ESAF was replaced with the Poverty Reduction and Growth Facility (PRGF), which is designed to allow more input in policy conditions from the government of the country in question – to promote greater "ownership" of programs – and to emphasize the importance of government accountability.

How does the Fund provide loans through these windows without encouraging moral hazard? To address the problem of moral hazard, the Fund requires an arrangement by which the executive entering into the agreement promises to follow specific policy conditions in return for the loan. Thus, governments do not have unlimited access to foreign exchange. If a government finds itself in a deep financial crisis, it must sacrifice the sovereignty of the country and submit to Fund conditions in order to receive a loan. The government must change its "bad" policies to what the IMF views as "good" ones.

Because balance of payments deficits are viewed as problems of excessive demand, IMF conditions usually entail fiscal austerity (cutting government services and increasing taxes), tight monetary policy (raising interest rates and reducing credit creation), and currency devaluation (Taylor 1993: 41–2).[15] Programs are intended to involve first *stabilization*, the "removal of macroeconomically disabling balance of payments and fiscal gaps as well as inflation," followed by a presumed *adjustment* period which creates "conditions for sustainable growth" (Taylor 1993: 41–2).

Governments entering into an IMF program are required to follow these conditions and thus sacrifice some sovereignty in return for the IMF loan. They are often viewed by domestic constituencies as "selling out" (Remmer 1986: 7). Hence, "Policy conditionality can be interpreted as a . . . penalty, as

---

[14] The latter arrangements provide loans at below market rates, whereas the former arrangements carry loans at "essentially market interest rates" (Polak 1991: 6).

[15] Officials at the IMF have come to believe that some balance of payments crises are purely the result of random shocks and are not due to bad policy. Hence, the Fund has created facilities which provide unconditioned currency, such as the Compensatory Financing Facility and the Oil Facility. Arrangements under these facilities involve no policy prescriptions, so are not treated in this study as IMF "programs."

seen from the viewpoint of the borrower country's policy makers" (Fischer 1999). Governments, it is assumed, do not want to pay these "sovereignty costs" and have conditions imposed upon them.

In sum, one can think of an IMF arrangement as composed of two parts: a "loan" and a set of "conditions" imposed by the IMF in return for the loan. When an executive of a country enters into an IMF arrangement, the Fund sets aside a certain amount of hard currency. The country can draw on the currency at specified intervals as long as it lives up to certain conditions set by the Fund. Note that while the IMF enters into agreements with the national executive alone, policy changes required to comply with conditions are made *ex post*. Disbursements of IMF loans are made over the course of the agreement only if the Fund observes what it deems as sufficient policy change.

IMF arrangements are a strange and rare breed of international agreement. "Ratification" of the agreement is not required *ex ante*. The IMF recognizes the finance minister appointed by the executive as the country's "authority." Thus, the Fund enters into agreements with this branch of government alone, even if the approval of other parties, such as a legislature, are required for the policy changes laid out in the agreement.

WHY DO GOVERNMENTS AND THE IMF ENTER INTO AGREEMENTS?

Conventional wisdom holds that governments enter into these agreements with the Fund for a straightforward reason: They need foreign exchange (Payer 1974; Haggard and Kaufman 1992; Taylor 1997; Bird 2001). They do not want to sacrifice their sovereignty and have conditions imposed, but they need the IMF loan and therefore accept IMF conditions because they have no choice.

Thus, the emerging literature on selection into Fund programs has considered potential economic determinants of the decision to accept IMF conditions. Significant disagreement exists, however, over the role of many of these variables. For example, whereas Knight and Santaella (1997), Conway (1994), and Edwards and Santaella (1993) do not find that the balance of payments matters in determining selection, Santaella (1996) and Goldstein and Montiel (1986) find that increasing the balance of payments deficit significantly predicts participation. Regarding inflation, Edwards and Santaella (1993) and Goldstein and Montiel (1986) find that higher inflation makes countries more likely to participate in IMF programs. Yet, Santaella (1996), Conway (1994), and Knight and Santaella (1997) find the rate of inflation does not affect the chance of program participation. There is also disagreement regarding the importance of terms of trade. Conway (1994) and Santaella (1996) find that it is a predictor of participation, but Knight and Santaella (1997) do not.

Reviewing previous studies, Bird (1996b) reports that there is consensus regarding development, foreign reserves, exchange rate, and GDP growth.

Low levels of development increase the likelihood of an agreement, as do low foreign reserves. An overvalued exchange rate is reported to make an agreement more likely. And low GDP growth makes a country more likely to enter into an IMF program. High debt is also associated with agreements (Santaella 1996; Knight and Santaella 1997; Conway 1994), and high deficits in tandem with credit expansion are cited by Edwards and Santaella (1993) and Santaella (1996) as making IMF programs more likely.

The only noneconomic variable which has received attention is *recidivism*. Knight and Santaella (1997) report that the dummy variable for a past agreement increases the likelihood of another agreement; Conway (1994) finds that previous participation lowers participation in subsequent years.

What about the political determinants of the decision of governments to participate in IMF programs? Contrary to the conventional view that governments turn to the Fund for a loan and do not want conditions imposed, some scholars have observed that governments may *want* specific conditions to be imposed upon them (Spaventa 1983; Remmer 1986; Vaubel 1986; Putnam 1988; Kiondo 1992; Stein 1992; Edwards and Santaella 1993; Bjork 1995; Dixit 1996).

One argument for why governments desire conditionality is that they can blame the IMF for unpopular policies. Remmer (1986: 7, 21) contends that the presence of the IMF "allows authorities to attempt to shift blame for austerity to the Fund" and that the "power of the IMF remains a useful myth to explain difficult economic decisions." Edwards and Santaella (1993: 425) argue that governments facing domestic opposition to devaluation get the IMF to do their "dirty work": "By involving multinational bodies in the decision-making process, local politicians can shield themselves from the political fallout associated with unpopular policies." Generally, Vaubel (1986: 45) states, international organizations enable politicians "to shirk domestic responsibility for unpopular policies."

Note that "trust," although perhaps not easily observed, is a factor in this argument. A government can effectively use the IMF as a scapegoat only if the population believes it. A skeptical constituency may not readily accept that bad outcomes are entirely the fault of the Fund. Mistrusted governments may therefore be less likely to turn to the IMF to use it as a shield.

A separate, but related argument, is that the IMF is used to "tip the balance" in favor of economic reform. In Putnam's (1988) seminal piece on two-level games, he notes that "International negotiations sometimes enable government leaders to do what they privately wish to do, but are powerless to do domestically . . . this pattern characterizes many stabilization programs that are (misleadingly) said to be 'imposed' by the IMF."[16] An executive may enter into IMF agreements to push through unpopular

---

[16] Putnam's argument about the IMF followed the work of Spaventa (1983) who was the first to make this observation about IMF agreements.

domestic policies – a phenomenon Gourevitch (1986) calls "the second image reversed."

How exactly does an IMF agreement help to push through unpopular reforms? My argument follows Schelling's (1960: 22) contention that "the power to constrain an adversary may depend on the power to bind oneself." Suppose a reform-oriented executive faces opposition. By entering into an IMF agreement, an executive ties its preferred policies of economic reform to the conditions of the IMF. Note that the executive of a country can enter into an agreement with the IMF unilaterally, but changing policy to comply with IMF conditions may require the approval of other actors with veto power ("veto players," Tsebelis 1995, 2002). Bringing in the IMF raises the cost of rejecting the executive's proposals, because a rejection is no longer the mere rejection of an executive but also of the IMF. A total rejection of the IMF not only limits the credit that the IMF will extend to the country, it also sends negative signals to creditors and investors. So politically, the IMF is brought in to "tip the balance" (Bird 2001).

Note that the costs of rejecting IMF conditions are imposed on the country as a whole, and they may be even higher for the executive than for the opponents of economic reform. Thus, the strategy may be risky. But as long as there are sufficient costs that the opponents of economic reform must also bear, the strategy may be effective. The executive can push through more of its reform program with the additional bargaining leverage that an IMF agreement brings.

Note the role of "rejection costs" for this argument. It must be true that failure to comply with an IMF agreement is costly to the opponents of economic reform – in particular those with power to veto policy changes. The argument does not require one hundred percent enforcement on IMF conditions. There are many anecdotes suggesting the IMF may relax conditions or continue to extend credit to a country that has not fully complied with an IMF agreement.[17] Still, noncompliance is often sanctioned. The most obvious sanction imposed on a country is the restriction of access to the IMF loan. This is a direct cost that a country risks when it does not comply with an IMF agreement. One indirect sanction for rejecting IMF conditions involves creditors. As Callaghy (1997, 2002) notes, organizations such as the Paris Club, an informal group of creditor countries that reschedules country debt, almost always require that countries be in good standing under an IMF agreement if any debt negotiations are to take place.[18] Rejecting IMF conditions may, therefore, preclude debt rescheduling desperately needed in many developing countries. A third form of sanction for noncompliance occurs if investors withhold support from a country with a failed IMF

---

[17] For a discussion of the problems of measuring compliance with international agreements, see Simmons (1998).

[18] See also Lipson (1986).

arrangement.[19] Thus, the IMF can punish countries for failing to live up to conditions.

Note that the strategy of using the IMF to push through unpopular policy is only credible without perfect collusion between the executive and the IMF. The IMF must be independent and willing to punish noncompliance. Therefore, the decision making of the IMF must be independent of the government's decision for the threat of sanctions to be credible. Hence the question, what motivates the Fund? With which countries does the IMF choose to sign agreements? According to the "Conditions governing use of the Fund's general resources," found in Article V, Section 3 of the IMF *Articles of Agreement*:

(a) The Fund shall adopt policies on the use of its general resources, including policies on stand-by or similar arrangements, and may adopt special policies for special balance of payments problems, that will assist members to solve their balance of payments problems in a manner consistent with the provisions of this Agreement and that will establish adequate safeguards for the temporary use of the general resources of the Fund.
(b) A member shall be entitled to purchase the currencies of other members from the Fund in exchange for an equivalent amount of its own currency subject to the following conditions: . . . .
(ii) the member represents that it has a need to make the purchase because of its balance of payments or its reserve position or developments in its reserves.

Thus, the IMF is conventionally thought of as a technocracy. Its task is to sign agreements with countries facing low reserves or balance of payments deficits and impose best policies to address the problems. A loan is held out as the carrot, with conditionality as the stick. Some argue, however, that the Fund may seek only to aggrandize its influence in the world without concern for its mandate. Vaubel (1986: 52), for example, argues that "international bureaucracies . . . try to maximize their power in terms of budget size, staff and freedom of discretion and appreciate some leisure on the job." The IMF may simply seek to sign agreements with as many countries as it can to extend its budget to the limit. If this is the case, the IMF may have little incentive to punish noncompliance.

IMF officials are not shy about their desire to protect the budget. Boughton, a historian for the IMF explains, "The main challenge for the future is safeguarding the [IMF's] identity *and its resources*, so that it can continue to provide adequate support to its now universal membership" (*IMF Survey 1994*: 222, emphasis added). IMF officials stress the importance of safeguarding Fund resources and providing loans. And the fact noted

---

[19] As Stone (2000: 2) observes, an IMF program "creates a focal point for investors to coordinate their expectations." Edwards (2000) finds that while increased investment is not associated with compliance with an IMF agreement, decreased investment is associated with a failed IMF arrangement.

above – that balance of payments problems do not always precede IMF agreements – indicates that sometimes the Fund bends the rules.

This does not mean, however, that the IMF is completely unaccountable. Contrary to Vaubel's "hard core" public choice approach to the institution, Willett (2001b) argues in favor of a "soft core" approach, where the bureaucratic motivations of maximizing budgets are recognized, but so are mechanisms of accountability. The IMF is formally accountable to the 183 member countries that provide the organization with its resources. The G-5 countries alone control nearly 40 percent of the total votes: United States (17.16 percent), Japan (6.16 percent), Germany (6.02 percent), France (4.97 percent), and United Kingdom (4.97 percent). Such a vote share can amount to over 60 percent of voting power when the potential winning coalitions that can be formed are taken into account (Shapley and Shubik 1954: 791; see Vreeland 1997 for details). When the G-5 votes as a block, it wields tremendous power over the IMF as a whole. Thacker (1999) argues that Fund officials respond to pressure from its largest member, the United States, which has veto power over the decisions requiring an 85 percent majority. Noting that market approval is of central importance to the Fund, Gould (2001a) argues that the IMF responds mainly to the preferences of international financiers.

Fund officials do have private information about the negotiations held with governments signing agreements, and this informational asymmetry allows room for the Fund to extract rents. It may, in some cases, be able to extend loans and impose conditions on countries that do not need them, or to extend loans to governments that fail to comply with conditions, as Vaubel contends. Accountability is far from perfect, and the bureaucratic motivations of budget and leisure maximization that Niskanen (1971) describes certainly drive Fund activities to an extent. But the Fund also faces constraints and is ultimately held accountable at least by its most powerful members. Otherwise, one might never observe cases of the IMF limiting access to credit or imposing harsh conditions. Yet, in a study of fifty-nine IMF agreements, Schadler (1995) found that the IMF restricted access to the agreement loan thirty-five times. In other cases, notably Nigeria and Tanzania (described in Chapter 2), the IMF has demanded such strict conditions that governments have refused to sign an agreement.

As long as opposing veto players believe there is some possibility that the IMF will impose "rejection costs," a proreform national executive can use this threat to push through unpopular policies. Once such an executive signs an IMF agreement, opponents of economic reform face a new trade-off between rejecting the IMF and accepting policy changes. When the trade-off is stark, they may prefer the latter, and the proreform government can push through more of its own preferred policies. Governments with high "political will" to engage in economic reform thus have an incentive beside the IMF loan to participate in IMF programs. Simply put, they may want conditions to be imposed.

THE DATA

This story of selection into IMF programs will be explored in greater detail in the next three chapters, culminating with a statistical story of selection. These statistical results can then be used to evaluate the effects of IMF agreements on economic growth. As noted above, I use a statistical technique to address these questions of selection and performance because it allows me to account for both observed and unobserved variables that may influence program participation and program outcomes.

The statistical approach requires data from countries that both have and have not participated in IMF programs under different conditions. A complete list of the countries, years, and variables used in this study is available in the appendixes to this book. Here, I describe the main variables of interest for my two questions: Economic growth and participation in IMF programs.

Economic Growth

I take the data for economic growth from Przeworski, Alvarez, Cheibub, and Limongi (2000). These data cover 135 countries from 1951 (or date of independence) to 1990, and are derived from Heston and Summers' (1995) earlier work. Observations are organized into "country-years": An observation is a measure of economic growth in a country for a particular year. Economic growth is measured as percent change (from the previous year) in gross domestic product (GDP). GDP is standardized in 1985 international "purchasing power parity" (PPP) dollars. PPP dollars are normalized to ensure that the GDP of different countries are comparable. As of this writing, the Przeworski et al. (2000) data stop in 1990. Although economic growth data are available in PPP format for the 1990s from the World Bank, for the period before 1990 the World Bank series is not highly correlated with the data used in the Przeworski et al. (2000) study ($\rho = 0.6$). Thus, it is questionable whether such data are reliable and I use data only up to 1990 in the main part of my analysis. Limited analysis of data from the 1990s is included in Chapter 5.

Participation in IMF Programs

The main variable used throughout this study is participation in IMF programs. It is the dependent variable for the question of selection, and the key explanatory variable of interest for the question of performance. This measure was collected from *IMF Annual Reports* and *IMF Survey*, a biweekly publication of the Fund.

Unlike previous studies, which consider a "spell" of participation as the duration of a single IMF agreement, I consider consecutive agreements as part of the same "spell." The reason for this is that governments almost always enter into more than one consecutive agreement with the Fund. Although Stand-by Arrangements (SBAs) usually last about a year and the other agreements are signed for one to three (or at most four) years, such time limits on participation are arbitrary. The vast experience of countries has been to sign consecutive agreements. The 678 agreements from my "large sample" (described below) make up only 226 separate spells of consecutive agreements. Only 9 of these spells span a single year.[20] On the other hand, 145 spells span 3 years or more. For example, South Korea spent 13 years under consecutive agreements from 1965 to 1977, Zaire 14 years straight (1976–89), Liberia 15 (1963–77), Peru participated in consecutive agreements from 1954 to 1971 (18 years), and Panama from 1968 to 1987 (20 years of consecutive agreements). And after a stint of 7 years (1961 to 1967), Haiti entered into agreements again from 1970 to 1989, for a total of 27 out of 29 years. During the entire period between 1952 and 1990, an average completed spell lasted 4.7 years; between 1971 and 1990 these spells were longer, lasting on average 5.3 years. Consecutive agreements are thus the rule, not the exception.

This study does not differentiate between type of agreement: SBA, EFF, SAF, or ESAF. Polak (1991: 6) notes that sometimes an insufficient planning period precludes one of the three long-term arrangements, and the Fund prescribes a temporary SBA program, even though a longer program is more appropriate and subsequently should be applied. Furthermore, he describes the differences between the arrangements as they relate to the conditions, timing, and size of the loan disbursements, but argues that the fundamental objectives of these programs do not differ. Thus, in this study I consider only whether countries are under or not under agreements without differentiating between type of agreement, following Santaella (1996) and Knight and Santaella (1997). Note that out of 678 agreements, 598 of them are SBAs (88 percent).

The IMF participation variable, like the growth variable and all other variables used in this study, is organized into country-years, and is coded 1 if the country is participating during any part of a year and 0 otherwise. Measuring this variable in terms of country-years introduces some error – if a country enters a program on December 31, it is considered to have been participating for the entire year. Other studies, however, using quarterly data when coding IMF programs (such as Knight and Santaella 1997), produce observations highly correlated with my variable. Only 46 out of the 1,584 observations in common between the two samples are coded differently due to timing.

The total number of country-year observations available from the Przeworski et al. (2000) study is 4,126. This includes 102 countries that

---

[20] The nine instances are: Finland 1953, Iran 1956, Mexico 1959, Australia 1961, Yugoslavia 1961, Syria 1962 and 1964, Congo 1977, Nicaragua 1979, and China 1981.

have signed 678 agreements and cumulatively spent 1,080 years participating in IMF programs. Obviously, other variables are used in the statistical stories of selection and performance (see Appendix 1 to the book), but unfortunately, the coverage of these other variables is much less extensive. If all the relevant selection variables are used, the sample size drops to 1,024 observations from 1970 to 1990 on 79 countries that have cumulatively participated in IMF agreements for 465 country-years. Regarding the years lost, some would argue that this is actually a more appropriate sample because during the 1950s and 1960s the IMF was primarily engaged in monitoring exchange rates and did not become extensively involved in the developing world until the 1970s. Of the countries lost, most of them are from the Communist world, where many countries were not even members of the IMF, and the industrialized world, where participation in IMF programs has been rare. So, perhaps this is an appropriate sample, but I would actually prefer to use all the observations and drop them only when data are missing. Thus, where possible, I use "stripped" or "large sample" models, where variables with missing observations are stripped from the specification so that more observations can be used (n = 4,126). Otherwise, I use a "full" model, where all relevant variables are included, but the sample size is reduced (n = 1,024).

PLAN OF THE BOOK

Evaluating the effects of IMF programs entails understanding selection. In the next three chapters, I build a story of selection using narrative (Chapter 2), formal (Chapter 3), and statistical (Chapter 4) approaches. I use the results to control for nonrandom selection when I estimate the effect of IMF programs on economic growth (Chapter 5). The surprising result is that the selection-corrected effect of IMF programs on growth is negative. This finding is simply too intriguing to forgo further analysis. Thus, I address the distributional consequences of IMF programs, finding that the negative effects are not evenly distributed (Chapter 6). This finding implies that IMF programs offer a trade-off for some groups: growth decreases but share of income increases. The worst-off in society, however, are certainly hurt in terms of income: IMF programs lower growth and redistribute income away from them.

2

Analytically Significant Cases

How should cases be selected? Exciting stories about new IMF agreements unfold every week. When I first drafted this chapter in 1999, IMF agreements with Russia, Brazil, Korea, and Indonesia filled the headlines. As I revise this chapter in 2001, agreements with Argentina, Turkey, Kenya, and Guatemala have emerged as top stories. From all the hundreds of IMF agreements that have been signed in all the regions of the world, how does one select a few instances to provide insight on the question of selection?

Note that a few anecdotes do not amount to much. To control for selection when estimating the effects of IMF programs, a general, systematic story of selection is required. But even though the ultimate test of the selection story will be a statistical one, one may gain greater insight to the process of IMF participation by selecting particular types of cases.[1]

If one were starting from scratch, one might want to start with a case selected randomly, to find the most typical characteristics of participating countries. But one does not have to start from scratch regarding IMF participation. The conventional story of participation is that governments turn to the Fund when they need an IMF loan. This assumption has led researchers to consider the economic determinants of IMF participation. As Chapter 1 describes, there is some consensus about the economic determinants of IMF programs, but disagreement over some key factors remains. Perhaps, therefore, consideration of cases that do not fit what might be expected from specific economic indicators would shed light on different aspects of selection.

Suppose one could measure the "need" a country has for foreign exchange. One could imagine different types of cases presented in Table 2.1.

---

[1] For an excellent discussion on the purposes and limitations of case studies, see Huber (1996, Chapter 6). Although Huber is mostly in agreement with King, Keohane, and Verba (1994), there are some key areas of difference. Also see Geddes (1990) and Bates, Greif, Levi, Rosenthal, and Weingast (1998).

TABLE 2.1. *Participation in IMF agreements according to need for an IMF loan*

	Participating	Not Participating
Need for loan	Cell 1	Cell 3
No need for loan	Cell 2	Cell 4

TABLE 2.2. *Participation in IMF agreements according to lagged foreign reserves*

		Country-Year Observations		
		Participating	Not Participating	Total
Reserves	Low	414	413	827
lagged one year	High	260	577	837
	TOTAL	674	990	1664

"Reserves" are foreign reserves measured in terms of monthly imports. "Low" reserves is set at less than 2.4 times monthly imports. This arbitrary cut-off point is the median level of reserves of the 1,664 observations available on the 135 countries considered in this study, and also is the average level of reserves for countries participating in agreements.
Source: World Bank (1998).

Cases found in Cells 1 and 4 of Table 2.1 would support the conventional understanding that governments turn to the Fund when they need a loan. Cases in Cells 2 or 3 would not: Countries that do not need foreign exchange should not participate in IMF agreements, and countries that need foreign exchange should participate. These latter cases, if they exist, may introduce new factors about participation in IMF programs that should be considered. Such cases may provide new analytical leverage over the question of IMF participation.

To get a rough idea of where actual cases may lie in this matrix, I start with "level of foreign reserves" as a proxy for the need for an IMF loan. There are other measures of a country's need for foreign exchange that the IMF uses, such as the country's balance of payments position, but the foreign reserve position, measured in terms of monthly import requirements, is a good starting point. Ultimately what matters to governments is whether they have on reserve enough foreign exchange to continue to purchase necessary imports. Other factors matter as well, and I address these when exploring the specific cases below. The main test for all indicators is in the statistical evaluations of participation in Chapter 4.

Table 2.2 divides 1,664 country-year observations of lagged foreign reserves available from the World Bank for 135 countries from 1951 to 1990 into four types: country-years with high and low reserves observed participating or not participating in IMF agreements.

Note that 60 percent of the observations in Table 2.2 are consistent with the view that governments sign when facing a foreign exchange crisis (those observations along the downward sloping diagonal). In 414 country-year observations, reserves are low and the government participates in an IMF agreement. In 577 observations, reserves are high and the government does not participate in an IMF agreement.

But what about the remaining 673 observations? Why are there 260 country-years where governments have strong foreign reserves but choose to participate in an IMF program the following year? Why are there 413 country-years with low reserves and no IMF agreement? The need for an IMF loan may not be sufficient to explain these observations. Government preferences over IMF conditionality may have been the deciding factor. To gain analytical leverage over how the desire for IMF conditions may enter into the decision-making process, I choose two stark examples from sets of observations noted above.

Consider Table 2.3. This table identifies three types of cases (for countries observed participating and those not participating): countries with extremely low reserves, countries with typical reserves, and countries with extremely high reserves. If one wanted to gather evidence in favor of the view that governments turn to the IMF because they need a loan, one might start with cases such as Nigeria, which is listed in Table 2.3 as having extremely high foreign reserves and no agreement, or cases like Guyana, which appears as one of the countries with extremely low reserves while under agreement.

Other cases may more clearly demonstrate different stories of participation: countries with extremely low reserves and no program, and countries with a program despite high reserves. For example, Table 2.3 identifies Myanmar, Portugal, Turkey, and Uruguay as the most extreme cases of countries participating despite strong foreign reserves. Myanmar participated in an IMF agreement in 1975 even though its reserves were extremely high in 1974: 9.1 times monthly imports. The Portuguese government signed an IMF agreement in 1977 despite having reserves of 15.2 times monthly imports the preceding year. Turkey had an overall balance of payments surplus in 1969 and reserves of 11.7 times monthly imports and signed an agreement in 1970. All of these are good cases to study because none of the governments faced the dire circumstances consistent with the foreign exchange crisis explanation of IMF agreements. In fact, they did not even meet the requirements laid out in the IMF *Articles of Agreement* for the use of Fund credits (Article V, Section 3).

Uruguay is the most interesting case. In my "large sample" (n = 4,126), I observe 102 countries that participated in 226 separate spells of IMF agreements from 1952 to 1990. Uruguay in 1990 had the sixth strongest foreign reserve position of all countries to enter into a spell of IMF agreements, and *the strongest* reserves of any country ever to enter, with both a balance of payments and current account surplus.

TABLE 2.3. *Typical and extreme levels of foreign reserves*

Lagged Reserves for Country-Years not Participating in IMF Programs		
Extremely Low (0.0–0.1)	**Typical** (3.8)	**Extremely High** (12.0–18.7)
Central African Republic 1972	Central African Republic 1982	Argentina 1980
Chad 1974	Colombia 1986	Botswana 1987–9
Congo 1984–5, 1989	El Salvador 1988	Colombia 1980–1
Guyana 1989	Ethiopia 1971	Iran 1980
Senegal 1975	Guatemala 1975	Jordan 1971
Sudan 1986	India 1989	Malta 1968–84
Tanzania 1983	Jordan 1982, 1984	Nepal 1974
	Malaysia 1982, 1986, 1990	Nigeria 1975
	Myanmar 1989	Portugal 1969–71, 1976
	Nigeria 1978	Trinidad & Tobago 1978–9, 1982
	Papua New Guinea 1979–80, 1983	Uruguay 1974
	Paraguay 1990	Venezuela 1975–6, 1986
	Somalia 1976	
	Thailand 1984	
	Tunisia 1972	
	Turkey 1975	

Lagged Reserves for Country-Years Participating in IMF Programs		
Extremely low (0.0–0.1)	**Typical** (2.4)	**Extremely high** (8.6–15.2)
Benin 1989	Central African Republic 1980, 1984	Myanmar 1975
Congo 1986–8, 1990	Ecuador 1990	Portugal 1977, 1979, 1983–4
Côte d'Ivoire 1981–90	Guatemala 1983	Turkey 1969–70
Gabon 1978–88	Honduras 1980	Uruguay 1973, 1975–84, 1986–7, 1990
Guinea-Bissau 1987	Hungary 1984	
Guyana 1982	South Korea 1977	
Liberia 1981, 1983, 1985–6	Mauritania 1977	
Madagascar 1980–1	Mexico 1984	
Panama 1982–3	Niger 1985	
Senegal 1982, 1985–6	Romania 1976, 1983	
Somalia 1985	Turkey 1983	
Sudan 1982–5	Uganda 1984	
Uganda 1981		

Regarding the other type of interesting case, where countries do *not* participate in IMF programs despite low reserves, Table 2.3 identifies the most extreme cases: Central African Republic, Chad, Congo, Guyana, Senegal, Sudan, and Tanzania. Congo, for example, averaged reserves of 0.1 times monthly imports in 1983 and went without the IMF in 1984 and 1985. In 1988, Guyana also had reserves of 0.1 times monthly imports and survived 1989 without the IMF. Chad did not turn to the IMF despite reserves averaging only 0.1 times monthly imports in 1973.

Of the remaining four examples from Table 2.3, the worst-off cases are the Central African Republic and Tanzania which both averaged foreign reserves of less than 0.1 times monthly imports in 1971 and 1982, respectively. I study Tanzania in what follows because of greater availability of data about this country than for Central African Republic, a country with a particularly erratic government.

Because participation in an IMF program is a joint decision between the government and the Fund, the reason that the government of Tanzania does not participate may be because the IMF does not have a strong interest in the country. The health of the Tanzanian economy does not have pivotal consequences for world economic stability. In order to study a country in which the IMF has a strong interest, I include an additional case: low foreign reserves and high absolute balance of payments deficit.

Countries with large economies and balance of payments deficits have a stronger negotiation posture with the IMF because their economic problems may have a greater impact on the world economy. Of the 413 observations of countries with low reserves and no IMF agreement from Table 2.2, some come from countries that also had large balance of payments deficits. Among these observations, the largest balance of payments deficits in absolute terms occurred in Brazil 1982; Egypt 1975–6, 1990; Mexico 1982; Nicaragua 1989–90; Nigeria 1982; and Poland 1981–6. From these cases, I choose Nigeria to study because it stands out as an interesting case in other respects. It appears twice in Table 2.3 as having extremely high reserves in 1975 and typical reserves in 1978 without an IMF agreement.

The two main cases used to explore how the utility of IMF conditions can influence the decision to enter into an IMF agreement are:

1. The case observed with the *highest* level of foreign reserves *participating* in an IMF program: Uruguay 1990.
2. The case observed with the *lowest* level of foreign reserves *not participating* in an IMF program: Tanzania 1983.

Can one generalize from such cases? Only statistical tests can establish typical patterns about the population (see Chapter 4), but the analytically significant cases presented in this chapter indicate that governments entering into IMF agreements derive some benefit from IMF conditionality. The case of Tanzania 1983 sets a minimum bound on the advantages derived from IMF conditions, and the case of Uruguay 1990 indicates a range. Governments that enter into IMF arrangements derive more utility from conditionality imposed by their IMF agreements than the governments with the strongest need for an IMF loan with no IMF agreement (Tanzania), and they may desire conditionality to be imposed, as the case of an agreement with no need for a loan illustrates (Uruguay).

Perhaps this seems trivial. Governments that turn to the IMF get something out of conditionality. This is consistent with the claims of IMF officials that programs are successful when governments have "political will." But if political will is systematically related to both participation in programs and the effects of programs, then one should account for this selection effect when determining the inherent effects of IMF programs. Note that although the governments' desire for conditions may be discernible in detailed cases, it may not be obvious how to quantify this desire across thousands of cases. This does not mean that this unmeasured factor does not play a role in selection and performance.

The purpose of exploring these cases in detail is to establish that in fact the preferences of the governments over IMF conditionality were decisive. The next section considers the case of Tanzania, followed by the case of Nigeria, and finally the case of Uruguay. A brief conclusion follows.

TANZANIA

The case of Tanzania is the starkest example of a government that has a strong need for an IMF loan but does not sign an IMF agreement. Such a case is a clear illustration of a government that decides not to sign an IMF agreement because it does not want conditions to be imposed.

Consider Figure 2.1. According to the level of foreign reserves in 1983, Tanzania would appear to be a prime candidate for an IMF loan. Indeed, the first part of Figure 2.1 illustrates that the early IMF experience of Tanzania closely follows the conventional story of participation: Foreign reserves dropped in 1974, and the government signed an IMF agreement the next year. Reserves dropped again in 1978 and 1979, and the government signed in 1980. What is strange about the case of Tanzania is that reserves continued to drop, reaching an all time low in 1982, and yet the government allowed its three-year agreement with the IMF to expire without signing another agreement in 1983. Reserves remained extremely low in 1983, 1984, and 1985, and the country ran a balance of payments deficit straight through this period. It is even more remarkable that reserves could hit such a low when one considers that Tanzania received much more foreign aid than other developing countries (see Lancaster 1999). From 1983 to 1985, the country was truly in dire straits. The government did not return to the Fund, however, until 1986.

Why did the government not sign when it needed the IMF loan? Was it because of conditionality? This question is particularly puzzling since Tanzania had entered into previous agreements submitting to IMF conditions when it needed foreign exchange.

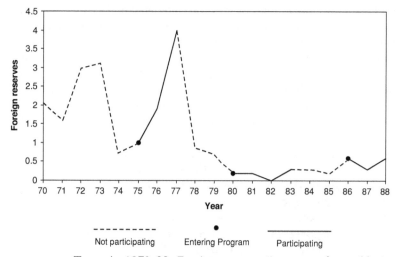

FIGURE 2.1. Tanzania 1970–88: Foreign reserves (in terms of monthly imports). *Note:* In all of the country-specific graphical figures throughout this chapter, a *dashed line* indicates periods of time when the country was not participating in an IMF agreement. *Solid lines* indicate the country was participating in an IMF agreement. The *dot markers* (•) indicate the years in which IMF agreements (for Uruguay, sometimes consecutive agreements) were signed by the country. Unless otherwise noted, the source of the data in all figures is *World Development Indicators*.

The 1975 Agreement

According to Campbell and Stein (1992: 1), "The IMF and the World Bank's stated goal of economic liberalization was publicly resisted in Tanzania until 1986." Independence leader and President Julius Nyerere based his regime on advocating a particular form of Tanzanian socialism that stressed independence from world powers. His famous Arusha Declaration, issued in 1967, called for egalitarianism, socialism, and self-reliance. The government was accordingly reluctant to enter into IMF agreements.

When the government needed foreign exchange in the early 1970s, it avoided IMF conditions for as long as possible by taking out loans from the IMF that did not entail conditionality.

First, the government drew down the maximum amount of foreign exchange allowed without entering into a special arrangement. Recall from Chapter 1 that all IMF member countries keep a specified amount of their national currency – called the country's quota – on deposit at the Fund. The general view of the Fund is that the ebbs and flows of reserves due to trading-as-usual may lead to small balance of payments deficits, causing a government to draw on no more than 25 percent of its quota. Thus, a member can freely draw on other countries' currency up to an amount equivalent to 25 percent of its quota. If a government needs to draw on more than this amount, the Fund assumes that the balance of payments deficit must be due to bad policy, so it usually calls for policy changes as a condition of the loan of foreign exchange.

When Tanzanian reserves plummeted in 1974, the government drew down 10.5 million SDR[2] from the Fund – exactly 25 percent of its quota (*IMF Survey 1974*: 86). This was the limit of what the government could take without signing an agreement.

When the government faced further need of foreign exchange, it negotiated an agreement from the Oil Fund Facility of the IMF for 6.3 million SDR. The Oil Facility was designed to provide foreign exchange to countries facing shortages due to the impact of increased petroleum prices (*IMF Survey 1974*: 86). Because rising oil prices were viewed as a random shock and not the result of bad policy, these agreements entailed no conditions. Thus, the Tanzanian government was able to obtain foreign exchange through this agreement without having the Fund impose conditions. The government made a second Oil Facility purchase for 3.15 million SDR in 1975 (*IMF Survey 1975*: 77). In total up to this point, Tanzania had obtained nearly 20 million SDR in loans from the IMF without submitting to conditionality.

Economic problems persisted, however, and Tanzania finally entered into a one-year stand-by arrangement for 10.5 million SDR in August 1975. The IMF press release stated that the program was "in support of the government's economic and financial policies of expanding output and tightening fiscal and monetary measures" (*IMF Survey 1975*: 254). Stein (1992: 63) reports, however, that the actual conditions associated with the arrangement were weak. The IMF required only that domestic credit usage by the public sector be constrained. The government did not want any conditions imposed, but it desperately needed foreign exchange. The IMF granted an agreement with soft conditions, and the government accepted.

The 1980 Agreement

Four years later, foreign reserves plummeted again because of the Tanzanian intervention in Uganda. Thus, the government returned to the Fund for assistance in 1979.

This time, however, the Fund offered a severe package that the government refused despite its shortage of foreign reserves. The IMF insisted on restrictions over imports, foreign exchange and price controls, devaluation of the national currency, and an end to the growth of the sizable public sector.

[2] SDR stands for "Special Drawing Right." This is a pseudo-currency used as a common denomination for the foreign exchange held on deposit at the Fund. It is currently valued at $1.25.

Tanzania refused the agreement and walked away from the negotiation table (*New York Times*: December 20, 1979):

Tanzania summoned its firmest socialist resolve and told the International Monetary Fund to think again if it thought the country would compromise ideology for 300 million desperately needed dollars.

President Nyerere announced, "People who think Tanzania will change her cherished policies of socialism because of the current economic difficulties are wasting their time" (*New York Times*: December 20, 1979). He criticized the IMF for attempting to take advantage of the economic crisis to cut public expenditures, freeze wages, promote the private sector, and reduce the size of the state (Kiondo 1992: 24). In 1980, Nyerere cohosted, along with President Michael Manley of Jamaica, a conference called the Arusha Initiative, where governments criticized the Fund for forcing them to follow austerity measures.

The need for foreign exchange continued, however. President Nyerere used his prominence as a world figure to negotiate an IMF agreement with weaker conditions. He also took advantage of a move by the new Managing Director of the Fund, Jacques de Larosière, to reach out to Africa. Following a series of personal communications between Nyerere and de Larosière, negotiations resumed (*New York Times*: September 4, 1980). The government succeeded in getting extremely soft conditions.

According to the three-year arrangement, Tanzania would receive access to 179.6 million SDR, equivalent to 327 percent of Tanzania's quota (*IMF Survey 1980*: 328). In return, the government had to do very little. It got around devaluating the national currency by agreeing to "a joint Tanzanian-IMF study of the exchange rate" (*New York Times*: September 4, 1980). The other previously demanded conditions regarding foreign exchange and price controls were abandoned.

The only actual demand the Fund made was that a ceiling be placed on government borrowing. Yet, even this single condition was too much for the government. It exceeded the limit on public borrowing, the IMF suspended disbursement of loans, and the program fell apart by November 1980 (Stein 1992: 64).

At this point, Tanzania had only drawn on 25 million of the 179.6 million SDR set aside by the 1980 agreement. As a condition for Tanzania to regain access to the foreign exchange remaining under the arrangement, the Fund demanded that the country meet a new list of conditions: a currency devaluation of 50 to 60 percent, reductions in the government budget deficit, a freeze on wage increases, the removal of subsidies on gas and petroleum products, increased interest rates, increased producer prices, and the removal of import controls (Stein 1992: 65). Tanzania rejected these conditions and allowed the agreement to expire in 1982 without entering a new IMF program.

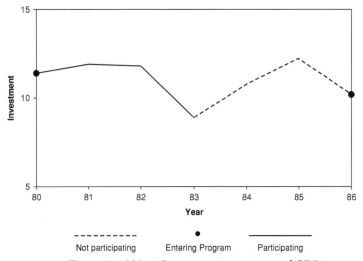

FIGURE 2.2. Tanzania 1980–6: Investment (percentage of GDP)

Tanzania did not participate in an IMF program in 1983 despite shortages in reserves because the IMF demanded more conditions than the government was willing to accept.

Note that rejecting the IMF appears to have been costly. Figure 2.2 shows that once it became clear Tanzania would not renegotiate a new program, investment dropped from 11.8 percent of GDP to 8.9 percent, the lowest level since 1964. Still, the government preferred this alternative to complying with IMF conditions.

The fact that Tanzania survived from 1982 to 1985 – at times with foreign reserves of *zero* – without signing an IMF agreement shows that if a government is strongly enough opposed to IMF conditions, it will go the crisis alone. The 1975 and 1980 agreements called for conditions that were soft enough for the government to sign, but when the IMF demanded more, the government abandoned ship.

The Negotiation Posture of the IMF

An IMF agreement involves a joint decision between a government and the Fund. Tanzania did not participate in an IMF program in 1983 despite shortages in reserves because the IMF demanded more conditions than the government was willing to accept. Why did the negotiation posture of the IMF become more severe after the 1980 agreement fell apart?

One reason is that in 1975, the Fund faced a loose budget constraint. The number of countries participating in IMF programs had dropped from thirty-two in 1969 to twenty-one in 1974. Recall that the IMF faced a crisis of

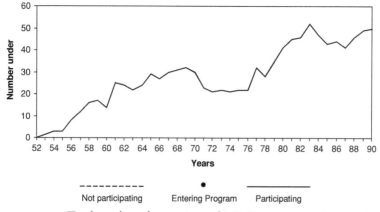

FIGURE 2.3. Total number of countries under IMF agreements. *Source:* Appendix 2.

purpose when the United States went off the gold standard. During this period the negotiation posture of the IMF was weak, and it was willing to grant soft conditions to the government of Tanzania. Essentially, the Fund needed business.

In the late 1970s, the Fund gradually changed its major operations from regulating currency to more strictly managing balance of payments difficulties. The organization became more involved than ever before in national policies. By 1980, the number of countries with IMF agreements had climbed back up. The negotiation posture of the Fund was tougher, so Tanzania had to work harder for lenient conditions. In 1981 and 1982, the number of countries participating in IMF programs went up even further. By 1983, the number of countries had reached an all time high. Figure 2.3 illustrates the number of countries under IMF agreements from 1952 to 1990.

Furthermore, after the 1982 world debt crisis, the Fund was under more scrutiny than ever before. Critics of the Fund began to argue that the stabilization programs sponsored by the IMF did not go far enough – deeper structural adjustment was needed. Thus, not only was the budget tighter, the technocratic position of the IMF also became more severe.

When Tanzania failed to live up to the lenient conditions granted in the original 1980 agreement, the Fund insisted on stricter conditions than Tanzania had ever faced. The government considered these conditions too severe and bailed out of the agreement.

Changing Views of Reform

When the 1980 IMF program fell apart, Nyerere undertook his own economic initiative called the "National Economic Survival Program." This program, however, relied on mere directives to state entities and on moral exhortations to peasants and workers (Kiondo 1992: 23–4). The program failed and Tanzania's economic problems deepened.

Over the years from 1982 to 1985, the government of Tanzania changed its views on economic reform. In 1982, it introduced a much more aggressive program, the Structural Adjustment Program (SAP). Under the SAP, the government implemented many of the measures called for by the IMF. The currency was devalued, first by 12 percent in March and then by 20 percent in July (Kiondo 1992: 24). By 1984, the government had removed subsidies, raised producer prices, introduced new taxes to finance the budget deficit, frozen certain civil service hiring, and devalued an additional 26 percent (Stein 1992: 68–9).

Another important area of reform involved trade liberalization. The government allowed people to import goods with their own foreign exchange and sell these imports domestically. This move opened an important area for compromise between the IMF and the government since it effectively opened a second window allowing the Tanzanian currency to operate on a dual exchange rate (Kiondo 1992: 26). Hence, this reform represented a further real devaluation.

Other reforms were envisioned: adjusting marketing and produce prices, cutting back government expenditures, reducing monetary expansion, and improving the efficiency of the state sector. Yet, unable to garner enough support from the members of the ruling (and only) political party, the Chama Cha Mapinduzi revolutionary party (CCM), supporters could not push these reforms through (Kiondo 1992: 24). As Kiondo explains,

One of the contradictions of the liberalization process in Tanzania was the constant tug of war between those leaders in the government and party who wanted to remain true to the spirit of [Tanzanian socialism] and those who pushed for reforms. (1992: 28)

This tug of war manifested itself in the struggle for leadership of the country. With the 1985 elections, Nyerere stepped down as president after more than two decades. Ali Hassan Mwinyi became the new president. Although he came from the same political party (the CCM) as Nyerere, Mwinyi – who favored deeper economic reforms – represented a shift in the agenda of the government.

Although the reform-minded Mwinyi was elected president of the country, the members of CCM reelected Nyerere – who still opposed economic reform – as president of the party (*New York Times*: November 1, 1987). Furthermore, they voted out two members of the CCM central committee who supported economic reform (Matthews 1998: 1036).

Facing such resistance, Mwinyi was unable to bring about his reforms. As Figure 2.4 shows, whereas the government deficit had been steadily reduced with the implementation of the SAP from 1982 to 1985, the deficit shot up in 1986, after Mwinyi took office.

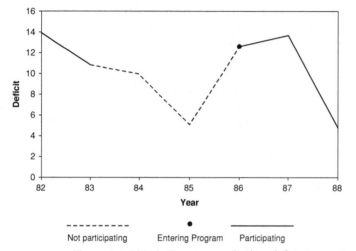

FIGURE 2.4. Tanzania 1982–8: Government budget deficit (percentage of GDP)

Bringing in the IMF

Lacking support in his party to bring about further reform, Mwinyi brought in the IMF. In September 1986, the president signed an 18-month agreement with the Fund for 64.2 million SDR (60 percent of Tanzania's quota at the time).

Kiondo (1992) argues that the Fund was brought in to help push through reform. The IMF acted as an ally for those supporting economic reform. Its influence was used against the elements in CCM that opposed Mwinyi's program. Over time, "The owners of [foreign exchange]...gained supporters in the party and the government while forging an alliance with the IMF and the World Bank" (Kiondo 1992: 26). Therefore,

> by the time of the IMF agreement [in 1986] there were elements in Tanzanian society with an objective interest in the reforms. However, because they did not yet dominate the state there was subterfuge in the approach taken by Tanzania in implementing the reforms. Indeed, Tanzania's reforms are implemented in secretive, unplanned, and nondemocratic ways. (Kiondo 1992: 35)

Kiondo goes on to argue that "the IMF found domestic allies who in turn found supporters within the state" (Kiondo 1992: 35).

How could an alliance with the IMF help push through the reforms? On the one hand, the government could still argue that the country needed foreign reserves. The need, in fact, was desperate (recall Figure 2.1). Furthermore, the IMF agreement increased the pressure to reform, since a failure to do so would no longer be a mere rejection of Mwinyi, but a rejection of the IMF. A rejection of the IMF would send a negative signal to creditors and investors. Recall from Figure 2.2 how investment dropped when the 1980

IMF agreement fell apart. A drop in investment would hurt all of Tanzania, including those opposed to the IMF.

So even though Tanzania turned to the Fund because it needed foreign exchange, the government also wanted IMF conditions to be imposed. As Stein puts it,

Critics typically argue that the [IMF]'s policies tend to come at the expense of 'socialist' and nationalist governments' autonomy to pursue their own agendas. [However,] the IMF agreement with Tanzania is not inconsistent with the agenda of the state. (1992: 59)

Tanzania did not sign in 1983 because, although it was able to get lenient conditions in 1975 and 1980 when the IMF budget constraint was less binding, it could not get the conditions it wanted in 1983. The government lacked the negotiation strength to get conditions from the Fund that were acceptable. When the country needed an IMF loan but did not want IMF conditions (1982–5), the government rejected Fund agreements. When the government of Tanzania finally returned to the IMF, it did so not only because it wanted foreign exchange but because it wanted conditions. The government sought political support through IMF conditionality to push through its preferred policies. The government finally signed in 1986 because its preferences over conditions changed.

The question of negotiation strength raises another factor one should consider when looking at countries without a program: How much does the IMF care? According to the Fund *Articles of Agreement*, the IMF is charged with facilitating "the expansion and balanced growth of international trade." Countries like Tanzania have a relatively small impact on the world economy. The average GDP of Tanzania during the period 1983 to 1988 was 3.3 billion dollars (in constant 1987 U.S.$).[3] The largest balance of payments deficit that Tanzania had ever reported was 398 million in constant 1987 U.S. dollars, which occurred in 1988. Such deficits are not likely to upset world trade the way a large deficit will. This may have contributed to the decision not to enter an agreement: the government could not negotiate for good terms.

I now briefly consider a second case of a country with low reserves and no IMF agreement, but a country with a strong negotiation posture, Nigeria.

NIGERIA

In 1981, Nigeria faced its worst balance of payments crisis ever: The current account deficit and the overall balance of payments deficit had never been

---

[3] For 1983–8. These are the only years for which the World Bank has data on this variable for Tanzania. See World Bank (1998).

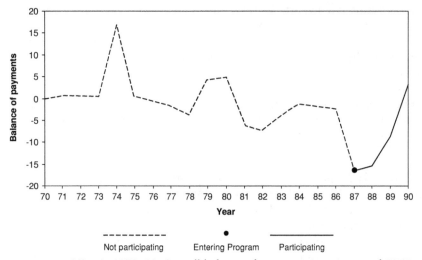

FIGURE 2.5. Nigeria 1970–90: Overall balance of payments (percentage of GDP)

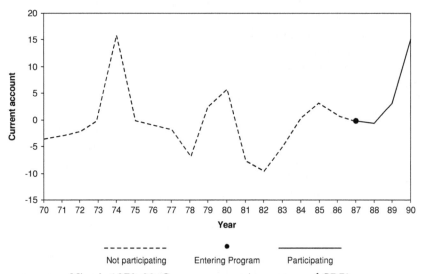

FIGURE 2.6. Nigeria 1970–90: Current account (percentage of GDP)

higher, and foreign reserves were at the lowest level in almost a decade (see Figures 2.5, 2.6, and 2.7).

In 1982, things really fell apart. The current account and balance of payments deficits widened, and foreign reserves continued to drop. As Callaghy describes, "With the advent of the world oil surplus, oil production dropped from 2.4 million barrels a day in 1979 to 1.2 million in 1982" (1990: 305). Production had dropped to 370,000 barrels a day by February 1983. Like many other countries in such dire straits, Nigeria had no choice but to turn

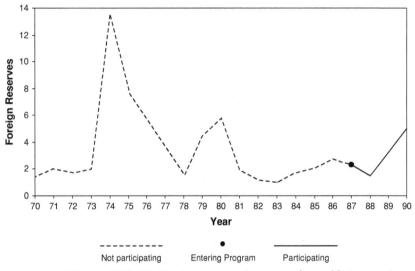

FIGURE 2.7. Nigeria 1970–90: Foreign reserves (in terms of monthly imports)

to the IMF for currency, accepting whatever conditions demanded. But it did not. Why did the Nigerian government choose not to enter an IMF program?

Nigeria had never turned to the IMF. When British rule ended in 1960, agricultural exports accounted for 70 percent of export earnings in Nigeria (*New York Times*: December 13, 1986). Then Nigeria struck oil. Agriculture was left by the wayside and by the 1980s petroleum accounted for 95 percent of exports. Earnings from oil drove up the stock of foreign reserves in Nigeria so that in 1974, Nigeria held the fourth highest ratio of foreign reserves to imports in the world.[4] Due to changing oil prices, the reserves level dropped to a level typical in the world in 1978 (recall Table 2.3), but the country still held a strong external position.

This kind of independence, as well as Nigeria's status as the most populous country in Africa, was a great source of national pride. By 1983, out of 115 developing countries in my whole sample of data (n = 4,126), Nigeria is one of only 27 countries that had never signed an IMF agreement. Submitting to IMF conditions at this point would have been extremely unpopular. Callaghy describes "vehement popular antipathy for the IMF" (1990: 269) throughout Nigeria. The government would have taken severe criticism from all segments of society for being the first Nigerian government to submit to the Fund.[5]

---

[4] In 1974, only Malta, Venezuela, and Uruguay had higher reserves in terms of monthly imports.

[5] Even military dictatorships avoided the IMF. No government entered into an IMF agreement until 1987, and when one finally did, it made certain to demonstrate that it was not bowing to IMF conditionality. As Lewis (1996: 110), citing Olukoshi, notes, the government "publicly repudiated the Bretton Woods institutions and unveiled a 'home-grown' package" before finally turning to the Fund.

The Nigerian government in the early 1980s was extremely vulnerable to shifts in public opinion. The government that faced the decision of signing an IMF agreement in 1983 was democratically elected and faced severe electoral constraints. This government followed a military regime that began in 1966 and had been fraught with plots, coups, violence, and a civil war. The period of dictatorship finally ended in 1979 when the military held elections. Fragile democratic rule returned with the election of President Alhaji Shehu Shagari.

When oil prices dropped in 1981 and 1982, Shagari proved reluctant to go down in Nigerian history as the first leader to submit to the conditions of the IMF. Recall that when economic problems first hit Tanzania, the government accepted funding from the IMF that did not entail conditions. Nigeria did the same. First, the government turned to its unconditioned reserves tranche at the Fund (25 percent of its quota). Then the government obtained additional foreign exchange from the unconditioned Oil and Supplementary Financing Facilities designed to help countries through crises caused by random shocks (*Financial Times*: June 10, 1982). These facilities did not entail conditionality.

Although the government was reluctant to submit to IMF conditions, it made some policy changes consistent with what the IMF would have required. For example, the president introduced sweeping import restrictions (*New York Times*: August 22, 1983) and the central bank stopped issuing letters of credit (*IMF Survey 1982*: 103). Shagari hoped that his limited reforms and the unconditioned loans from the IMF would be enough to help the country weather the crisis. The crisis continued in 1983, however, and the government finally approached the IMF for a stand-by arrangement in April "despite the fact that all major sociopolitical groups were vehemently opposed to doing so" (Callaghy 1990: 305).

The Fund was eager to sign an agreement with Nigeria because its balance of payments deficit was so great: 2.989 billion 1983 dollars. Only Sweden (5.481 billion 1983 dollars) and Poland (4.918 billion 1983 dollars) had larger overall balance of payments deficits and no IMF program. The average balance of payments position for the 119 observations available in my data for 1983 was only 301 million 1983 dollars. The balance of payments deficit in Nigeria was large enough in absolute terms to matter to many other countries, and the IMF wanted the country under a program.

The IMF offered Nigeria two options: (1) a one-year stand-by arrangement for 810 million SDR or (2) a three-year extended fund facility arrangement for 2.43 billion SDR. Both these options entailed IMF conditions, however. Negotiations broke down over three main issues: elimination of petroleum subsidies, trade liberalization, and devaluation (Callaghy 1990: 305). The national currency of Nigeria, the naira, was considered by many as a symbol of national sovereignty (*Financial Times*: August 16, 1983) and was a particularly important issue.

Because Shagari faced elections in August 1983 and the race was close, the government had no intention of actually signing an IMF agreement at this time. Entering into the IMF agreement, it was believed, would have doomed Shagari's reelection bid. Thus, while Nigeria and the IMF entered negotiations and spelled out potential arrangements, the government made it clear that it would not enter an agreement until after the elections. Refusing to sign, in spite of the economic crisis, demonstrated national strength which helped Shagari. The austerity measures that Shagari implemented might have been otherwise unpopular, but because he did so without actually entering into an IMF agreement, he won support for his program.

Shagari won reelection. The elections were accompanied by violence and corruption, and Shagari's margin of victory appeared inflated, but observers agreed that it was a legitimate victory (*New York Times*: August 10–11, 1983). The first priority of the reelected government was to conclude an IMF agreement (*Financial Times*: August 16, 1983). One month later the government reached a preliminary agreement on a three-year extended fund facility program.

With the reforms that Shagari had put forth on his own, only two stumbling blocks remained before this arrangement could be finalized: (1) the continuing reluctance on the part of the government to devalue the naira and (2) the budget constraint of the IMF.

With more countries under IMF agreements in 1983 than ever before (forty four, according to my data), the Fund had exhausted its resources and needed to put any new arrangements on hold until it had increased member contributions (*New York Times*: October 5, 1983). As the Fund lobbied for an increased budget, the economic crisis deepened and the Shagari government ran out of time. Shagari was deposed by the military on December 31, 1983.

There appear to be three major factors that prevented the conclusion of the agreement before the Shagari government was toppled: the history of IMF agreements, the elections, and the budget constraint of the Fund.

Note that as time ran out for the Shagari administration, the president seemed to be coming closer to acquiescing to the Fund. But ultimately he resisted because he opposed the conditions proposed by the Fund. This appears to differ from what happened in 1986 when the government of Tanzania finally entered into an agreement. In that case, the government wanted both the loan and the conditions from the IMF agreement. Shagari publicly announced, however, that Nigeria would "not be dictated to" by the IMF (*Financial Times*: August 16, 1983). He seemed to be in opposition to Fund conditionality.

Privately, however, Shagari administration officials admitted to the *Financial Times* that "the whole idea of bringing in the IMF is to get the alibis to persuade the politicians of what we need to do" (*Financial Times*:

August 16, 1983). The Nigerian government needed a loan, but, like the Mwinyi administration in Tanzania, it also wanted conditions imposed. By bringing in the Fund, certain members of the Shagari administration hoped to put pressure on those elements within the government that resisted the economic reforms.

Thus, once again, a government that is in economic crisis seeks an IMF agreement not only for a loan but also for conditions to push through policies that it prefers. In this case, the government seems to have wanted some conditions imposed, but not devaluation.

Note that this may have been fortunate for the IMF, as this government may have been a particularly bad one to have an agreement with. Callaghy describes the policies of this government as "largely ad hoc and based on political expediency" (1990: 305). As Foltz (1985: 5) argues, the proximate reasons for the coup against the Shagari government "were the regime's corruption, economic mismanagement, and rigging of . . . elections – all three at levels scandalous by even Nigeria's tolerant standards." The new leader of the country, Major General Muhammadu Buhari, announced that the coup was necessary because "the former regime did not have the discipline or the will to arrest the deterioration of the economy" (*New York Times*: January 18, 1984). It seems that this nonparticipant in IMF programs had low levels of trust and political will and probably would have had inherently poor performance with or without the IMF.

SUMMARY

The Tanzanian and Nigerian experiences of nonparticipation in IMF programs illustrate three factors which explain why some countries facing financial crises choose not to enter IMF arrangements. First of all, governments may decide against an IMF arrangement if no previous government has submitted to the IMF in the country's history. The penalties for sacrificing a country's sovereignty by submitting to IMF conditions are high when earlier governments have not done so. Second, governments may prefer to wait until after elections before incurring sovereignty costs. The third factor relates to the IMF's decision. The Fund may be constrained by its budget when attempting to sign an additional country.

The existence of these types of cases indicates that the mere need for a loan is not sufficient for a country to turn to the IMF. But is it a necessary condition, or do some governments turn to the IMF for other reasons? The cases of Tanzania and Nigeria have demonstrated that governments not only sign IMF agreements for the foreign exchange they provide, but also for conditions.

To learn more about why governments turn to the IMF to have conditions imposed, I turn to a different type of case study: governments that enter into IMF agreements even though they have no need for an IMF loan.

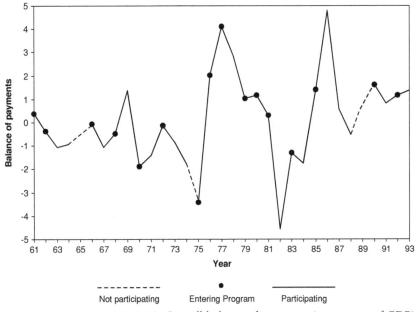

FIGURE 2.8. Uruguay 1961–93: Overall balance of payments (percentage of GDP)

URUGUAY

In 1975, Uruguay's balance of payments deficit doubled and the government entered into an agreement with the IMF. This arrangement granted the country access to foreign exchange, provided the country comply with specific conditions set by the IMF. Over the next decade, Uruguay remained under IMF conditions, signing consecutive agreements. The balance of payments position improved and in 1987, the government allowed its last agreement to expire without entering into a new arrangement. After nearly twelve years, Uruguay was finally free of IMF conditions.

Three years later, the overall balance of payments was in surplus, as was the current account. Foreign reserves were also strong. The country had no impending financial crisis requiring foreign exchange. But on December 12, 1990 the Uruguayan government signed a new agreement with the IMF. Uruguay did not need an IMF loan. Why did the government sign?

Uruguay did not need foreign currency when it signed the 1990 agreement. Of the $136.7 million provided by the fifteen-month stand-by arrangement, Uruguay drew down less than 10 percent of the credit provided. This amounted to about one-tenth of one percent of gross domestic product (GDP). The overall balance of payments of Uruguay was in surplus in 1989 and 1990 (see Figure 2.8) as was the current account balance (see Figure 2.9). Uruguay also held a strong foreign reserves position. The 1988 reserves were 10.2 times the average monthly import requirements. This level dropped to

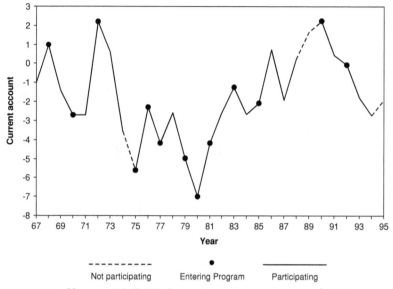

FIGURE 2.9. Uruguay 1967–95: Current account (percentage of GDP)

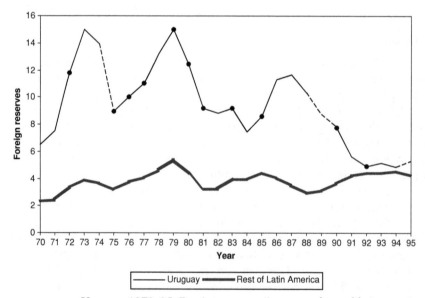

FIGURE 2.10. Uruguay 1970–95: Foreign reserves (in terms of monthly imports)

7.7 by 1990 but remained strong by developing country standards. The rest of Latin America held reserves of only 3.7 times average monthly import requirements; reserves in Uruguay were more than double this (see Figure 2.10).

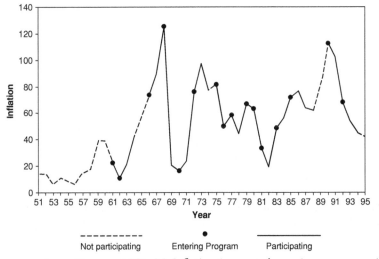

FIGURE 2.11. Uruguay 1951–95: Inflation (percent change in consumer price index)

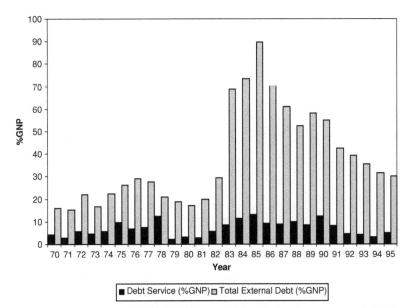

FIGURE 2.12. Uruguay 1970–95: Debt and debt service (percentage of GNP)

But Uruguay faced other economic problems. From 1951 to 1990, inflation averaged 47.9 percent per annum. In 1990, it was more than double this, reaching 112.5 percent, the highest level since 1968 (see Figure 2.11). Uruguay also faced severe foreign debt which had shot up in the early 1980s, reaching 89.7 percent of GNP in 1985 (see Figure 2.12). Investment also

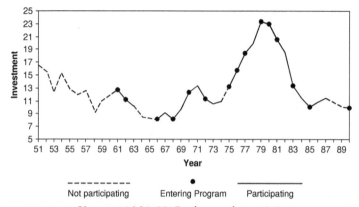

FIGURE 2.13. Uruguay 1951–90: Real gross domestic investment, private and public (percentage of GDP). *Source: Penn World Tables 5.6.*

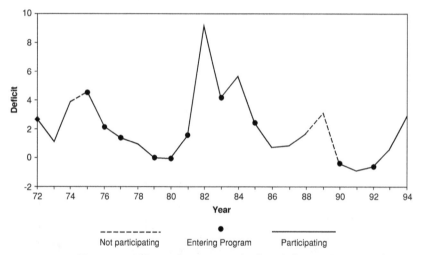

FIGURE 2.14. Uruguay 1972–94: Government budget deficit (percentage of GDP)

suffered. After reaching a high point of 23.3 percent of GDP in 1979, investment fell almost every year thereafter (see Figure 2.13). By 1990, it had dropped to 9.9 percent of GDP – the lowest level since 1969.

Uruguay faced low investment, high debt, and the worst inflation it had seen in more than two decades. These economic indicators prompted the push for economic reform from the newly elected (1989) administration of President Luis Alberto Lacalle Herrera.

Under the IMF programs of the late 1970s, the budget deficit had been eradicated (see Figure 2.14). However, no sooner had the budget gone into surplus than government consumption began to rise. By 1981, government expenditures once again outpaced government revenue. Still under IMF programs, the government brought the deficit down again to less than 1 percent of GDP in 1986, but it left IMF programs in 1987. After the country left IMF programs, the deficit again began to grow. By 1989, it had reached 3 percent, the highest deficit since 1984. Thus, the government sought to reduce the size of the public sector – but it faced opposition.

Why Did Lacalle Need the IMF?

To understand why President Lacalle faced tough opposition, it is useful to review the historical development of the welfare state in Uruguay as well as the political institutions and parties that supported the large role of the state in the economy.

Early in the twentieth century, Uruguay became one of the first welfare states in the world and the first in Latin America (Mesa-Lago 1978, 1985; cited in Filgueira and Papadópulos 1997: 363). Cattle and sheep products drove export-led prosperity from the 1870s to the 1950s. The flourishing economy generated government surpluses which "helped finance the development of protected import substitution industries and the expansion of the state apparatus" (Filgueira and Papadópulos 1997: 369).

A client-patron system developed where the political parties used the state to redistribute resources to their constituencies. Filgueira and Papadópulos (1997: 381) define this system as one "of redistribution of political goods sustained by the material and regulatory resources of the state." Thus, both main parties, the Blancos and the Colorados, advocated a strong role for the state in the economy, promoting state-owned enterprises, protectionist policies, and generous social benefits.

Large segments of the population came to have a vested interest in maintaining the welfare state due to "high levels of incorporation" (see Filgueira and Papadópulos 1997: 368, 379). Labor unions, for example, lobbied for high levels of labor protection. And the beneficiaries of the strong state were not limited to labor. The percentage of public employment was high compared to the rest of Latin America, and coverage from state service was largely based on equal distribution, not concentrated on any particular group.

Thus, when the economy stagnated in the late 1950s and crisis exploded in the 1960s, large blocs of voters opposed the austerity measures suggested to cope with the difficulties. Both the Blanco and the Colorado parties found it more convenient to continue doling out rewards to their political clientele than to reduce state spending. With the resources of the state diminished, the government turned to the IMF, entering austerity programs from 1961 to 1963 and 1966 to 1973.

The austerity measures suggested by the IMF mobilized opposition to these reforms. Small left wing parties began to work together in the early 1960s (Gonzalez 1995: 152). In 1971, the "Frente Amplio" – a coalition of the parties of the left – was born and took 18 percent of the national vote (Gonzalez 1995: 152). In addition to this success at the polls, outright insurrection of the left wing in the late 1960s and early 1970s pressured the government to resist austerity.

In the face of economic crisis and rising demands from the left, the military took over in 1973, restricting legal political activities. The military government slashed the budget deficit when it signed an IMF agreement in 1975, and it continued to sign IMF agreements until stepping down in 1985. When the military held elections for a new civilian regime, in November 1984, the fiscal deficit had risen again. By this time, both the Blanco and the Colorado parties had changed their views on the state's role in the economy – they wanted it reduced. The Colorado party won the presidency and pressed for rapid liberalization, signing with the IMF in September 1985.

But with the end of dictatorship, opponents of IMF-style austerity were allowed to organize legally again (Filgueira and Papadópulos 1997: 365). Labor leaders called general strikes opposing the influence of international organizations in domestic politics. The Frente Amplio reemerged. And thirteen of the most important associations of retirees formed the Plenary of Associations of Retirees and Pensioners of Uruguay (Filgueira and Papadópulos 1997: 365). Overall, organizations representing retired persons and pensioners constituted about 20 percent of the total population, and an additional 10 percent were public servants (Rial 1986: 136).

In November 1989, in the first fully free election since 1972, the opponents of economic reform did well at the polls. Frente Amplio gained a presence in Congress and its candidate was elected mayor of the capital city, which included 42 percent of Uruguay's 3.2 million people. Nevertheless, the reform-oriented Lacalle of the Blanco party took the presidency. Upon election, Lacalle announced plans of economic reform "if necessary" (*New York Times*: November 28, 1989). He talked of raising taxes and cutting public spending. He wanted to privatize national industries, reform the state pension system, and reduce the size of the state.

But Lacalle had hardly received a mandate. His party received only 37 percent of the presidential vote (Schooley 1997), and Lacalle himself received only 22 percent (*Financial Times*: November 8, 1994).[6] The Colorados received 30 percent of the presidential vote, and Frente Amplio received 21 percent. The main opposition party received nearly as many votes as Lacalle himself, and overall, 78 percent of the electorate had not voted for Lacalle.

In congressional elections, the Blanco party only won 40 percent of the seats (Schooley 1997). The main opposition party, Frente Amplio, had

---

[6] Until recent elections, Uruguay had a rare electoral system in which primaries and elections were combined. The party with the most votes won the election, and the candidate with the most votes from that party took office.

enough seats in Congress to force Lacalle to form a coalition government between his Blanco party and the Colorado party. This coalition was tentative
at best: Lacalle "obtained... a vague agreement that did not create politically binding obligations, with non-political Colorado cabinet ministers. ...
[T]he loose agreement was termed the *coincidencia nacional*, or 'national
coincidence' " (Gonzalez 1995: 161).

There were three further reasons why the newly elected president needed
an international ally to get past domestic opposition: (1) institutional factors
leading to a lack of party discipline, (2) the patron-client promotion system
that failed to reward technocrats, and (3) the institution of the national
referendum.

Lack of Party Discipline. Lacalle could not depend on the loyalty of his
governing coalition. Gonzalez (1995: 147) explains that the electoral voting
system of "double simultaneous vote" weakened party discipline because
the system allowed for the expression of intraparty preferences at the voting
booth. Primaries and elections were held simultaneously. The party with the
most votes won the election and the candidate with the most votes from that
party took office. Thus, Gonzalez argues, "Candidates cannot rely solely on
their party; they must distinguish themselves from competitors within their
own party. They must develop at least a minimal organizational base of their
own" (Gonzalez 1995: 147).

Note this does not imply that there was no discipline or loyalty within the
party system. The intraparty preferences exacerbated by the double simultaneous vote system led to many distinct factions within the party.[7] Since a
candidate not only depended on his party, but on his faction within the party,
ultimately legislators voted along "faction" lines (see Buquet, Chasquetti,
and Moraes 1999).

Patron-Client Promotion. Furthermore, Lacalle could not look to national
technocrats for support because there were so few of them in positions of
power. Promotion within political parties was based not on merit or train-
ing, but on patron-client relationships (Filgueira and Papadópulos 1997:
380). Thus, unlike other developing countries, the system did not promote
Western trained economists (IMF-style economists) to the upper echelons of
the parties.

National Referendum. Lacalle was also up against an additional institution
that could work against his reform efforts: the national referendum (Filgueira
and Papadópulos 1997; Lupia and McCubbins 1998). Opponents could
petition to have legislation put to a national plebiscite that could override

---

[7] I am grateful to Juan Andrés Moraes for pointing this out.

any reforms pushed through Congress. As Huber and Stephens (2000: 20) point out, "the institution of the referendum constituted a veto point where opponents of privatization could successfully mobilize."

Not surprisingly, Lacalle faced difficulties right from the start of his administration. Labor leaders called four general strikes and numerous smaller strikes to oppose Lacalle's policies, promising him "not one day of truce" (*New York Times*: August 24, 1990).[8] Six months into their terms, while Frente Amplio's mayor of Montevideo enjoyed 55 percent approval rating in the capital, Lacalle's nationwide approval was a mere 18 percent (*New York Times*: August 29, 1990). Frente Amplio, labor leaders, and even members of Lacalle's coalition government opposed his program. Even members of Lacalle's own party publicly denounced parts of his economic policy.

By mid-1991, one of the president's cabinet ministers resigned in protest to the economic program. In January 1992, Lacalle decided to reorganize his cabinet to increase support from within his government. The plan backfired. No one was willing to participate in the government, and the president could fill only three cabinet positions. Neither the Blanco nor the Colorado party wanted to be associated with Lacalle's program.

The administration correctly feared that so many compromises would be necessary that economic restructuring would be diluted (*New York Times*: August 24, 1990). Lacking the domestic political support to promote his program of economic reform, Lacalle turned to an international ally: the IMF.

The 1990 IMF Arrangement

The Lacalle government proved extremely eager to have IMF conditions imposed. Less than two weeks into his term of office, Lacalle announced the preparation of a new letter of intent for an IMF agreement. He said he expected to sign the agreement within two weeks (*Busqueda*: February 28, 1990, *Financial Times*: March 13, 1990). This was mid-March. In July, the Lacalle administration announced that the government had clinched an eighteen-month stand-by arrangement for $150 million (*Financial Times*: July 2, 1990). The arrangement had still not been signed, however. It was not signed until December and it was for less money and fewer months than the government had announced when it declared the deal "clinched." Thus, the statements of the government were premature and misleading. By announcing the agreement with the IMF early, however, Lacalle was able to use IMF conditionality to push through reforms right away.

Note that the strategy of bringing in the IMF to help push through policy is effective because the president can enter into the IMF agreement unilaterally. So although the opponents of reform policies with veto power

---

[8] By the end of his term, Lacalle had faced eight general strikes.

("veto players") may be able to block policy change, they cannot block the IMF arrangement. And once the IMF conditions have been imposed, failure to change policy becomes more costly for the country as a whole. Even for a case such as Uruguay where the IMF loan was not needed, there were costs associated with rejecting the IMF. Besides limiting access to IMF credit, rejecting the IMF sends negative signals to creditors (Callaghy 1997: 2001) and investors (Stone 2002; Edwards 2000). Debt negotiations are virtually impossible in the light of a canceled IMF agreement. Investors also pull out of the country. As Stone (2000: 2) argues, IMF programs create "a focal point for investors," coordinating their expectations about a country. To avoid these costs, opponents with veto power may be willing to accept more economic reform than they would if they were not facing the costs of rejecting the IMF.

The original announcement of the IMF letter of intent revealed specific conditions attached to the loan. The Lacalle administration reported that the IMF-sponsored program required increasing the value added tax by 1 percent to 22 percent, raising the basic income tax from 17 percent to 20.5 percent, and increasing the basic import duty from 10 to 15 percent (*Financial Times*: March 13, 1990). A major goal of the program was to cut the fiscal deficit to 2.5 percent of gross domestic product. Under the guise of conditionality, the government exceeded this goal, pulling off a budget *surplus* of 0.37 percent for 1990 (recall Figure 2.14).

By effectively putting the country under IMF conditions ahead of schedule, Lacalle successfully changed the balance of the budget by 3.4 percent of GDP. Meanwhile, the IMF itself made no press announcement regarding the stand-by arrangement until it actually began on December 12, 1990.

What did the IMF say about Uruguay's need for a loan? The IMF made no mention of the reserve position of Uruguay – perhaps because Uruguay's reserves were conspicuously strong. Regarding the balance of payments situation, the IMF highlighted that the agreement would help the government to continue "strengthening the balance of payments" (*IMF Survey 1991*: 12–13). The Fund did not point out that Uruguay had maintained a balance of payments surplus for the past two years and a current account surplus for the past three.[9]

What did the IMF announce regarding Uruguay's need for conditions? The Fund "stated that its intention was to assist the government's efforts to strengthen public finances and tighten credit policy" (*Economist Intelligence*

---

[9] The press release was misleading in other ways. Reviewing Uruguay's economic history, it stated that subsequent to strong growth and balance of payments surpluses in the 1970s, economic performance in Uruguay had declined in the early 1980s. The press release leads one to believe that the IMF addressed Uruguay's economic problems for the first time with the 1983/4 program. It fails to mention that Uruguay was under IMF programs straight through the period from 1975 to 1987.

Unit Uruguay, Paraguay Country Report 1, 1991: 11). Officials attributed
the economic problems in Uruguay to a rising government budget deficit
(*IMF Survey 1991*: 12–13). Hence, a key element of the program was reducing the size of the public sector. The agreement also called for improving public finances, linking public sector wages to the projected decline in inflation,
deregulating and privatizing public enterprises, greater reliance on market
forces to determine interest rates, and reorganizing the social security system
(*IMF Survey 1991*: 12–13). The last condition was not met during Lacalle's
administration, but Uruguay complied with the other conditions of the
agreement.

The IMF never announced that the main reason for the arrangement was
to give Lacalle political leverage, but this was apparent to observers. *The
Economist Intelligence Unit* reported, for example,

having lost the support of the Partido Colorado [Lacalle] is likely to face much more
concerted opposition to his policies. Nevertheless, economic policies are likely to be
strengthened, not watered down. No longer needing to placate the Colorados, Sr
Lacalle will be able to be more forthright. *He will be encouraged to be so, moreover,
by the IMF, now supporting the government's policies with a stand-by agreement.*
(*Economist Intelligence Unit Uruguay, Paraguay Country Report 1*, 1991: 6, emphasis added)

The "encouragement" of the IMF was a useful tool for the president.
When the 1990 agreement ended, the IMF declared the 1990/1 program a
success (*IMF Survey 1992*: 238–9). By raising taxes and cutting spending,
the government built on its 1990 budget surplus, increasing it to 0.91 percent
of GDP for 1991, the highest surplus recorded in Uruguay's history (recall
Figure 2.14).

Despite ultimately giving Uruguay its seal of approval, the IMF stepped
up the pressure to reform the economy over the course of the arrangement.
For example, during the first half of 1991, the Fund withheld its approval
of the disbursement of $65 million in World Bank loans and $800 million in
Inter-American Development Bank loans that were to be used to buy
back foreign debt (*Economist Intelligence Unit Uruguay, Paraguay Country
Report 3*, 1991: 13). This increased the pressure on Congress to approve Lacalle's proposed new taxes and adjustments to public and private
wages (*Economist Intelligence Unit Uruguay, Paraguay Country Report 4*,
1991: 14). Even though the Fund approved of the 1990/1 program, it noted
that public wages had gone over target by 5 percent, and insisted that they be
cut before it would enter into further agreements with Uruguay (*Economist
Intelligence Unit Uruguay, Paraguay Country Report 1,2*, 1992).

Some of Lacalle's measures were not successful. He won the approval
of Congress for the controversial privatization of the last state-owned telephone company. This measure was so unpopular that after it was passed,
opponents gathered the signatures necessary to hold a national referendum

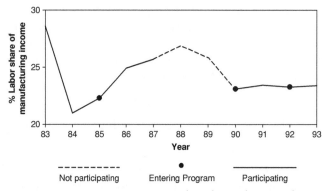

FIGURE 2.15. Uruguay 1983–93: Labor share of income from manufacturing

on the legislation. When put to the national electorate, the motion to repeal the privatization legislation carried with a 70 percent majority of the voters.

This referendum highlights just how unpopular Lacalle's policies were and shows why he wanted IMF conditionality to be imposed. Lacalle needed allies. The fact that he won the approval of Congress for a measure opposed by more than 70 percent of the voters indicates that the IMF alliance may have helped. The increased leverage from the IMF may not have been enough to push through policies when put "directly to citizens on the basis of specific policy preferences" (Filgueira and Papadópulos 1997: 380), but it was enough to get it past substantial opposition in Congress.

And note that 30 percent of the electorate voted yes in the referendum. Lacalle was not entirely without supporters. Some groups actually benefited immediately under the IMF program. Unfortunately – due to lack of data – it is not easy to ascertain the distributional consequences of the 1990 IMF agreement. The UNDP World Income Inequality Database (WIID) does not report income inequality data for Uruguay after 1989. There is evidence, however, that IMF programs in general redistribute income from the poor to the rich (a finding treated more thoroughly in Chapter 6). In his 1987 study of IMF programs in Latin America, Pastor finds that "the single most consistent effect the IMF seems to have is the redistribution of income away from workers" (1987a: 89). Recently, Garuda (2000) confirmed this finding, showing that the income distribution deteriorates for most countries participating in IMF programs. This, in fact, was the case in Uruguay 1990. Figure 2.15 illustrates the pattern using data from the labor share of income from manufacturing.

In 1989, labor share of income from manufacturing was 25.8 percent.[10] In 1990, the government entered into the IMF program. The economy experienced a contraction of −1.03 percent and earnings from manufacturing

---

[10] Data on labor share of earnings from manufacturing were taken from World Bank (1995).

dropped from $3,722 million to $3,667 million.[11] Labor share of income from manufacturing dropped to 23.1 percent. Thus, the income going to the owners of capital increased from $2,762 million to $2,820 million. Despite negative growth for the economy as a whole, the income of the owners of capital increased by 2 percent. This group seems to have been better off with the changes in policy.

The defeat in the referendum was a major defeat for Lacalle's reform program. It indicated extremely low public support for the continuation of reforms. Yet, when the 1990 agreement with the IMF expired, Lacalle signed another agreement in July 1992. This arrangement provided Uruguay with $72 million, but nearly 70 percent of this loan went untouched. The government used an amount equivalent to less than two-tenths of a percent of GDP. Once again the government signed even though it did not need foreign exchange.

For this agreement, although there was no immediate need for the loan, the case can be made that there was a *prospective* need.[12] The IMF explained that certain policies of the program would hurt the current account surplus because they called for opening the economy to imports (*IMF Survey 1992*: 238–9). By 1992, export duties were cut by more than half of what they were in 1990 and import duties were also reduced. Recall, however, that this prospective need was not the reason for the first IMF loan. Under the 1990 agreement, import duties were increased 5 percent.

Beyond the opening of the economy, the Fund reported frankly that the goal of the 1992 program was to "consolidate gains made in the fiscal area" (*IMF Survey 1992*: 238–9). And despite the lack of domestic support, Lacalle implemented much of the reform program. In addition to what had already been forced through, the president succeeded in ending the state monopoly on insurance and pushed through port reform, as well as reprivatizing all four banks absorbed by the previous administration and selling the last state-owned meat packing plant (*Financial Times*: May 25, 1994). Lacalle lost the big battles over social security[13] and the sale of the telephone company, but he won many other unlikely victories.

By the end of his term, Lacalle's policies had gained the approval of investors and creditors. In May 1994, the *Economist Intelligence Unit* improved the political risk rating of Uruguay. The change was issued because of "continued efforts at structural reform by the Lacalle administration – and its partial success – despite a hostile congress" (*The Economist Intelligence Unit* cited in *Financial Times*: May 25, 1994).

---

[11] Data on earnings from manufacturing were taken from World Bank (2000).

[12] I am grateful to Beth Simmons for raising this possibility.

[13] Social security reform was given up by this administration after four attempts to push it through Congress achieved only minor changes in the system (*Financial Times* May 25, 1994).

In particular, foreign direct investment experienced a dramatic increase going from less than 0.01 percent of GDP in 1991 and 1992 to 0.74 percent of GDP in 1993 and nearly 1 percent of GDP in 1994. Overall investment grew every year after 1990, going from 12 percent of GDP in 1991 to 13 percent in 1992 to over 14 percent in 1993 and 1994. Economic growth (percent of GDP) went from less than 1 percent in 1990 to 3 percent in 1991 and nearly 8 percent in 1992. Growth slowed to about 2.4 percent in 1993 but then shot back up to over 6.5 percent in 1994. (These figures come from *World Development Indicators 1997*.)

As for the causal link between the IMF agreement and the economic improvements, consider the following counterfactual: Had the IMF program been rejected in its entirety, these improvements would not have come to fruition. The IMF would not have issued the 1992 press release declaring the 1990 program a success, and a negative signal would have been sent to creditors and investors. Investment and growth would have suffered from a rejected IMF program. This is not to say that growth and investment were helped by the agreement, only that – given that an agreement was in place – failure to meet the IMF conditions would have hurt. Whether growth would have been higher or lower without any participation in an IMF arrangement is the subject of Chapter 5.

CONCLUSION

In this chapter, I show that the need for a loan is neither sufficient nor necessary for a country to enter into an IMF agreement. Countries in economic crisis with dire need for foreign exchange may negotiate with the IMF, but governments must weigh the domestic audience costs of surrendering national sovereignty to the Fund. These costs may depend on easily observable measures such as a country's history, the prospect of an election, or whether other countries are participating in IMF programs. "Trust," although not easily measured or quantified, may be another factor. Despite an economic crisis, a government will weather the storm without the Fund, as did Tanzania from 1982 to 1985 and Nigeria from 1983 to 1986, if the costs of the agreement outweigh the benefits.

The most important lesson of this chapter is that governments have an ideal level of conditions that they want the IMF to impose. Some governments will only negotiate for and accept agreements with weak conditions, as did Tanzania in 1975 and 1980. Sometimes governments want more stringent conditions to be imposed. Entering IMF agreements enables governments to increase the cost of rejecting unpopular economic policies, particularly for slashing the government budget deficit by raising taxes, cutting spending, and privatizing state enterprises. This was seen in Tanzania 1986, Nigeria 1987, and throughout Uruguayan modern history. In 1990 the Uruguayan government had no need for the IMF loan and signed purely for the conditions.

This desire for conditionality may be exactly what IMF officials mean by their common references to strong "political will."

The IMF may or may not grant the ideal level of conditions the government seeks. The Shagari administration tried to bring in the IMF to push through certain policies, but the Fund insisted on one condition – devaluation – that the government did not want and no agreement was reached. If a government is willing to take on enough conditions, however, the IMF will overlook its charge in the *Articles of Agreement* which states that agreements are to be extended only to countries with balance of payments difficulties or shortages in foreign reserves. In these cases, the Fund – seeking to maximize its influence around the world – is a willing accomplice in pushing economic reform past domestic resistance.

Thus, one can tell a richer story of participation in IMF programs than one based purely on a need for an IMF loan: Governments face sovereignty costs for submitting to IMF conditionality. These are the domestic audience costs a government must pay when it turns to the IMF for assistance. They depend on what past governments have done vis-à-vis the IMF, as well as what contemporary governments around the world are doing. If sovereignty costs are not too high, a government may turn to the Fund if it needs an IMF loan. Whether the government actually signs depends on whether it can get the conditions that it wants. Thus, the negotiation posture of the IMF, which may depend on its budget constraint as well as on how important the IMF considers the country in question, also determines whether an agreement will be concluded.

Some governments want specific conditions to be imposed by the IMF. A government may want the IMF to impose policy that it prefers because it faces opposition. By attaching certain policies to an IMF agreement, the government raises the costs of failing to approve the policy because a rejection is no longer merely a rejection of the government, but of the IMF. Rejecting the IMF is costly since it sends a negative signal to creditors and investors. Thus, debt and investment also determine whether the government will bring in the IMF.

There are many factors involved in this story: preference over loans and conditions, the negotiation posture of the IMF, sovereignty costs, and rejection costs. Does the intuition about the interaction of this plethora of considerations hold up to rigorous logic? And, if so, what general implications can one draw from their interaction? To examine these questions carefully, I use formal models to spell out this story in the next chapter.

3

An Analytical Approach to the Politics of IMF Agreements

The narratives in the previous chapter illustrate that, although some governments enter into IMF agreements because they need a loan, they also have an ideal level of conditions they want to have imposed upon them as part of the IMF agreement. Some governments, like Tanzania 1976 want a loan and only weak conditions imposed. Others want both a loan and conditions, as seen in Tanzania 1986 and possibly Nigeria 1983. Still others, like Uruguay 1990, do not need a loan and enter into the IMF agreement purely for the conditions.

Why would a government want conditions to be imposed? I have argued that by entering into an IMF agreement, a reform-oriented executive makes it more costly for domestic actors with veto power over policy ("veto players") to reject his preferred policies. Rejecting the IMF is costly – to the executive as well as to potential opponents – because it limits access to IMF credit (Schadler 1995) and sends negative signals to creditors (Callaghy 1997, 2002; Aggarwal 1996) and investors (Stone 2002; Edwards 2000). Callaghy explains that debt negotiations are virtually impossible with a canceled IMF agreement. Regarding investors, Stone (as noted before, 2000: 2), contends, "When the Fund negotiates a stabilization program with a government that imposes policy conditions, it creates a focal point for investors to coordinate their expectations." The country as a whole may suffer if the IMF is rejected. To avoid these rejection costs, opponents with veto power over policy may be willing to accept more economic reform than they would otherwise.

This argument draws on the literature on two-level games. In Putnam's (1988) seminal piece on this subject, he draws attention to the "Schelling conjecture": by tying its hands domestically, a government may gain bargaining leverage in international negotiations (Pahre and Papayoanou 1997: 9). Many scholars have studied this phenomenon from the bottom up. They have found that domestic constraints can influence negotiations at the international level.[1] But what about the flipside of the two-level game? I consider the two-level game from the other direction; top down. Just as domestic constraints increase bargaining leverage at the international level, international constraints can increase bargaining leverage at the domestic level. An executive may enter into IMF agreements to push through unpopular domestic policies – a phenomenon Gourevitch (1986) calls "the second image reversed."[2]

Note, however, that the case studies of the previous chapter also show that there are constraints on using this strategy. Sovereignty costs matter. Opponents can accuse governments that turn to the IMF of bowing to the forces of international capitalism or "selling out" (Remmer 1986: 7). This is the other edge of what Remmer calls the "double edged sword" of bringing in the Fund. Measuring "sovereignty costs" is not straightforward, but it may have something to do with what other governments in a country's history have done, or other countries around the world do. When few other countries enter IMF agreements or when a particular country does not have a history of entering into IMF agreements, the domestic political costs for "selling out" to the Fund and submitting to conditionality are greater. In Nigeria, sovereignty costs were high enough to keep the country from entering an agreement for many years, despite a desperate need of foreign exchange. In Uruguay, where repeated participation in IMF agreements dated back to the early 1960s, the sovereignty costs were lower.

The negotiation posture of the IMF also plays a role. At certain times in its history, when few countries had IMF programs, the Fund has taken a soft stance. When the IMF faces a tighter budget constraint, it may demand more conditions from a government. The Fund also takes a tougher negotiation posture with smaller countries than with those that have large, destabilizing balance of payments deficits.

Thus, several factors play a role in the decisions of a government and the IMF to enter into an agreement. What are the implications of the claim that governments want conditions to be imposed upon them? How much can increasing the "rejection costs" help a government seeking economic reforms? When does this benefit outweigh the penalty of "sovereignty costs"? How does the negotiation posture of the IMF mediate this?

---

[1] For some examples, see Iida (1993, 1996), Mo (1995), Frieden (1995), Milner and Rosendorff (1997), Pahre (1997), Gilligan and Hunt (1998), Leeds (1999), Mansfield, Milner, and Rosendorff (2000), Martin (2000), and McGillivray (2002).

[2] For more examples of tying hands arguments, see Elster (2000, 1990). Note that in my story (below), an executive can use the IMF to push through economic reform because rejecting the IMF is costly. Reinhardt (2002) shows that international institutions (in particular, the World Trade Organization) may be used as commitment devices even if enforcement is not forthcoming. Wolf (1999) argues that international institutions in general can increase executive autonomy.

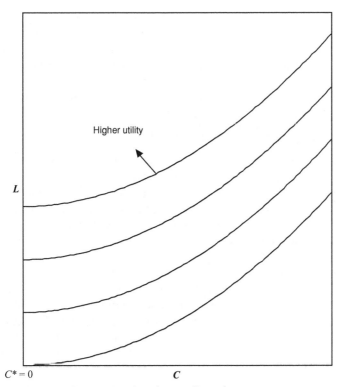

FIGURE 3.1. Conventional understanding of agreements

To consider these questions carefully, I develop formal models in this chapter. Like the narrative work in the previous chapter, the models further develop the story behind participation in IMF programs. The implications are tested statistically in Chapter 4.

PREFERENCES OVER LOANS AND CONDITIONS

One can think of an IMF arrangement as composed of two parts: a loan of foreign exchange (L) and the conditions attached to the loan (C). The utility, U, that a government derives from entering into an IMF program is therefore a function of L and C: $U = U(L, C)$. Conventional wisdom holds that governments signing IMF agreements need foreign exchange, but do not want to take on conditions. Hence, the government's utility is increasing in $L(U_L > 0)$ and decreasing in $C(U_C < 0)$ (subscripts denote partial derivatives).

To make these relationships clear, consider the map of government indifference curves presented in Figure 3.1.[3] The curves in Figure 3.1 represent

---

[3] I assume that governments derive quadratic utility in Figures 3.1, 3.2, 3.3, and 3.5.

iso-values of utility for the government. Along any single curve, the government is indifferent between combinations of L and C. But to maintain indifference, the size of the loan must increase as conditions increase. Thus, the government is indifferent between a small loan with low conditions and a large loan with high conditions. As one moves up from curve to curve, the government is better off, with the highest utility being obtained in the upper left hand part of the figure. The government prefers an agreement with a high loan and weak conditions attached. It is willing to accept more conditions only if it can get a larger loan.

Under what conditions will countries enter into IMF agreements according to this framework? Assume that the utility the government derives from L depends on how badly the government needs the loan, or in other terms, how low are its foreign reserves. The government gets more utility from the IMF loan when its reserves are low because it is desperate for foreign exchange. Therefore, one should expect only countries with low reserves to enter into IMF agreements.

The problem with this framework is that many countries which enter into IMF programs may want conditions to be imposed. Hence, this framework needs changing. Suppose a government wants some degree of conditionality to be imposed by the IMF to gain domestic bargaining leverage. The government does not want the IMF to impose conditions that are too strict, but there exists some ideal level of conditions that the government prefers. Let the government's ideal level of conditions be denoted by C^*. The utility the government derives from an IMF program depends on L and C, as above, but now U_C is positive up to C^*, and negative beyond this point:

$$U_C \quad \begin{matrix} \geq 0 & \text{if} & C \leq C^* \\ < 0 & \text{if} & C > C^* \end{matrix}$$

As in the first framework, the government prefers to enter into agreements when foreign reserves are low and prefers a larger loan to a smaller one ($U_L > 0$). In this framework, however, the government also prefers a certain level of conditions to be imposed. The ideal arrangement is one that provides a large loan and imposes conditions equal to C^*.

Figure 3.2 serves to illustrate how the introduction of an ideal level of conditions changes the shape of the government's indifference curves. As in Figure 3.1, the curves represent iso-utility values. Here, however, the government is happiest when C is set to C^*. Thus, in Figure 3.2, the government's utility increases as it moves upward and toward C^*. According to this framework, a government with low reserves will still seek an IMF loan, but a government desiring an IMF arrangement need not face a reserves crisis. The government may seek an agreement simply because it offers conditions close to the government's ideal point, C^*.

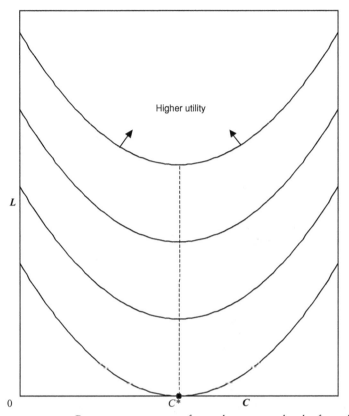

FIGURE 3.2. Governments may prefer to have some level of conditions imposed upon them

Note that the framework in Figure 3.2 is just a generalization of the framework in Figure 3.1. The previous framework simply represents a government with an ideal level of conditions equal to 0: $C^* = 0$. Yet, one could envisage a continuum of governments with ideal points ranging across the spectrum. Figure 3.3 illustrates four governments with different ideal points.

Now consider the preferences of the IMF over loans and conditions. Recall from Chapter 1 that the IMF may have technocratic concerns (Gould 2001a, 2001b) and bureaucratic motivations (Vaubel 1986). If the IMF seeks to maximize its technocratic influence in the world and its budget, it prefers to impose as many conditions as possible for the least amount of money. Let us suppose the IMF offers a simple linear menu of arrangements according to $L = b + qC$, where L represents the size of the loan and C represents the conditions associated with the loan.

The intercept-parameter b represents the budget constraint that faces the Fund. The higher the value of b, the more foreign exchange the IMF has

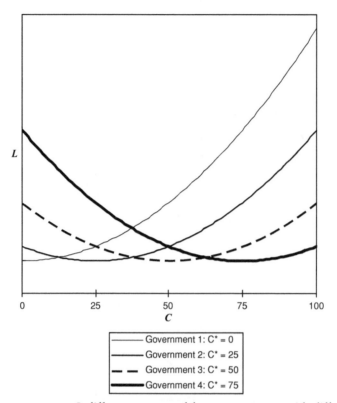

FIGURE 3.3. Indifference curves of four governments with different ideal levels of conditions

available to loan. For simplicity I have left out subscripts, but *b* should in fact be subscripted for time, since the budget constraint of the IMF changes as member contributions increase and as more or fewer agreements are signed.

The slope-parameter *q* characterizes the technocratic position of the Fund. The intuition behind this parameter is that the IMF is willing to pay for more conditions. If a country is willing to take on more conditions, it will get a bigger loan. Countries that want fewer conditions get a smaller loan. The *q* parameter determines just how much more foreign exchange the IMF will loan as a government takes on more conditions. Again, for simplicity the subscripts have been dropped, but *q* should be subscripted for time, country, and government. The technocratic position of the Fund varies with changes in its leadership and as criticism of the Fund waxes and wanes. The technocratic position toward individual countries also varies depending on changes in government and on the size of balance of payments deficits. In particular, large countries with important economies will be able to get more out of the Fund than smaller countries. This is because large economies have more of an impact on world financial stability. Moreover, governments with

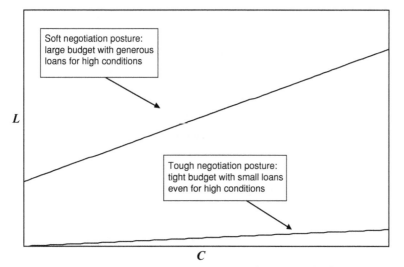

FIGURE 3.4. Two separate negotiation postures the IMF may adopt

more experience with the IMF may be able to negotiate for better terms than governments new to IMF negotiations.

Figure 3.4 illustrates two different negotiation postures the IMF might take. The higher line represents a particularly soft negotiation posture. The budget constraint is weak, so the Fund has a lot of money to loan (b is high). The technocratic position of the Fund is also weak, so the Fund concedes very large loans as a country takes on more conditions (q is high). The lower line represents a tough negotiation posture. The b parameter has been set at 0, indicating that the budget constraint is binding. The low q indicates that governments must take on extreme conditions to get bigger loans.

Suppose there are two countries seeking IMF agreements facing the same negotiation posture of the IMF. The government of one country prefers $C = 0$ and the government of the other prefers $C = C^*$. Figure 3.5 represents an illustration consistent with these assumptions, demonstrating the types of arrangements the two types of governments will choose.

The government which prefers no conditions ($C = 0$) will choose an arrangement at point x, with low conditions and a small loan. The government which prefers a higher level of conditions ($C = C^*$) will choose an arrangement at point y with more conditions and get a larger loan.

Note that the government which prefers $C = 0$ will only turn to the IMF if it needs a loan. Thus, this type of government will certainly have low reserves. The government which prefers $C = C^*$ may or may not have low reserves. Despite having high reserves, it may seek an IMF arrangement simply because it wants conditions. The counterintuitive prediction which follows is that governments with stronger reserves may get larger loans from the IMF.

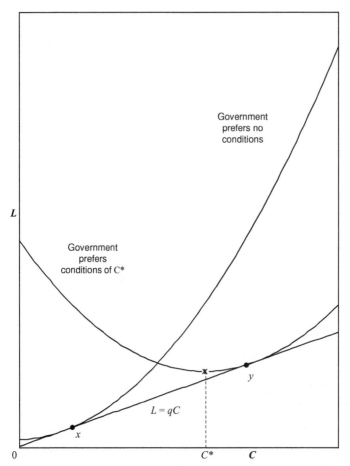

FIGURE 3.5. Governments that prefer more conditions get higher loans

This is exactly what is observed. I use a simple OLS regression to explain the size of an IMF loan on country-year observations for cases where a country signed an IMF agreement.[4] I expect that countries with stronger foreign reserves positions get larger loans than countries with weaker reserves positions. Table 3.1 presents the results.[5]

---

[4] Data on foreign reserves and balance of payments are available for 334 out of the total of 678 separate agreements.

[5] Clearly the set of countries receiving IMF loans is not a random sample. To correct for the nonrandom nature of my sample, I estimate the expected size of the IMF loan *given* that the government and the IMF want the agreement. I draw on the statistical results presented in Chapter 4 and use the method of correcting for selection bias presented in the appendix to Chapter 5. Essentially, I include an instrument to control for the government's decision to sign the agreement and a separate instrument to control for the IMF's decision to enter

TABLE 3.1. *Size of IMF loan according to foreign reserve position*

Variable	Specification 1	Specification 2	Means
CONSTANT	149.77**		1.0
	(40.35)		
RESERVES	24.30**	24.59**	2.2
	(12.48)	(9.76)	
BOP		−0.28**	−361.4
		(0.02)	
E(LOAN)	204.18	207.80	
(standard deviation)	(534.25)	(539.35)	
Observations	334	327	
Likelihood ratio test		0.003	
F-test		0.005	
Adjusted R-squared	0.01	0.47	

* indicates significance at the 90% confidence level.
** indicates significance at the 95% level.
Note: Standard errors in parentheses. Independent variables are lagged one year.

The counterintuitive prediction is supported by the data. According to the first specification in Table 3.1, RESERVES (the average annual foreign reserves in terms of monthly imports) has a significant positive effect on the size of the loan. Recall, however, that the negotiation posture of the Fund may vary between countries and over time. Thus, in the second specification I include in the regression the value of the country's balance of payments deficit in constant 1987 U.S. dollars. The second variable is included because the mandate of the IMF is to promote stable international trade. I assume that the Fund will provide larger loans to countries whose deficits are more destabilizing. In other words, countries with larger balance of payments deficits in absolute terms should get more money. This is intended to control for different postures the IMF may take with different countries. To control for possible time effects, I run the regression for fixed panel effects by year. (Year-specific constants are not reported.)

The second specification shows that the result on foreign reserves holds when one controls for balance of payments and time effects. On average, for every additional unit of foreign reserves (in terms of average monthly imports), a government will get an IMF loan larger by SDR 24.59 million. The more intuitive prediction, that countries with larger absolute deficits in the balance of payments get larger loans, is also supported by the data.[6]

into the agreement. These instruments are called hazard rates (Inverse Mill's Ratio). See Chapter 5 for details. The coefficients when hazard rates are included do not qualitatively differ from what is reported here. They are available from the author upon request.

[6] Statistical tests (both F-test and likelihood ratio tests) indicate that the sample is heterogeneous and exhibits fixed, year effects. There are not enough observations for the

If one thinks of the IMF as a bank, one might not find it surprising that the IMF provides access to larger amounts of foreign exchange to countries that are better able to pay for their imports. Private lending institutions prefer clients that are better credit risks. The IMF, however, is not a private lending institution, and its mandate is to provide foreign exchange to countries that have no other option. To counteract the moral hazard that this introduces, the IMF imposes conditions that one presumes governments do not want. If this is the case, then countries with stronger reserves should look for loans elsewhere. The fact that they do not – as seen from the above regressions – implies that governments do not always see conditionality as a deterrent. Thus, this preliminary statistical evidence supports the hypothesis that governments enter agreements because they want conditions to be imposed upon them.

Why do governments want conditions imposed? Although many have argued that governments enter into IMF arrangements to pursue their own preferred policies (Spaventa 1983; Vaubel 1986; Putnam 1988; Kiondo 1992; Stein 1992; Edwards and Santaella 1993; Bjork 1995; Dixit 1996; Brooks 1998: 23), it is not clear that such a move can always be effective. Bringing in the Fund may increase a government's bargaining leverage, but the government must be willing to accept the penalties for sacrificing sovereignty. Entering into an arrangement so that conditions can be imposed is thus a "double-edged sword" (Remmer 1986). If the sword cuts both ways, when is it worthwhile for a government to pursue such a strategy?

THE LOGIC OF USING IMF CONDITIONALITY

Suppose an executive wishes to lower the budget deficit,[7] but needs the approval of a domestic constituency which prefers to maintain public spending at the status quo level. This constituency can be thought of as any actor with veto power (de facto or de jure) over policy. In a democracy, it may be either chamber in the parliament or congress, as in the case of Uruguay. In a one-party state, it may be the party leadership, as Kiondo (1992) and Stein (1992: 81) argue about Tanzania. In a military dictatorship, the actor advocating lower spending may be the finance minister, whereas the "veto player" may be the defense minister. Pauly (1997: 163–4) tells the story of a finance minister of a developing country who "specifically requested the

---

year 1975 to control for these effects for this year. Thus I drop the observations for 1975.

[7] One could consider any of the number of policy areas where the IMF imposes conditions such as interest rates, exchange rates, privatizations, and so on. The argument holds for any policy area where the approval of another actor, different from the executive who signs the IMF agreement, is required for changes in policy.

managing director of the IMF to include in the routine surveillance report on his country a reference to the need to cut military expenditures.... [T]he ruse apparently achieved its objective of adding weight to the views of the minister."

Putnam (1988: 457) cites IMF negotiations with Italy in 1974 and 1977 as instances where "domestic conservative forces exploited the IMF pressure to facilitate policy moves that were otherwise infeasible internally." He follows the work of Spaventa (1983) who argues that even "the unions and the Communists actually favored the austerity measures, but found the IMF demands helpful in dealing with their own internal [domestic] constituents" (Putnam 1988: 454). Bjork (1995) makes a similar observation about Poland. He contends "that most of the macroeconomic program imputed to IMF conditionality can be more accurately traced to economic imperatives or to domestic Polish political factors" (1995: 89). Edwards and Santaella (1993: 425) argue that, in general, governments facing domestic opposition get the IMF to do their "dirty work." Dixit (1996: 85) sums up the situation nicely:

Most countries, particularly less developed ones, in need of fiscal and monetary restraint are able to make a commitment by using international organizations such as the World Bank or the International Monetary Fund as "delegates" for this purpose. When their domestic constituents press for protection, subsidies, or inflationary finance, the treasuries can point to the conditions imposed by these bodies in return for much needed project loans or foreign currency.

This argument is similar to Schelling's (1960: 22) contention that "the power to constrain an adversary may depend on the power to bind oneself."

How exactly does an IMF agreement help to push through unpopular reforms? Suppose a reform oriented executive faces opposition. By entering into an IMF agreement, an executive ties its preferred policies of economic reform to the conditions of the IMF. For opponents of economic reform, this move raises the costs of rejecting the executive's proposals, because a rejection is no longer the mere rejection of an executive but also of the IMF. A total rejection of the IMF not only limits the credit that the IMF will extend to the country but it sends out costly negative signals to creditors and investors. So, politically, the IMF is brought in to "tip the balance" (Bird 2001).

Note that these costs are imposed on the country as a whole, and they may even be higher for the executive than for the opponents of economic reform. Thus, the strategy may be risky. But as long as there is some positive cost that the opponents of economic reform face as well, the strategy may be effective. The executive can push through more of its reform program with the additional bargaining leverage that an IMF agreement brings.

The role of rejection costs is obviously pivotal for this argument. It must be true that failure to comply with an IMF agreement is costly to the veto players opposing reform. This does not mean that enforcement of conditions must be one hundred percent. In fact, it is not. There are many anecdotes of the IMF relaxing conditions or continuing to extend credit to a country that has not fully complied with an IMF agreement. On the other hand, noncompliance is often sanctioned:

1. The most obvious sanction imposed on a country is the restriction of access to the IMF loan. In a study of fifty-nine IMF agreements from 1988 to 1992, Schadler (1995) found that the IMF restricted access to the agreement loan thirty-five times (cited in Edwards 1999). This is a direct cost that a country risks when it does not comply with an IMF agreement.

2. One indirect sanction for rejecting IMF conditions involves creditors. As Callaghy (1997, 2002) notes, organizations such as the Paris Club, an informal group of creditor countries that reschedules country debt, almost always require that countries be in good standing under an IMF agreement if any debt negotiations are to take place. Rejecting IMF conditions may, therefore, preclude debt rescheduling desperately needed in many developing countries.

3. A third form of sanction for noncompliance may come through investors. As Stone (2000: 2) argues, an IMF program creates a "focal point" for investors: "Investors benefit from following IMF signals because the threat of IMF sanctions for noncompliance helps to protect the value of their investments." Edwards (2000) finds that whereas increased investment is not associated with compliance with an IMF agreement, decreased investment is associated with a failed IMF arrangement. Investors do not rally to countries in compliance with an IMF agreement, but they do withhold support from a country with a failed IMF arrangement. When an IMF agreement is canceled due to noncompliance, investment is hurt.

It can, therefore, be costly in several ways for countries to reject the policies imposed by the IMF. Facing the trade-off between rejection costs and policy changes, opponents of economic reform may prefer the latter.

A Simple Game

To make the argument more concrete, suppose that IMF agreements are negotiated over only one dimension – the budget deficit – and that the budget deficit can be set anywhere on the interval $[0,1]$. Suppose that a relevant opponent of the executive's program of economic reform – call him a "veto player" (Tsebelis 1995) – has standard Euclidean preferences over the single dimension of deficit and has an ideal point at 1. The logic of the argument below holds for any Euclidean preferences (such as quadratic utility). To make the algebra as simple as possible, however, assume the actor has a linear "tent-shaped" utility function so that the utility is measured as the negative of the distance from the actor's ideal point.[8]

Let the level of deficit in the IMF agreement (set by the executive and the IMF) be a, and let r denote the cost to the veto player of rejecting the IMF. Obviously, the decision-making context is more complicated than I lay out in this simple model. There is some uncertainty as to whether the IMF will impose rejection costs or not. Still, one can think of r as the expected cost of rejecting the IMF. As long as there is some positive probability of punishment that can negatively affect the veto players or their constituents, the logic holds.

Assume that the status quo deficit is 1 – the veto player's ideal point. Rejecting the IMF agreement will give the veto player a payoff of $-r$. Accepting the level of deficit set by the IMF agreement will give the veto player a payoff of $-|1 - a| = a - 1$. The veto player will prefer the agreement level of deficit to the status quo provided $a > 1 - r$. If the executive can convince the IMF to set the agreement level of deficit to $a \geq 1 - r$, the veto player will approve and the deficit will be reduced.[9] Without the IMF, the veto player will veto any deviation from the status quo. Recall that the executive himself will also suffer if the IMF is rejected. The country as a whole suffers, and the executive may even pay a higher price than the veto players. This may make the strategy of bringing in the IMF more risky for the executive, but as long as the veto players also suffer sufficiently from rejecting the IMF, the winset will increase in the direction of more economic reform.

Figure 3.6 illustrates the decision-making context. The figure shows that if the executive proposes deficit cuts without bringing in the IMF, the veto player will always reject because $0 > a - 1$. If the government brings in the IMF, however, rejection becomes more costly. The veto player will accept the new deficit level if rejection costs are high: $r \geq 1 - a$.

This simple model merely illustrates how an IMF agreement may be used to push through economic reform. It ignores the fact that by bringing in the IMF to change policy, the executive runs certain risks. What risks does the executive face? First of all, because the opposition will accuse it of "selling out," the executive will pay "sovereignty costs," the penalty of sacrificing sovereignty to the IMF. Second, the executive faces an unknown negotiation posture of the IMF. The Fund may require drastic cuts to the deficit that go beyond even what a reform oriented executive is willing to accept. I show below that, given low enough sovereignty penalties and high enough rejection costs, the executive will gamble on negotiations with the IMF to push through a new budget that otherwise would have been rejected.

---

[8] The argument holds under less restrictive assumptions about the preferences and number of veto players. See Vreeland (2001).

[9] The other root, $a \leq 1 + r$, lies outside the interval [0,1]. At any rate, it is assumed that the IMF imposes conditions that reduce the deficit.

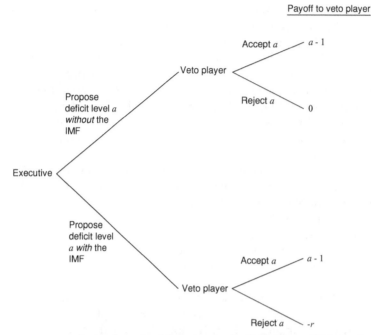

FIGURE 3.6. A simple logic of bringing in the IMF. *Note:* Without the IMF agreement, the veto player will always reject the executive's proposal because $a < 1$. If the executive signs an IMF agreement, the veto player will accept the executive's proposal when rejection costs are high enough: $r > 1 - a$.

Introducing Negotiation Postures and Sovereignty Costs

Consider the game presented in Figure 3.7. The game involves three actors: the executive, represented by G for "government," the veto player, V, and the Fund, F. G can approach F to negotiate an agreement. An agreement consists of setting a new government budget deficit. For convenience, let d denote the value of the deficit, where d is normalized to range over the interval from 0 to 1 ($d \in [0,1]$). The status quo size of the deficit is 1. If G and F agree to a package, G submits the proposed agreement value of deficit, denoted by $d = a$, to V for its approval. If V approves, d is set to a. If not, d remains at the status quo, 1.

Each actor $i, i \in \{V,G,F\}$, derives linear utility from the deficit, d: $U_i(d) = -|d - d_i|$, where d_i denotes the ideal deficit of actor i. To keep the game simple, let the ideal point of V be 1 ($d_V = 1$) and the ideal point of F be 0 ($d_F = 0$). Let the ideal point of G, d_G, be a random variable uniformly distributed over the interval from 0 to 1 ($d_G \in [0,1]$). The intuition behind these assumptions is that V wants to keep the deficit at the status quo level, F wants to eradicate the deficit, and G wants some change in between the two. For example, if G's ideal point is 0.5, it wants to cut the deficit in half (0.5 times the status quo). The values of d_V and d_F and the probability distribution of d_G are commonly known to V, G, and F at the beginning of the game.

Note that the way I have laid out the utility of the Fund so far, it will be made better off by any reduction of the deficit and should be willing to help any government that wants to reduce the deficit. The IMF, however, does not simply enter into agreements with every country. With some countries it has a tough negotiation posture, demanding high levels of economic reform. With other countries, the IMF is more lenient.

To represent the negotiation posture of the IMF in a simple way in this game, I include the term $-(1 - n)$ in the payoff of F if an IMF agreement is signed. Thus, instead of a payoff of $U_F(d) = -|d - d_F|$, the payoff of F is $U_F(d) = -|d - d_F| - (1 - n)$ which is equivalent to $-d - (1 - n)$. This "negotiation posture" constraint is designed so that n is the maximum deficit that F will accept in an agreement. If G is unable or unwilling to set $a \leq n$, there can be no IMF arrangement because F will be better off with the status quo payoff. The status quo payoff is -1. The payoff to F after entering into the agreement (paying negotiation costs and setting up the loan) is $-d - (1 - n)$. F will only be better off if $-d - (1 - n) > -1$, which is true only when $d < n$. So F will never agree to setting the deficit higher than n. This is simply a way of structuring the game such that F is willing to impose only specific conditions. F will not provide an IMF agreement for very small changes in policy. G must agree to lower the deficit to at least n to gain F's support.

Although n is treated as exogenous, the negotiation posture can be thought of as a function of the technocratic stance of the IMF and of the resources available to the IMF. From the technocratic perspective, the IMF may care about a country's economic indicator variables such as its foreign reserves position. Regarding its own budgetary concerns, the Fund may be more demanding of countries when IMF resources are tight. Given that the IMF's mandate is to maintain international trade stability, the Fund may also be more willing to provide arrangements to countries with large balance of payments deficits. If a country is small and its balance of payments deficit has little impact on international trade, the IMF will take a tough posture. With larger countries that have balance of payments deficits with larger ramifications, the IMF will make concessions. Since information about the resources of the IMF is generally kept secret, only F knows the value of n at the beginning of the game, although the probability distribution of n is common knowledge. Let n be uniformly distributed over the interval $[0,1]$.

Figure 3.7 presents an extensive form model of G's and V's decisions and lists the payoffs to all three actors from each of four possible outcomes labeled 1 through 4. The game is played as follows:

G observes $d_G \in [0,1]$, which becomes G's private information, and chooses to "Approach" or "Not Approach" F to negotiate an IMF

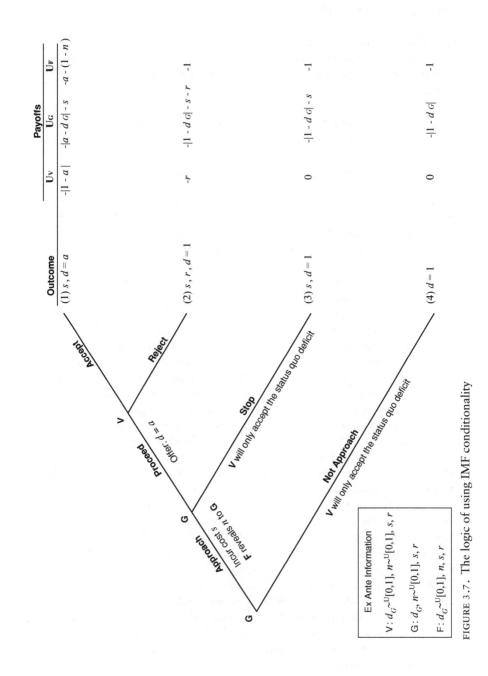

The following payoff table appears in the figure:

Outcome	Payoffs		
	U_V	U_G	U_F
(1) $s, d = a$	$-\|1 - a\|$	$-\|a - d_G\| - s$	$-a - (1 - n)$
(2) $s, r, d = 1$	$-r$	$-\|1 - d_G\| - s - r$	-1
(3) $s, d = 1$	0	$-\|1 - d_G\| - s$	-1
(4) $d = 1$	0	$-\|1 - d_G\|$	-1

Tree labels: Accept; Reject; V; Offer: $d = a$; Proceed; Stop — V will only accept the status quo deficit; F reveals n to G; Incur cost s; G; Approach; Not Approach — V will only accept the status quo deficit; G

Ex Ante Information

V: $d_G \sim^U [0,1]$, $n \sim^U [0,1]$, s, r

G: d_G, $n \sim^U [0,1]$, s, r

F: $d_G \sim^U [0,1]$, n, s, r

FIGURE 3.7. The logic of using IMF conditionality

agreement. If G chooses not to approach, it accepts the status quo deficit, $d = 1$, and the game ends. If G chooses to approach, F reveals the value of $n \in [0,1]$ to G, but G must pay a sovereignty penalty, $s \in [0,1]$, for involving the international organization in domestic politics. The value of s is known to all actors.

G can choose to "Proceed" with negotiations or "Stop" after observing n. If G decides to stop, the deficit remains at the status quo level and the game ends. If G proceeds, F and G put together an IMF package which stipulates an agreement value of deficit, $d = a$. F agrees to any value of a that G proposes, provided $a \leq n$. If the negotiation posture of F is weak (n is high), there is a wide range of acceptable values of a. If F is tough (n is low), this range is smaller. G publicly announces the IMF package, with $d = a$, to V.

V may "Accept" or "Reject" the agreement. Rejecting an IMF agreement which has been publicly supported by G and F sends a strong negative signal to investors and creditors. Observing that the country lacks the political will to undergo economic reform, creditors refuse to reschedule debt and investors pull out. Because the entire country is hurt by this, both G and V suffer a penalty when an agreement is rejected. Thus, if V chooses to reject, deficit remains at the status quo and both V and G bear cost $r \in [0,1]$. The value of r is known to all actors.

The Decision of a Veto Player (V) to Accept or Reject Policy Change

I use backwards induction to identify an equilibrium. Consider the decision of V. When would V rather accept the lower deficit associated with an agreement than reject an agreement and pay cost r? Note that V's utility from accepting the agreement (Outcome 1) is U_V (Accept) $= -|1 - a|$, while V's payoff from rejecting (Outcome 2) is U_V (Reject) $= -|1 - 1| - r = -r$. V will accept any agreement such that $-|1 - a| \geq -r \Rightarrow a \geq 1 - r$ (assuming V accepts when indifferent). Let m denote the minimum agreement value of deficit V will accept: $m = 1 - r$.

For any agreement value of deficit less than m, V would be better off rejecting the agreement and suffering the penalty r rather than accepting. Thus, for an agreement to be accepted, the deficit must be set no lower than m. Note that the greater the costs of rejecting an agreement, the lower the minimum deficit V will accept. If the costs of rejecting are 0 ($r = 0$), then V will accept only an agreement which maintains the deficit at the status quo: $m = 1$. At the highest possible cost of rejecting ($r = 1$), V will accept any agreement: $m = 0$.

The Decision of the Executive (G) to Continue Negotiations

Moving backwards to G's decision to stop negotiations or proceed, note that because G also faces the cost r if V rejects, G prefers Outcome 3 to

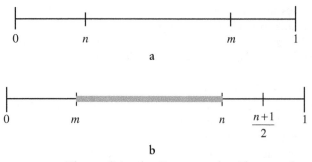

FIGURE 3.8. The condition for G to proceed. a. If $n < m$, there will be no agreement. b. If $m \leq n$, there can be an agreement in the shaded area.

Outcome 2. Provided r is greater than 0, G would rather stop negotiations than propose an agreement that V will reject. Because G knows the value of m – the minimum value of deficit that V will accept – G will only proceed with negotiations if it can offer $a \geq m$. Recall, however, that the IMF agreement value of deficit must also satisfy F's constraint: $a \leq n$. Therefore, G will proceed with negotiations only if the maximum deficit acceptable to F is greater than or equal to the minimum deficit acceptable to V: $n \geq m$. If this condition does not hold, there can be no agreement and G will stop negotiations. Figure 3.8 illustrates this point.

In Figure 3.8a, the maximum deficit that F will accept (n) is smaller than the minimum deficit that V will approve (m). Any deficit that G can get F to agree to will be rejected by V. Hence, if G observes $m > n$, G will stop negotiations and take Outcome (3): The deficit will remain at the status quo even though G incurred cost s. Note, however, that m may be smaller than n, as in Figure 3.8b. Any deficit in the shaded region in Figure 3.8b will be accepted by both V and F. Call this set of points from m to n the "acceptable set."

If d_G lies in the first region, between 0 and m, then the best value of deficit within the "acceptable set" that G can hope for is m. Here G is austere and would like to cut the budget as much as possible. Thus, G will negotiate for an agreement with the minimum deficit possible: $a = m$. Note that this goes beyond what F demands. If d_G lies in the second region, within the "acceptable set," G can negotiate for $a = d_G$ and set the agreement deficit level to its ideal point. G goes beyond what F demands but stops short of the minimum deficit V would accept. If d_G lies in the third region, between n and $(n + 1)/2$, G can do no better than propose an agreement with $a = n$. F insists on a lower deficit than G's ideal point. Here G is the victim of IMF policy. If d_G lies in the fourth region, between $(n + 1)/2$ and 1, then F's negotiation posture is too tough to make an agreement worthwhile. G prefers the status quo ($d = 1$) to an agreement with $a = n$. Hence, G chooses to stop negotiations.

To summarize, if $m > n$ or $d_G > (n + 1)/2$, there can be no agreement. If $m \leq n$ and $d_G \leq (n + 1)/2$, then there can be an agreement. The agreement value of deficit will be m if $d_G < m$, or it will be d_G or n, whichever is smaller:

$$a = \begin{cases} \{\max m, \min\{d_G, n\}\} & \text{if } m \geq n \text{ and } d_G \leq \dfrac{n + 1}{2} \\ \{\emptyset\} & \text{otherwise.} \end{cases}$$

Governments often claim that IMF austerity goes beyond their preferences. Note that this is the case when $a = n < d_G$. However, governments may make this claim to shirk the blame for their preferred policies. Since outsiders only observe a, it is unknown if a is set to the government's ideal point (d_G), or the maximum deficit the IMF will accept (n). To the degree that there is uncertainty, governments may get away with blaming the IMF.

The Decision to Turn to the IMF

Finally, consider the first node of the game tree in Figure 3.7. At the beginning of the game, G does not know the value of n (the negotiation posture of F) and must decide whether or not to approach F based on its knowledge of d_G (G's ideal point), s (sovereignty costs), r (rejection costs), m (the minimum acceptable deficit to V), and the probability distribution of n. Thus, G compares his expected utility of "approaching" to the utility of "not approaching" and chooses the better option.

The expected utility of approaching negotiations depends on which of four exogenous situations G may observe:

Situation I: $d_G < m$,

Situation II: (a) $d_G > m, d_G \leq 0.5$

(b) $d_G > m > 2d_G - 1, d_G > 0.5$,

Situation III: $m < 2d_G - 1 < d_G, d_G > 0.5$.

Given the situation, G determines the expected value of approaching IMF negotiations. The expected utility for not approaching is always: $U_G(\text{Not Approach}) = -|1 - d_G| = d_G - 1$. If G's expected utility of approaching negotiations is greater than the utility from not approaching, G approaches, gambling on the value of n. Otherwise, G does not approach.

The appendix to this chapter proves that in equilibrium there exists some d_G^* below which it is worthwhile for G to approach negotiations and above which it is not. Moreover, in equilibrium, the following holds:

1. The lower d_G, the more likely G is to benefit from approaching negotiations with F. In other words, the lower the ideal deficit of a government – relative to the status quo – the more likely the government will turn to the IMF. Although one cannot directly observe the preferences of a government,

one can expect this condition is more likely to hold as the deficit goes up. When the deficit is high, governments will be more likely to turn to the IMF to have fiscal discipline imposed.

2. The lower s, the more likely G is to benefit from approaching negotiations with F. A government is more likely to enter into an IMF agreement when the penalty associated with sacrificing sovereignty is low.

What determines the sovereignty penalty? Recall from the cases of Nigeria and Uruguay that the penalties from sacrificing sovereignty may be related to a country's history of IMF agreements. If a country has never in its history participated in an IMF agreement, the penalties for being the first government to do so are high. As a country signs more and more agreements, the penalties for a particular government signing decrease, since the government can argue that, as so many times in the past, the country has no choice. A government can also point to other countries around the world and argue that, like them, it too must submit to the IMF. Hence, the number of other countries around the world participating in IMF programs may also lower sovereignty penalties. Finally, the penalties for sacrificing sovereignty are most severe right before an election. Thus, one should expect governments to wait to sign IMF agreements until after elections.

3. The higher r, the more willing V becomes to accept an agreement (recall that higher r implies lower m). Consequently, G becomes more likely to approach F. Governments are more likely to enter into IMF agreements if rejection costs are high. The rejection cost depends on how much the country will be hurt by the negative signal sent to creditors and investors for failing to live up to IMF conditions. If a country has high debt, a negative signal may preclude a needed debt rescheduling. If investment is low, a negative signal may completely destroy the fragile confidence of investors. Thus, countries with high debt and low investment will be more sensitive to rejection costs and governments can hold this over opposition forces to push through their preferred policies.

4. A final implication of the game involves the negotiation posture of F. The higher the value of n, the more likely G will proceed with negotiations. In the model, the value of n is an exogenous parameter, but as stated above, n might depend on the budget constraint of F, or on the absolute size of the balance of payments deficit of a given country. The IMF is likely to pursue a tougher negotiation posture when it is close to its budget constraint and be more flexible when it has more resources available. The Fund is also likely to be tough in negotiations with small countries whose balance of payments deficits carry little weight in the world economy. It is likely to grant more concessions to countries with larger, more destabilizing balance of payments deficits. Thus, from the IMF point of view, agreements are more desirable with countries with large balance of payments deficits and when its budget constraint is not binding. The negotiation posture may also depend on the technocratic views of the Fund and thus be shaped by variables such as

foreign reserve position, budget deficit, debt, and investment rates. These different variables are tested to see if they matter to the IMF in Chapter 4.

EXTENSIONS

The value of n might also depend on the cost of negotiations to the IMF. Some executives may be more difficult for the IMF to negotiate with than others. Suppose the game is changed such that the IMF wants to impose the lowest deficit possible, but it does not know the minimum deficit that veto players will accept (F does not know how badly r will hurt V). If an executive claims in negotiations that the veto players will only accept a certain level of deficit, the IMF will not know if this is really the lowest acceptable deficit or if, in fact, it is the executive's own ideal level of deficit.

Executives who can point to more binding constraints (from V) can try to get more out of the Fund, claiming that domestic constituencies will not accept a tough agreement. The ability to play such a card may vary according to regime. As Schelling (1960: 28) argues: "the possibility of commitment . . . is by no means equally available; the ability of a democratic government to get itself tied by public opinion may be different from the ability of a totalitarian government to incur such a commitment." Accordingly, democracies can play this game more readily and make for more difficult negotiation partners. Thus, the IMF may prefer to sign agreements with dictatorships. As Bandow (1994: 26) argues, "the IMF has rarely met a dictatorship that it didn't like."

Note that if the IMF wants to negotiate for the agreement that is closest to its ideal point, the game presented in Figure 3.7 changes. In the simple game presented above, the IMF (F) does not push for the most austere agreement possible. It merely sets a maximum deficit it will accept. Similarly, the veto player (V) can merely "accept" or "reject" – there is no "amend" option to get an agreement that is closest to its ideal point.

A more realistic game would allow for these moves by F and V. This would complicate the already tedious math, so I have left the game as it stands. In a truly two-level setup, however, G would still be able to enter into an IMF arrangement to bring about the policy it prefers. G would have private information about V's preferences that F does not have and private information about F's negotiation posture that V does not have. The government could use this information to bind itself on both fronts to increase its bargaining leverage.[10] Thus, the main results of the game would hold.

But how could negotiations between G and F and between G and V take place under such asymmetric information? If G were to announce to F a

---

[10] This is precisely what Stiglitz (2000: 551) argues has occurred. Governments take advantage of informational asymmetries "both between themselves and the citizenry and between the international aid community and themselves."

certain minimum deficit that V will accept, this signal would not be credible. F would believe that G is merely announcing its own ideal point. Similarly, if G were to announce to V the maximum deficit that F will accept, V would not believe it, thinking that G is merely announcing its own ideal point.

Can information be transmitted in such "cheap talk" situations? Crawford and Sobel (1982) show in their seminal piece, "Strategic Information Transmission," that it can. Although a precise signal of the minimum deficit that V will accept reveals no information, G can send a "noisy" signal of "high" or "low" to F which is credible and transmits some information.

The intuition is the following: With no information transmitted, F only knows the probability distribution of the minimum deficit which V will accept (denoted by m). If m is distributed uniformly over the [0,1] interval, then F's best guess of the value of m is 0.5.

If G tells F the precise value of m, F will believe that G is merely revealing its own ideal point, and F will gain no new information. However, F knows that while G's ideal point is higher than F's own, G still wants to negotiate an agreement that will be accepted by V and will successfully lower the deficit. Thus, depending on the configuration of F's and G's preferences, G may be able to signal to F that m is either in the range 0 to 0.5 or in the range 0.5 to 1. If the former, F will update its beliefs about the value of m and estimate it at 0.25. If the latter, F's best guess becomes 0.75. Again, depending on the configuration of F's and G's preferences, both actors may be made better off by F choosing to set the deficit at 0.25 or 0.75, rather than F setting the deficit at 0.5. If F and G have preferences that are close together, then more refined signals can be sent ("high," "medium," and "low," etc.).

Thus, some information can be shared in such "cheap talk" settings. If V had the option of "amending" the agreement of the deficit, V might choose a deficit that is too high and F would cancel the agreement. V and G would have to accept painful rejection costs. Thus, if V could "amend," G would play a "cheap talk" game with V so that both could be better off than V's guessing too high a value of n and incurring rejection costs.[11]

Thus, under certain configurations of preferences and values for s and r, the results of the original game would hold even with these extensions. A government could use an IMF agreement to push through economic reforms that otherwise would not be accepted by domestic constituencies.

WHY DO AGREEMENTS CONTINUE?

When a government enters into a Stand-by Arrangement (SBA), the program is designed to last twelve to eighteen months. Other types of conditioned

---

[11] Note one significant change to my original game for the Crawford and Sobel setup to work between G and V: V would have to know what G's ideal point is. For more details, see Crawford and Sobel (1982).

arrangements (EFF, SAF, or ESAF) are supposed to cover one to three (or at most four) years. But such time limits are arbitrary. Once an agreement expires, countries usually enter into a consecutive arrangement to extend the program. An average stint under IMF agreements lasts about five years, and often they last much longer. During the period from 1960 to 1990, Bolivia, Costa Rica, Jamaica, Kenya, Liberia, Madagascar, Morocco, Paraguay, Senegal, South Korea, Togo, Turkey, Uruguay, Zaire, and Zambia remained under consecutive IMF agreements for more than ten years. Colombia, El Salvador, Guyana, Peru, and Yugoslavia remained in agreements for more than fifteen years straight. Haiti and Panama stayed under IMF agreements for twenty years.

Why do governments and the IMF typically sign consecutive agreements? The reason that the Fund wants to keep countries under agreements seems straightforward according to the Vaubel argument. To the extent that the Fund wants to maximize its budget, it wants to keep all countries under agreement (Vaubel 1986, 1991). Note that the budget constraint the Fund faces is a soft one: The more resources it uses, the more it can demand from its members through increased contributions. If the Fund does not keep countries under agreements, staffers cannot justify increasing their budgets.

Of course, the Fund must justify the loans it extends. Note, however, that there are several layers of principal-agent problems which present enormous informational asymmetries. IMF staffers are the agents of the Managing Director, who is the agent of an Executive Board, and each member of the board is the agent of at least one member country. At each of these levels, accountability may be weakened (see Stiglitz 1994, Macho-Stadler and Perez-Castrillo 1997, and Laffont and Tirole 1994 for formal arguments of how principal-agent problems allow for rent seeking on the part of agents). This may explain why the Fund can sign agreements such as the 1990 arrangement with Uruguay, where the country did not seem to meet the formal requirements. Nevertheless, to the extent that the Fund is accountable to its funders, one would expect it to continue agreements with countries that have persisting balance of payments problems. Thus, the IMF may continue agreements with countries that continue poor economic performance.

Why do governments continue? Once an IMF arrangement is in place, a government has already paid sovereignty costs, so the government may prefer to continue agreements with the Fund to maintain conditionality. Otherwise the political forces in favor of high government consumption may once again drive up the budget deficit.

Staying under IMF agreements may involve penalties as well, however. Recall from the above game that the veto players do not observe if the deficit set by the IMF agreement is above or below the ideal point of the executive. Sometimes the executive gets its ideal point, and sometimes the IMF imposes a lower deficit than the executive would like. If the population trusts that the executive should be following IMF policies, it may tolerate continued agreements. If the executive does not enjoy the trust of the population, however, it may risk resistance to continued participation. Under these circumstances, the executive may allow IMF arrangements to expire.[12]

The executive or the IMF may also allow an arrangement to expire if the conditions demanded are two harsh. Recall from the game that sometimes the executive negotiates for conditions that match his ideal point, but sometimes the IMF demands more reform than the executive would like. If the executive does not have the political will to follow through with harsh demands, he or the IMF may discontinue participation.

Any time a country leaves the IMF, however, it faces rejection costs. If many countries are participating in IMF agreements, a country that unilaterally abandons the Fund may appear to lack the political will necessary to continue agreements. Suppose there are no other countries participating in IMF agreements. Leaving the IMF may not be particularly costly. But if many countries around the world are currently cooperating with the Fund under the auspices of an official program, then it may be costly for an individual government to defect on the IMF. Thus, one might observe countries ending spells of IMF agreements in groups or when no other countries are participating (as in the early years of the IMF). Otherwise, one should expect agreements to continue.

CONCLUSION

The implications of the formal work in this chapter are consistent with the evidence presented in Chapter 2. The formal models point to three intuitive implications. The first is that the greater the discrepancy between the status quo and the executive's ideal level of budget deficit, the more the executive has to gain from negotiating with the IMF. Second, the higher the sovereignty costs for the executive, the less incentive it has to negotiate with the IMF. Finally, when a country is more dependent on investors and creditors, and the costs of rejecting the IMF are high, the executive has more to gain by bringing in the IMF because domestic constituencies are in no position to reject whatever agreement it works out.

The implication about sovereignty costs is evident in a number of cases. On the one hand, Nigeria did not enter into an IMF agreement in the early 1980s because sovereignty penalties were high: It had never had an agreement in its history and elections were right around the corner. Tanzania also avoided signing its first IMF agreement. Only when economic problems persisted did it accept one with weak conditions. Uruguay, on the other hand, signed its first agreement early in Fund history, before sovereignty penalties had become apparent – it was during this period that the Fund's

---

[12] I address how one can capture the effects of something unobservable like "trust" in Chapter 5.

primary activities involved monitoring exchange rates. Subsequently, IMF agreements became business as usual in Uruguay.

Chapter 2 presented anecdotal evidence supporting the implications of the formal model. The next chapter completes the work on selection, testing whether this anecdotal evidence holds up systematically. In this way, one can see whether or not this story is generalizable.

APPENDIX: THE DECISION OF THE EXECUTIVE
UNDER UNCERTAINTY

G must decide whether or not to approach F (and pay cost s) without observing value of n. The expected utility of approaching negotiations depends on which of four situations G observes. Given the situation, G determines the expected value of approaching IMF negotiations. If G's expected utility of approaching negotiations is less than the utility from not approaching, U_G (Not Approach) $= d_G - 1$, G does not attempt to bring F into negotiations. Otherwise, G approaches.

Situation I

In Situation I, d_G is less than or equal to m. Though G does not know the value of n at the beginning of the game, once n is observed, G will proceed with negotiations only if $n \geq m$. If $n < m$, G will not proceed. Thus, G's expected utility from approaching negotiations can be calculated according to the diagram of Situation I in Figure 3.9.

If n lies between 0 and m, no agreement is possible because the maximum deficit F will accept is less than the minimum deficit V will accept. Because n is assumed to be uniformly distributed over $[0,1]$, the probability that $n < m$ is m: $\Pr(n < m) = m$. When this happens, G will opt for Outcome (3) and obtain utility $U_G = -|1 - d_G| - s = d_G - 1 - s$. If n lies between m and 1, F and V are both willing to accept a deficit equal to m. Since there is no other value of deficit acceptable to V that is closer to G's ideal point of d_G, G will negotiate for an IMF package with $d = m$, and V will accept it. The outcome of the game will be (1), and G will receive $U_G = -|m - d_G| - s = d_G - m - s$. The probability that this will transpire is $\Pr(n \geq m) = 1 - m$.

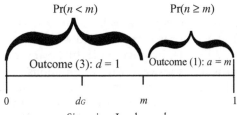

FIGURE 3.9. Situation I, where $d_G < m$

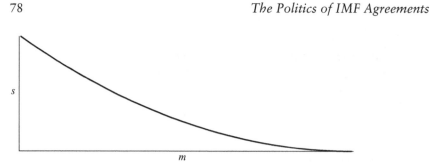

FIGURE 3.10. In Situation I, G "approaches" for values of m and s below this curve

Thus G's expected utility from approaching negotiations in Situation I is

$$E^I(U_G) = \int_0^m (d_G - 1 - s)dn + \int_m^1 (d_G - m - s)dn.$$

G approaches negotiations only if $E^I(U_G) \geq U_G$ (Not Approach), which holds when: $s \leq (1 - m)^2$. In this situation, if sovereignty costs are too high with respect to the minimum deficit that V will accept, it is not worth the risk for G to approach F. Note, however, that if there are no sovereignty costs at all $(s = 0)$, then G will always approach F. Intuitively, this is because without sovereignty costs, G loses nothing by observing n, and there is some possibility that n will be high enough to get V to accept an agreement. If, on the other hand, sovereignty costs are at their maximum $(s = 1)$, then G will never approach negotiations. As rejection costs go up and m goes down, G is more likely to approach F. The shape of the relationship between m and s is illustrated in Figure 3.10.

Situation II

In Situation II (a), d_G is again less than or equal to 0.5, so G will proceed with negotiations provided $n \geq m$. Unlike in Situation I, however, d_G is greater than m. G wants a lower deficit than V, but the costs of rejecting an agreement (r) are high enough that the minimum deficit V will accept is actually less than the ideal deficit of G: $m < d_G$. Thus, the agreement value of deficit (a) will not be set to m, rather it will be set to either n or d_G. G's expected utility from approaching negotiations in Situation II (a) is illustrated in Figure 3.11.

In Situation II (b), d_G is still greater than m but d_G is less than 0.5. Thus, there are values of n for which G would not want to proceed with negotiations even if V were willing (if $n < 2d_G - 1$). In Situation II (b), however, m is greater than $2d_G - 1$. Hence, G will not proceed with negotiations even when n is greater than $2d_G - 1$, that is, unless n is also greater than m. In Figure 3.12, G's expected utility from approaching negotiations in Situation II (b) is illustrated to have the same relevant regions as Situation II (a).

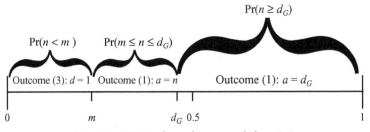

FIGURE 3.11. Situation II (a), where $d_G > m$ and $d_G \leq 0.5$

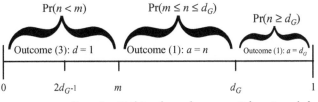

FIGURE 3.12. Situation II (b), where $d_G > m > 2d_G - 1$ and $d_G > 0.5$

In both Situation II (a) and (b), since n is distributed uniformly over its domain, the probability that n is less than m is simply m. When this occurs, there can be no agreement and deficit remains at the status quo ($d = 1$). The probability that n lies between m and d_G is ($d_G - m$). An n in this range results in an agreement with $a = n$. The probability that n is greater than d_G is $1 - d_G$. An n of this magnitude will allow G to set the agreement value of deficit to its ideal point: $a = d_G$.

G's expected value of approaching negotiations in Situation II is therefore

$$E^{II}(U_G) = \int_0^m (d_G - 1 - s)dn + \int_m^{d_G} (n - d_G - s)dn + \int_{d_G}^1 (-s)dn.$$

Again, as above, G will approach negotiations under Situation II if $E^{II}(U_G) \geq U_G$ (Not Approach), which holds when $s \leq \frac{1}{2}(2 - 2d_G - d_G^2 - 2m + 4d_G m - m^2)$. As this is a complicated expression, consider some specific points of reference. Suppose Situation II (a) is the case. If G is extremely conservative and has an ideal point just above 0, say $d_G = \varepsilon$ (where ε is infinitesimally greater than 0), and rejection costs are high enough that $m = 0$. Then G will approach negotiations provided that $s \leq 1 - \varepsilon - \frac{1}{2}\varepsilon^2 \Rightarrow s < 1$. If G is not so conservative, say $d_G = 0.49$, and $m = 0$, then sovereignty costs must be lower, $s < 0.39$, for G to approach negotiations. And if rejection costs are lower, such that $m = 0.48$, then sovereignty costs must be lower still, $s < 0.27$, for G to approach negotiations.

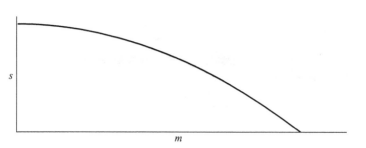

FIGURE 3.13 a. In Situation II, G "approaches" for values of m and s below this curve

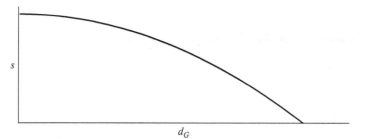

FIGURE 3.13 b. In Situation II, G "approaches" for values of d_G and s below this curve

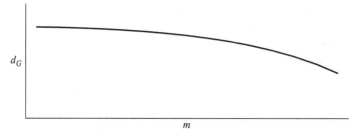

FIGURE 3.13 c. In Situation II, G "approaches" for values of m and d_G below this curve

Suppose Situation II (b) is the case, and $d_G = 0.75 + \varepsilon$ with rejection costs that are low enough to make $m = 0.75$. Then sovereignty costs must be low, $s < 0.06$, for G to approach negotiations. As one moves toward a less conservative G and a less accepting V, sovereignty costs must be practically equal to zero for G to gamble on approaching negotiations. For example, if $d_G = 0.95 + \varepsilon$ and $m = 0.95$, then there must be $s < 0.004$ for G to approach. Furthermore, if sovereignty costs are as high as possible, $s = 1$, even if V will accept any value for deficit ($m = 0$), there are no values of $d_G > 0.5$ which will satisfy this condition. If sovereignty costs are high enough, G will never approach F. Figures 3.13a, b, and c illustrate the relationship between m and s, d_G and s, and m and d_G for Situation II.

Situation III

In Situation III, d_G is situated as it is in Situation II (b): d_G is greater than m and greater than 0.5. However, unlike in Situation II (b), m is less than $2d_G - 1$. This implies that rejection costs are high enough that V will accept some levels of deficit that G will reject. If n is too low, G will prefer to stay with the status quo $(d = 1)$ rather than sign an agreement with $a = n$. G's expected utility in this situation can be illustrated as in Figure 3.14.

If n is less than $2d_G - 1$, G prefers to stop negotiations and keep $d = 1$. The probability of this is equal to $2d_G - 1$. If n is between $2d_G - 1$ and d_G, G will enter into an agreement with $a = n$. The probability of this is $d_G - (2d_G - 1)$. Finally, if n is greater than d_G, G will negotiate for an agreement with $a = d_G$. The probability of this is $1 - d_G$. One can therefore calculate G's expected value for approaching negotiations in Situation III as:

$$E^{III}(U_G) = \int_0^{2d_G-1} (d_G - 1 - s)dn + \int_{2d_G-1}^{d_G} (n - d_G - s)dn + \int_{d_G}^1 (-s)dn.$$

G will approach negotiations if $E^{III}(U_G) \geq U_G$ (Not Approach), which holds if $s \leq \frac{3}{2}(d_G - 1)^2$. Note that in Situation III, $d_G > 0.5$. So when G is at

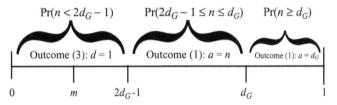

FIGURE 3.14. Situation III, where $m < 2d_G - 1 < d_G$ and $d_G > 0.5$

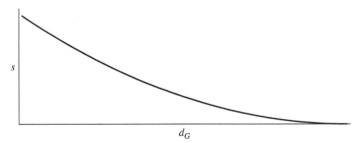

FIGURE 3.15. In Situation III, G "approaches" for values of d_G and s below this curve

its lowest for this situation, $d_G = 0.5 + \varepsilon$, it must be true that $s < 0.375$ for G to approach F. In Situation III, therefore, G will never approach negotiations if s is greater than 0.375. Also note that in Situation III only, the value of m is unimportant for G's decision. This is because in this situation $m < 2d_G - 1$ (r is sufficiently high). In general, for the relevant ranges of this situation, the lower s and the lower d_G, the more likely G will approach F. Figure 3.15 illustrates the relationship between d_G and s.

4

Testing the Selection Story

The following predictions are generated in Chapter 3: Governments turn to the Fund when their foreign reserve position is weak and they need an IMF loan; they also enter into arrangements when they want conditions to be imposed upon them, subject to sovereignty costs and rejection costs. They are more likely to enter when sovereignty costs are low and rejection costs are high. Governments continue participation in agreements if rejection costs remain high – if other countries are participating. Regarding the decision of the Fund, it is shaped by technocratic and bureaucratic concerns. The Fund is more likely to conclude agreements with countries that have large, destabilizing balance of payments deficits, and more likely to sign agreements when the budget constraint is less binding.

This story is consistent with the anecdotal evidence presented in Chapter 2, but it may apply more generally. To the extent that governments and the IMF enter into agreements according to some systematic patterns, selection is not random. And if selection is not random, then one must control for the possible effects that selection may have on economic growth when estimating the effects of IMF programs. Thus, the task of this chapter is to use a statistical model to test the story of participation in IMF programs to see whether the story applies in general. Results can then be used to control for selection effects in subsequent chapters.

Testing to see which variables drive selection into IMF programs is tricky. It is not merely a matter of measuring correlations between variables – whether the value of, say, *debt service* is high or low when countries are participating or not participating in IMF programs. The decision-making process of selection involves at least two separate actors (the government and the IMF), making at least two separate decisions (entering and continuing IMF programs). A complete test of the selection story requires a statistical model consistent with this decision-making setting. Thus, before turning to which variables best capture the elements of the story laid out in Chapter 3, one must build the appropriate statistical model to test the story.[1] This is the first task of this chapter. Following this, I describe the variables used to capture the different elements of the selection story: the need for an IMF loan, the desire for IMF conditions, rejection costs, sovereignty costs, and technocratic and bureaucratic goals of the IMF. The chapter concludes by presenting statistical tests of the selection story.

A STATISTICAL MODEL OF BILATERAL COOPERATION

The statistical model described in this section has a ponderous title: "dynamic bivariate probit with partial observability."[2] Each word, however, has an intuitive interpretation relating to the process of participation in IMF programs. Consider them word by word.

The model is "dynamic" because participation in IMF programs changes over time. Participation involves the decision to enter or not enter an agreement, and also involves the decision to remain under IMF arrangements or terminate participation. I argue that the determinants of these decisions may be different. By using a dynamic statistical test, I can identify not only the factors that matter for the decisions to enter into agreements, but also the factors that determine why participation continues or not.

The model is called "bivariate" because two sets of variables determine participation. An IMF arrangement is a joint decision between a government and the Fund. The analytical models in the previous chapter indicated that some factors matter to the government, whereas other factors influence the decision of the IMF. The bivariate aspect of the statistical model allows one to identify the effects of variables which matter to each actor, the government and the IMF, separately.

Thus, the statistical model addresses four separate questions:

1. Why does the government decide to seek an agreement?
2. Why does the IMF decide to seek an agreement?
3. Why does the government decide to terminate an agreement?
4. Why does the IMF decide to terminate an agreement?

Note that one does not usually observe the individual decisions of the government and the IMF. Even though there has been a move toward greater "transparency" at the Fund, arrangements are negotiated behind closed doors. This is why the statistical model must be "with partial observability."

---

[1] Context-specific statistical models are becoming more common in political science. For an excellent approach to this kind of statistical modeling, see Signorino (1999). Also see Smith (1996, 1999) and Reed (2000).

[2] This model was originally developed by Przeworski and Vreeland (2002). It combines approaches developed by Poirier (1980) and Amemiya (1985).

		Participation in IMF agreement at time t?	
		No$_t$	*Yes$_t$*
Participation in IMF agreement at time t–1?	*No$_{t-1}$*	Pr(not enter)	Pr(enter)
	Yes$_{t-1}$	Pr(not continue)	Pr(continue)

Pr(enter) = Φ (government variables) * Φ (IMF variables)

Pr(not enter) = 1 – Pr(enter)

Pr(continue) = Ψ (government variables) * Ψ (IMF variables)

Pr(not continue) = 1 – Pr(continue)

FIGURE 4.1. Illustration of dynamic bivariate probit model with partial observability

Ideally, one would have two sets of dependent variables: one for the government and one for the IMF. One could code them "1" if the actor wanted an IMF agreement, and "0" otherwise. Unfortunately, all one observes is participation, coded "1" if both actors have entered into an agreement, and "0" otherwise. When one observes "0," one does not know which actor – perhaps both – did not want the agreement.

One can get around this problem by estimating the probability that a country enters an agreement as the joint probability that the government wants the agreement and the IMF wants the agreement.[3] Obviously when an agreement is signed, both parties wanted it; otherwise at least one of them would not have signed. The probability that a country does not enter an agreement is simply estimated as the complement of the probability that it enters to 1. Similarly, the probability that a country continues participation is estimated as the joint probability that the government wants to continue and the IMF wants to continue. The probability that the agreement is terminated is the complement of the probability that it continues to 1. Thus, one can identify the determinants of the individual decisions of the government and the IMF solely on the basis of the observations of whether or not an agreement is in force.

The intuition behind the statistical model is the following: It takes two parties, the government and the IMF, for an agreement and the deal can be broken by either party. Thus, we take a pair of probits, where having an agreement means that the latent variable associated with both parties is positive. To distinguish between the decisions to enter into an agreement and the decisions to remain, the latent equations have a hierarchical structure indicating whether or not an IMF agreement was in force in the previous year. Figure 4.1 illustrates how the model works.

[3] This follows Abowd and Farber (1982) who follow Poirier (1980).

In sum, the statistical model involves four simple joint probabilities, two for observations of participation and two for observations of nonparticipation.

For countries not participating,

1. The probability that the country enters an agreement: the joint probability that both the government and the IMF want the agreement, given that the country is not currently under an agreement.
2. The probability that the country does not enter an agreement: the complement of the above to 1.

For countries participating,

3. The probability that the country remains under an agreement: the joint probability that both the government and the IMF want to continue.
4. The probability that the country ends participation: the complement of the above to 1.

Each of these probabilities is modeled as a joint decision. For example, the probability of a country entering into an agreement is a function of the probability that the government wants to enter and the probability that the IMF wants to enter. Thus, these probabilities are estimated according to two separate vectors (or lists) of variables, one consisting of variables that matter to governments and the other consisting of variables that matter to the IMF. The statistical model identifies the influence of the variables determining the government's decision to enter an agreement (or not), as well as the effects of variables influencing the government's decision to remain under agreements (or not). Similarly, it identifies the influence of the variables that matter to the IMF when signing an agreement, and the effects of variables that matter to the IMF when terminating them.

Note that if one includes the exact same set of variables for both actors, one cannot distinguish between the two actors, and the model is not identified. To identify the model it is sufficient in principle that at least one variable not be in common between the two actors. As long as at least one variable is assigned to the IMF that is not assigned to the government (or vice versa), the model can be identified. Hence, a strong prior belief that a single variable belongs to one actor and not the other is required to identify the parameters.

In all applications below, I assume that the IMF is the actor that cares about world economic stability. The mandate of the IMF includes maintaining global financial stability, so the IMF may give special attention to countries with large balance of payments problems in absolute terms, whereas governments care about the relative size of a foreign exchange crisis. Thus, I identify the model by assigning to the IMF the variable measuring balance of payments deficit weighted by the economic size of a country. All other variables are assigned to both actors.

FILLING IN THE STORY

The above statistical model reflects the process of participation in IMF programs as a dynamic one involving the decisions of two separate actors. With this model, I can use the information presented about the determinants of IMF agreements in Chapters 2 and 3 to fill in the vectors of variables that matter to the government and the IMF.

For the government, the following has been argued: Some governments seek agreements when they need foreign exchange. Thus, I expect governments to turn to the IMF when their foreign reserves (RESERVES) are low. Some governments bring in the IMF to have the specific condition of fiscal discipline imposed. This gives them the political muscle to push through unpopular spending cuts. One cannot strictly observe the government's ideal budget balance. This unobserved variable may be correlated with "political will" (such unobserved variables are addressed in the following chapter). Note, however, that the deficit is more likely to have surpassed the government's ideal point when the budget balance (BUDGET BALANCE) is low (when the budget deficit is high).

This strategy of bringing in the Fund for conditionality is effective only if the cost of rejecting the IMF is high. The cost of rejecting the IMF is that it sends a negative signal out to creditors and investors. A country particularly sensitive to the decisions of creditors and investors will face higher "rejection costs" from creditors and investors. Thus, I expect governments to bring in the Fund when debt (DEBT SERVICE) is high – when they are sensitive to the decisions of creditors – and when investment (INVESTMENT) is low – when they are sensitive to the decisions of investors.

Signing an IMF agreement is also costly to the government that does so, however, since it faces what I have called "sovereignty costs" for selling out the national patrimony. Sovereignty costs are highest in countries that have never participated in an IMF program, and they are reduced when a country has an extensive history of IMF programs (YEARS UNDER) and when many other countries are under IMF programs (NUMBER UNDER). This variable may also determine why governments continue agreements. I argue in Chapter 2 that it may be costly for governments to leave an IMF program when many other countries are participating. Hence, they may choose to leave only if other countries do so.[4] The sovereignty costs are also highest

---

[4] Similarly, Simmons (2000) argues that government compliance with IMF Article VIII – which requires governments to "keep their current account free from restriction" – increases as the number of other countries in the world and in the region also comply with Article VIII.

TABLE 4.1. *Government objectives*

Objective	Variable
Loan:	RESERVES
Conditions:	BUDGET BALANCE
Rejection costs:	DEBT SERVICE
	INVESTMENT
Sovereignty costs:	YEARS UNDER
	NUMBER UNDER
	LAGGED ELECTION

TABLE 4.2. *IMF objectives*

Objective	Variable
Mandate:	BOP × SIZE
Budget:	NUMBER UNDER
Negotiation costs:	REGIME

before elections, so one expects governments to wait to sign agreements until after elections (LAGGED ELECTION). Table 4.1 summarizes the variables used to approximate the objectives of the government.

Turning to the decision of the IMF, I argue the following: The negotiation posture of the IMF changes toward different countries at different times. In fulfillment of its mandate to maintain world financial stability, the Fund seeks out countries with large, destabilizing balance of payments deficits in absolute terms (BOP × SIZE).

The negotiation posture also depends on the budget constraint of the Fund. I expect the IMF to sign more agreements when its budget constraint (NUMBER UNDER) is less binding and to sign fewer agreements as it approaches the limit of the budget. The IMF may have a flexible constraint, as it can always lobby its members to increase their contributions, but at any given time, the Fund faces a limit to its resources.

Finally, the IMF may have more difficulty negotiating with democracies and thus may prefer to sign with dictatorships. Recall that "the ability of a democratic government to get itself tied by public opinion may be different from the ability of a totalitarian government to incur such a commitment" (Schelling 1960: 28). Dictatorships may more readily commit to harsher conditions and face fewer impediments to carrying them out. Thus, as we saw Bandow (1994: 26) claim, "the IMF has rarely met a dictatorship that it didn't like." Table 4.2 depicts the variables used to approximate the objectives of the IMF.

Regarding the decision of the IMF to continue agreements, I argue in Chapter 2 that the Fund may prefer to keep as many countries under agreement as possible to justify demands for greater member contributions. As long as a country has a balance of payments problem, the Fund can argue that the program should continue.

In sum, the government cares about foreign reserves, the budget balance, debt, investment, its history with IMF programs, other countries, and elections. The IMF cares about the balance of payments, the budget constraint, and regime. I use the following variables as proxies for these determinants of participation:

RESERVES is measured as the average annual level of foreign reserves in terms of monthly import requirements (*World Development Indicators*). BUDGET BALANCE is measured as government budget surplus as a proportion of GDP (*World Development Indicators*). DEBT SERVICE is measured as total debt service as a proportion of GDP (*World Development Indicators*). INVESTMENT is measured as real gross domestic investment (private and public) as a proportion of GDP (*Penn World Tables 5.6*). LAGGED ELECTION is a dummy variable coded 1 if the previous year was a legislative election year, and 0 otherwise (Przeworski et al. 2000). YEARS UNDER is the sum of past years a country has spent participating in IMF agreements. NUMBER UNDER is the number of other countries currently participating in an IMF arrangement for a given year. I also use this variable for the IMF *budget constraint*. If one could include an actual measure of the IMF budget constraint, one might get a better picture, but the IMF keeps such information secret. I use NUMBER UNDER as a rough proxy for the budget constraint with the intuition that as the number of countries under agreements grows, the budget is increasingly constrained. BOP × SIZE is the overall balance of payments as a proportion of GDP weighted by the economic "size" of the country measured as GDP in millions of constant 1987 dollars (*World Development Indicators*). Finally, REGIME is a dummy variable coded 1 for dictatorships and 0 for democracies (Przeworski et al. 2000).

The vectors of variables that matter to the government and the IMF, respectively, are thus:

$$x^G = \text{CONSTANT, RESERVES, BUDGET BALANCE, DEBT SERVICE,}$$
$$\text{INVESTMENT, YEARS UNDER, NUMBER UNDER, LAGGED ELECTION,}$$
$$x^F = \text{CONSTANT, BOP} \times \text{SIZE, NUMBER UNDER, REGIME.}$$

THE RESULTS

Data for the "full" selection model which uses all the variables described above include 1,024 country-year observations. I use the statistical model of bilateral cooperation to analyze these data.

Table 4.3 presents four sets of results: (1) the effects of the variables influencing the government's decision to enter an IMF program, (2) the effects

Testing the Selection Story

TABLE 4.3. *Determinants of participation in IMF programs*

| | Government | | |
Variable	Decision to Enter	Decision to Remain	Mean[†]
CONSTANT	−2.27**	−0.01	1.00
	(0.61)	(0.59)	
RESERVES	−0.83**	−0.26	3.01
	(0.42)	(0.48)	
BUDGET BALANCE	−0.95**	−0.29	−6.22
	(0.28)	(0.33)	
DEBT SERVICE	1.38**	0.65	5.15
	(0.52)	(0.68)	
INVESTMENT	−6.06**	−0.17	13.35
	(1.79)	(1.92)	
YEARS UNDER	0.36*	−0.36	6.91
	(0.21)	(0.27)	
NUMBER UNDER	0.44**	0.38**	36.70
	(0.18)	(0.19)	
LAGGED ELECTION	0.87**	−0.01	0.19
	(0.29)	(0.35)	

| | IMF | | |
Variable	Decision to Enter	Decision to Remain	Mean[†]
CONSTANT	2.14*	2.84	1.00
	(1.24)	(2.02)	
BOP × SIZE	−0.91**	−0.41*	−120.00
	(0.37)	(0.23)	
NUMBER UNDER	−0.73**	−0.39	36.70
	(0.27)	(0.43)	
REGIME	0.43*	0.33	0.74
	(0.26)	(0.27)	

Number of observations:	1024
Correctly predicted:	86%
Log likelihood function:	−355.77
Restricted log likelihood:	−705.46
Chi-squared:	699.39

* Indicates significance at the 90% level.
** Indicates significance at the 95% level.
† To facilitate convergence of the model, the variables have been divided by powers of 10 so that they are all of the same order of magnitude. Thus, RESERVES, BUDGET BALANCE, DEBT SERVICE, YEARS UNDER, and NUMBER UNDER were divided by 10; INVESTMENT was divided by 100; and BOP × SIZE (already measured in millions of 1987 dollars) was divided by 1000. This is true of all specifications in this chapter.
Note: Standard errors in parentheses. All variables are lagged one year.

of the variables influencing the government's decision to remain in an IMF program, (3) the effect of the variables influencing the IMF's decision to enter into an agreement, and (4) the effect of the variables influencing the IMF's decision to keep a country under an agreement.[5]

All the variables included in this specification have the expected effects on the decision of the government to enter into arrangements. RESERVES has a significant negative effect on the probability that the government will enter into an IMF agreement. Governments are more likely to participate in IMF arrangements when foreign reserves are low. Hence, governments seek IMF programs when they need an IMF loan.

BUDGET BALANCE has a significant negative effect on a government's decision to enter. A government facing a large budget deficit is more likely to turn to the Fund. Governments which spend more than they collect enter into IMF arrangements and have fiscal discipline imposed upon them. Hence, governments also seek IMF programs when they want IMF conditions.

Other economic conditions also have significant effects on the government's decision. Rejection costs matter: When DEBT SERVICE is high, a government is more likely to enter an IMF arrangement. And governments typically turn to the IMF when INVESTMENT is low. Hence, governments turn to the IMF when they are sensitive to the decisions of creditors and investors. This is because rejection costs are high and a government can more effectively use the IMF to push through economic reform when a country is vulnerable to creditors and investors.

Sovereignty costs also influence the decision of a government. When YEARS UNDER is high, the government is likely to turn to the IMF. NUMBER UNDER also has a borderline significant positive effect on the government's decision. When many countries are participating, a government is more likely to enter into an IMF program. The last variable which affects the government's decision to enter agreements is LAGGED ELECTION. As expected, governments are more likely to enter agreements early on in their electoral terms, after elections.

The effect of the above variables on the government's decision to remain under agreements is surprising. None of the economic variables matters. The only variable which has a significant effect on the government's decision to continue participation in an IMF agreement is NUMBER UNDER. It has a positive effect. Thus, when many other countries have IMF arrangements, a government is more likely to continue its own participation in an IMF program.[6]

---

[5] To facilitate convergence of the model, the variables have been divided by powers of ten so that they are all of the same order of magnitude. This is true of all specifications in this chapter.

[6] For further research on the duration of IMF agreements, see Joyce (2001).

The variables influencing the decision of the IMF to enter into an arrangement have the expected effects. BOP × SIZE has a significant negative effect on the decision of the Fund to sign an agreement with a country. The IMF is more likely to enter into arrangements with countries that have low balance of payments. Thus, the Fund wants to sign agreements with countries with large, destabilizing balance of payments deficits, in accordance with its mandate to maintain world financial stability.

NUMBER UNDER, the number of countries around the world participating in IMF programs, also matters to the IMF, but in the opposite way that it does to the government. When NUMBER UNDER is high, the IMF is less likely to sign an additional country. I take this to be the effect of the IMF's budget constraint. As more and more countries participate in programs, the IMF has fewer resources left for more agreements. Increasing NUMBER UNDER brings the IMF closer to its budget constraint. Hence, NUMBER UNDER has a negative effect on the IMF's decision.

The REGIME variable has a significant positive effect on the decision of the IMF to enter an arrangement with a country. Since this variable is coded 1 for dictatorships, the coefficient on this variable indicates that the IMF is more likely to sign with dictatorships than with democracies. This finding is consistent with Schelling's conjecture that the costs of negotiating with democracies are higher than with dictatorships.

Turning to the decision of the Fund to continue programs with countries, the only variable that matters is BOP × SIZE. This is not surprising. Once negotiations have been concluded, a loan has been earmarked for a country and negotiation costs have been met. Thus, NUMBER UNDER and REGIME are not significant for the continuation of a program. Once a country is participating in a program, what matters to the IMF is whether or not a destabilizing balance of payments deficit persists. The Fund is more likely to continue with countries that have large balance of payments deficits in absolute terms.

Statistical tests can indicate if a story is plausible or consistent with the data. These results indicate that the story of participation constructed in the previous chapters plausibly holds over a large number of cases. Governments may turn to the IMF for a loan and to have conditions imposed, subject to rejection costs and sovereignty costs. The IMF may seek to maintain world financial stability and to maximize its budget.

Statistical tests can also help to rule out some alternative stories. Some variables can be shown not to have a significant relationship with participation in IMF programs. For example, in this specification, no other variables I tested affected the decisions of *governments* to enter or continue participation: TERMS OF TRADE, BOP × SIZE, CURRENT ACCOUNT, INFLATION, FOREIGN DIRECT INVESTMENT, EXPORTS (as a capacity to import), EXCHANGE RATE, PER CAPITA INCOME, WORLD PER CAPITA INCOME GROWTH, OUTPUT GROWTH, CAPITAL STOCK GROWTH, LABOR FORCE GROWTH, and a dummy variable for post-1982 years. I also tested other variables for the *IMF* and found they were not significant in this specification: TERMS OF TRADE, CURRENT ACCOUNT, INFLATION, DEBT, FOREIGN DIRECT INVESTMENT, EXPORTS, EXCHANGE RATE, PER CAPITA INCOME, WORLD ECONOMIC GROWTH, CAPITAL STOCK GROWTH, LABOR FORCE GROWTH, and the post-1982 dummy variable.

This does not imply, however, that the story tested in Table 4.3 is the only story consistent with the data. When using a statistical model of bilateral co-operation, not only can one add new variables to test, one can also rearrange the variables assigning them to the two different actors. In the following section, I reassign the variables above, keeping only the variable BOP × SIZE as a consistent part of the objectives of the IMF to identify the models. The results are intriguing and lend more confidence to the view that governments turning to the IMF do so when they want conditions to be imposed.

LOANS VERSUS CONDITIONS

The results presented in Table 4.3 indicate that a story where governments care about their foreign reserves position as well as fiscal deficits, while the IMF cares about balance of payments problems on a global scale, is consistent with the available data. Suppose, however, that one wants to spell out the technocratic concerns of the IMF in more detail. I suspect that in addition to a concern for the overall size of a balance of payments problem, the IMF also cares about the relative foreign reserve position of individual countries. Hence, I assign RESERVES to both the government and the IMF. Consider the results presented in Specification 4.4a of Table 4.4.

Most of the results presented in Specification 4.4a are consistent with the results from Table 4.3. What is particularly interesting, however, is that when RESERVES is included for the government *and* the IMF, it is significant only for the IMF. This finding supports the "tipping the balance" story of why governments turn to the IMF: Governments turn to the IMF for political leverage to help reduce the deficit, regardless of their foreign reserve position; the IMF enters into agreements with the ones with the lowest foreign reserves.

To test how strong this pattern is, I include RESERVES and BUDGET BALANCE for both actors. Specification 4.4b of the same table presents the results. When RESERVES and BUDGET BALANCE are assigned to both actors, BUDGET BALANCE is significant for the government's decision to enter into agreements but not for the IMF. RESERVES is significant for the IMF's decision to enter, but not for the government. (Most of the other variables have the same effects as in Table 4.3.) This pattern of RESERVES being significant for only one actor, and BUDGET BALANCE being significant for the other actor holds for a whole range of specifications. Table 4.5 shows a "Minimal" specification, where only RESERVES and BUDGET BALANCE are included, as well as NUMBER UNDER to make clear which actor is which – NUMBER UNDER has a positive effect for the government to enter and a negative effect for the IMF to enter. BOP × SIZE

TABLE 4.4. *"Loans" and "conditions" assigned to both actors*

Variable	Specification 4.4a		Specification 4.4b	
	Government		Government	
	Decision to Enter	Decision to Remain	Decision to Enter	Decision to Remain
CONSTANT	−2.89**	−0.11	−2.67**	0.08
	(0.60)	(0.66)	(0.64)	(0.56)
RESERVES	0.12	−0.13	−0.01	−0.19
	(0.83)	(0.69)	(0.78)	(0.57)
BUDGET BALANCE	−1.06**	−0.26	−1.14**	−0.38
	(0.28)	(0.35)	(0.28)	(0.29)
DEBT SERVICE	1.29**	0.65	1.15**	0.55
	(0.52)	(0.72)	(0.44)	(0.50)
INVESTMENT	−6.11**	−0.08	−5.81**	−0.20
	(1.83)	(2.01)	(1.68)	(1.67)
YEARS UNDER	0.36*	−0.40	0.32*	−0.23
	(0.20)	(0.29)	(0.18)	(0.20)
NUMBER UNDER	0.56**	0.43*	0.44**	0.27*
	(0.18)	(0.22)	(0.18)	(0.15)
LAGGED ELECTION	0.87**	0.03	0.81**	−0.01
	(0.27)	(0.38)	(0.25)	(0.28)
	IMF		IMF	
Variable	Decision to Enter	Decision to Remain	Decision to Enter	Decision to Remain
CONSTANT	3.76**	2.98	5.15**	4.16
	(1.51)	(1.92)	(2.05)	(2.89)
RESERVES	−2.11**	−0.53	−2.29**	−0.81
	(0.79)	(1.01)	(1.08)	(1.51)
BUDGET BALANCE			0.37	0.31
			(0.31)	(0.24)
BOP × SIZE	−0.83**	−0.37	−0.89**	−0.34
	(0.29)	(0.25)	(0.35)	(0.31)
NUMBER UNDER	−0.98**	−0.40	−1.20**	−0.56
	(0.31)	(0.41)	(0.39)	(0.60)
REGIME	0.35	0.29	0.50	0.42
	(0.27)	(0.28)	(0.32)	(0.40)
Number of observations:	1024		1024	
Correctly predicted:	75%		77%	
Log likelihood function:	−349.80		−345.87	
Restricted log likelihood:	−705.46		−705.46	
Chi-squared:	711.33		719.19	

* Indicates significance at the 90% level.
** Indicates significance at the 95% level.
Note: Standard errors in parentheses. All variables are lagged one year.

TABLE 4.5. *"Conditions" matter to governments, "loans" matter to the IMF*

Variable	Minimal Specification		All-Variable Specification	
	Government		Government	
	Decision to Enter	Decision to Remain	Decision to Enter	Decision to Remain
CONSTANT	−2.71**	0.05	−2.00**	4.39**
	(0.55)	(0.48)	(0.64)	(2.21)
RESERVES	−0.51	−0.28	−0.18	−0.62
	(0.62)	(0.54)	(0.80)	(1.45)
BUDGET BALANCE	−1.02**	−0.40	−0.74**	−0.68
	(0.24)	(0.25)	(0.25)	(0.50)
DEBT SERVICE			1.13**	1.22
			(0.43)	(0.83)
INVESTMENT			−3.29*	−14.68**
			(1.80)	(4.60)
YEARS UNDER			0.81**	0.24
			(0.30)	(0.45)
NUMBER UNDER	0.54**	0.29*	0.05	−0.26
	(0.20)	(0.15)	(0.13)	(0.31)
LAGGED ELECTION			1.51**	−1.89**
			(0.41)	(0.65)
REGIME			0.17	0.95*
			(0.34)	(0.57)

(IMF Decisions continued)

is also included for the IMF so that the model is identified. Table 4.5 also shows an "All-variable" specification where all variables are assigned to both actors (with BOP × SIZE assigned to the IMF to identify the model).

The "Minimal" specification in Table 4.5 shows again that the government is more likely to enter into an IMF agreement when the budget deficit is high (indicated by the significant negative coefficient on BUDGET BALANCE). The reserves variable has no significant effect on the decision of the government. Conversely, the IMF is more likely to enter into agreements with countries with low foreign reserves (indicated by the significant negative coefficient on RESERVES). The BUDGET BALANCE variable has no significant effect on the decision of the IMF. The NUMBER UNDER variable helps to identify the actors. The government is more likely to enter into and continue agreements when many other countries are participating; the IMF is less likely to enter when other countries are participating because it faces a budget constraint. The BOP × SIZE variable also helps to identify the IMF: The Fund is more likely to enter into agreements with countries that have large balance of payments deficits in absolute terms.

TABLE 4.5. *(IMF Decisions continued)*

Variable	Minimal Specification IMF		All-Variable Specification IMF	
	Decision to Enter	Decision to Remain	Decision to Enter	Decision to Remain
CONSTANT	4.67**	5.14*	4.06*	−0.02
	(1.85)	(3.09)	(2.09)	(0.54)
RESERVES	−2.17*	−0.95	−1.81*	−0.39
	(1.13)	(1.41)	(1.05)	(0.47)
BUDGET BALANCE	0.30	0.32	0.24	0.14
	(0.30)	(0.26)	(0.34)	(0.12)
DEBT SERVICE			0.06	0.20
			(0.50)	(0.24)
INVESTMENT			−5.25*	4.86**
			(2.83)	(2.07)
YEARS UNDER			−1.12**	−0.33*
			(0.52)	(0.17)
NUMBER UNDER	−1.03**	−0.69	−0.50*	0.25**
	(0.34)	(0.62)	(0.26)	(0.10)
LAGGED ELECTION			−1.36*	0.94*
			(0.70)	(0.50)
REGIME			0.27	0.06
			(0.55)	(0.25)
BOP × SIZE	−0.81**	−0.29	−2.00**	−0.18
	(0.38)	(0.32)	(0.80)	(0.22)
Number of observations:	1024		1024	
Correctly predicted:	77%		80%	
Log likelihood function:	−365.61		−331.96	
Restricted log likelihood:	−705.46		−705.46	
Chi-squared:	679.70		747.01	

* Indicates significance at the 90% level.
** Indicates significance at the 95% level.
Note: Standard errors in parentheses. All variables are lagged one year.

The "All-variable" specification from Table 4.5 exhibits the same pattern: Governments care about the budget, the IMF cares about foreign reserves. The coefficient for BUDGET BALANCE is negative and significant for the government; it is not significant for the IMF. The coefficient for RESERVES is negative and significant for the IMF; it is not significant for the government.

Most of the other variables have the same effects as noted above. DEBT SERVICE has a significant positive effect on the decision of governments to enter into IMF programs, and INVESTMENT has a significant negative effect on the decision of governments to enter. In this specification, INVESTMENT also has a significant negative effect on the decisions of governments to continue participation. The YEARS UNDER variable, measuring the number of years in the past a country has participated in IMF programs, has a positive effect on a government's decision to enter into programs. The finding is more strongly significant in this specification than in previous specifications. NUMBER UNDER has a positive effect, as in previous specifications, although it is not statistically significant in the "full" specification. Elections have the same effect for governments: They are more likely to enter into IMF programs following elections. In this specification, elections have a negative effect on the decision to continue. This may be the result of participating governments being thrown out of office. REGIME does not have a statistically significant effect on the decisions of governments to enter, although dictatorships appear somewhat more likely to continue.

For the IMF, DEBT SERVICE is not significant, but INVESTMENT has a significant negative effect. The IMF is more likely to enter into agreements with countries that have low investment. INVESTMENT, however, has a positive effect on the decision of the IMF to continue agreements with a country. The IMF is more likely to keep countries with high investment.

The variables YEARS UNDER and LAGGED ELECTION have the opposite effects for the IMF as they do for the government. The IMF is less likely to enter into or continue an agreement with a country that has come to the IMF many times in the past and with countries that have held recent elections. This may be because the IMF doubts the ability of such countries to live up to their commitments. If a country is already participating, however, the IMF may continue with a country following elections.

For the IMF to enter, the coefficients of NUMBER UNDER and REGIME have the same signs as they do above in previous specifications, though they are not as statistically significant here. Note that NUMBER UNDER has a positive effect on the IMF decision to continue. This may indicate that the IMF is likely to hang on to countries already participating. BOP × SIZE has the same significant negative effect as above, indicating that the IMF is more likely to enter into agreements with countries that have high balance of payments deficits in absolute terms.

The results in the previous section (Table 4.3) show that a story of participation in IMF programs where governments care about the IMF loan (as indicated by the RESERVES variable) and about IMF conditions (as indicated by the BUDGET BALANCE variable) is plausible. The results in this section indicate, however, that this story is not plausible if we assume that the IMF also cares about the reserve position of individual countries. If RESERVES and BUDGET BALANCE are assigned to both actors, only BUDGET BALANCE matters to the government and only RESERVES matters to the IMF. This pattern, found in a wide range of different specifications, is robust.

The BUDGET BALANCE variable is a rough proxy for a government's desire to have the IMF impose fiscal discipline. Hence, one can interpret this variable as the a measure of a government's desire to have conditions imposed. Although this proxy is consistent with the "tipping the political balance" story of the previous chapter, this story could be better tested if other variables could be observed. The ideal point of the government on the budget, for example, would be the best variable to test if governments that want conditions imposed are more likely to turn to the IMF than other governments. Unfortunately, this variable is unobservable.

There is, however, an additional observable variable which also plays a role in the "tipping the balance" story that has not been tested: the number of "veto players" in a political system. An executive may bring in the IMF to push through policy if there exists a veto player who is opposed. The probability that such opposition exists increases with the number of veto players. Even if the ideal points of veto players are correlated, the probability that one veto player is opposed to the policies preferred by the executive never decreases as the number of veto players increases (see Tsebelis 1995, Proposition 1; also see Vreeland 2001). I predict that as the number of veto players increases, the probability that the government will turn to the IMF also increases.

For the IMF, I predict the opposite. Just as the IMF may prefer to negotiate with dictators over democracies, it may prefer to negotiate with governments that have fewer constraints in the form of veto players. When negotiating the conditions for an IMF loan, an executive facing several constraints in the form of veto players can plead, "I'd like to accept your proposal, but I could never get it accepted at home" (Putnam 1988: 440). Because countries with fewer veto players are less constrained, they make easier negotiation partners and are preferred by the Fund. Thus, although increasing the number of veto players increases the probability that an executive will find an IMF agreement useful, it may decrease the probability that the IMF will want to expend resources negotiating with the constrained executive. The number of veto players may have a positive effect on the decision of the executive to enter and a negative effect on the decision of the IMF to enter into an agreement.

I chose not to include the veto players variable (see Beck, Clarke, Groff, Keefer, and Walsh 1999) in the main specification in Table 4.3 because the data are new and, as of this writing, there may be some problems in measurement.[7] Nevertheless, including a variable measuring the number of veto players in a political system produces results that are of interest. The variable is measured as the sum of the number of legislative chambers for presidential systems (if multiple parties compete in legislative elections) and the sum of the number of parties in the government for parliamentary systems.[8] Because

---

[7] Personal communication with Philip Keefer, May 18, 2001.
[8] Beck et al. (1999) call this variable "Checks1a." The same qualitative results are obtained using their "Checks2a."

TABLE 4.6. *The effect of the number of veto players*

	Government	
Variable	Decision to Enter	Decision to Remain
CONSTANT	−0.01	2.06**
	(0.43)	(0.85)
RESERVES	−2.23**	−1.53
	(0.84)	(1.41)
BUDGET BALANCE	−0.48**	0.59
	(0.20)	(0.46)
DEBT SERVICE	1.57**	0.96
	(0.57)	(1.71)
INVESTMENT	−7.30**	6.30
	(2.38)	(5.65)
LOG(NO. OF VETO PLAYERS)	0.81**	−0.61
	(0.38)	(0.73)
	IMF	
Variable	Decision to Enter	Decision to Remain
CONSTANT	1.71*	0.79*
	(0.94)	(0.45)
BOP × SIZE	−1.21**	−0.29
	(0.43)	(0.20)
NUMBER UNDER	−0.43**	0.12
	(0.18)	(0.11)
LOG(NO. OF VETO PLAYERS)	−0.88**	−0.08
	(0.36)	(0.24)
Number of observations:	879	
Correctly predicted:	79%	
Log likelihood function:	−307.75	
Restricted log likelihood:	−608.41	
Chi-squared:	601.32	

* Indicates significance at the 90% level.
** Indicates significance at the 95% level.
Note: Standard errors in parentheses. All variables are lagged one year.

the ideal points of veto players may be correlated, there may be diminishing returns from adding additional veto players. Hence I use the natural logarithm of this variable. The results are presented in Table 4.6.

Table 4.6 shows that governments facing more veto players are more likely to bring in the IMF, as the significant positive coefficient for LOG(NUMBER OF VETO PLAYERS) indicates for the government. For the IMF, this variable has a negative effect. The IMF is less likely to enter into agreements with countries that have many veto players in the political system. These results hold under many specifications tested, but not when the noneconomic variables

(YEARS UNDER, NUMBER UNDER, and LAGGED ELECTION) are included for the government.[9]

THE "STRIPPED" OR "LARGE SAMPLE" MODEL

It will be useful to have a "stripped" specification of selection into IMF programs so that in subsequent chapters I can test the effects of IMF programs using the complete set of available observations. My "large sample" specification includes only variables for which there are no missing observations. Variables with missing observations are "stripped" from the specification.

Recall from Chapter 1 that the complete data set available on growth includes 4,126 observations for 135 countries from 1951 to 1990. Most of the variables used to predict selection, however, have missing observations, cutting the sample by three quarters. Some would argue that this is appropriate. Most of the missing observations happen to be for the 1950s and 1960s, when IMF programs may have been substantially different, or they are from developed and Communist countries, which have participated in IMF programs only rarely. I would prefer, however, not to use these theoretical blinders. Rather, I seek to include as many observations as possible at least for robustness checks when I evaluate the effect of IMF programs on economic growth in Chapter 5.

Hence, Table 4.7 presents a "large sample" model of selection which includes all available observations (only 135 observations are lost – one for each country – since there is no lagged observation for the first observation of each country: 4,126 − 135 = 3,991). I tested all variables with no missing observations and included in this specification all that had significant effects in the large sample. This less than ideal approach was used because of the data constraints. In Table 4.7, INVESTMENT, NUMBER UNDER, REGIME, and CAPITAL STOCK GROWTH are assigned to both actors. Identifying variables are assigned this time to the government (since BOP × SIZE has thousands of missing observations). The variables included for only the government are LAGGED ELECTION and YEARS UNDER. One additional variable is assigned to the government: PER CAPITA INCOME. Note that this is the first specification in which PER CAPITA INCOME had any significant effect (it was not significant when included in any of the previous selection specifications). The reason it has an effect here but did not in previous specifications is fairly straightforward. The samples used for previous specifications did not

---

[9] It is important to include the other variables for the government in this specification – RESERVES, BUDGET BALANCE, DEBT SERVICE, and INVESTMENT. Roubini and Sachs (1989) argue that divided political systems will have particular difficulty responding to a fiscal crisis. Including these variables is an attempt to control for "economic crisis." Even controlling for these factors, the number of veto players increases the probability that a government will turn to the IMF.

TABLE 4.7. *"Stripped" or "large sample" model of selection*

	Government	
Variable	Decision to Enter	Decision to Remain
CONSTANT	1.03	0.75
	(0.65)	(0.47)
INVESTMENT	2.61	4.12*
	(1.74)	(2.10)
LAGGED ELECTION	0.47*	0.69**
	(0.25)	(0.30)
YEARS UNDER	3.33**	−0.08
	(0.95)	(0.14)
NUMBER UNDER	−0.41	2.36**
	(1.04)	(0.84)
PER CAPITA INCOME	−3.21**	−0.87
	(0.73)	(0.71)
REGIME	−1.38**	−0.69*
	(0.46)	(0.40)
CAPITAL STOCK GROWTH	0.07	−0.06
	(0.12)	(0.05)
	IMF	
Variable	Decision to Enter	Decision to Remain
CONSTANT	−1.04**	2.09**
	(0.25)	(0.74)
INVESTMENT	−0.87	−5.07**
	(0.74)	(2.01)
NUMBER UNDER	0.25	−0.81
	(0.56)	(1.13)
REGIME	0.37**	0.70**
	(0.13)	(0.31)
CAPITAL STOCK GROWTH	−0.17**	0.11
	(0.07)	(0.08)
Number of observations:	3991	
Correctly predicted:	67%	
Log likelihood function:	−1156.34	
Restricted log likelihood:	−2324.23	
Chi-squared:	2335.78	

* Indicates significance at the 90% level.
** Indicates significance at the 95% level.
Note: Standard errors in parentheses. All variables are lagged one year.

include developed countries. In the large sample, all available countries are included. Developed countries have rarely entered into IMF programs (see Appendix 2 of the book), and PER CAPITA INCOME has a negative effect on participation.

Many of the results presented in Table 4.7 differ from those presented in previous specifications. There are two possible reasons for this: sample bias and omitted variable bias. The possibility of sample bias comes from the fact that the variable means differ between the two samples, mainly because of the inclusion of different types of countries and including observations from the 1950s and 1960s. The possibility of omitted variable bias comes from the fact that most of the important variables that determine selection – shown in the previous specifications – are not included here because of missing observations. This specification is therefore far from ideal. It will be useful, however, for work in subsequent chapters when attempting to control for selection bias using the large sample.

Note that some of the results are consistent with the results of previous specifications. LAGGED ELECTION, for example, has a positive effect on participation. Governments are more likely to enter agreements and continue participation following elections (or, interpreted another way, they are less likely to participate before elections). Governments are more likely to participate if YEARS UNDER is high. When many governments in a country's history have participated, a government is more likely to turn to the IMF. In countries with a less extensive IMF history, government may be more reluctant to bring in the Fund. The third "sovereignty cost" variable, NUMBER UNDER, does not have a significant effect on the decision to enter agreements for the government, as it did in previous specifications, but it does have the same significant positive effect on the decision to remain. Governments are not likely to terminate participation when other governments are participating.

There are two other notable findings consistent with the story that governments seeking conditions are more likely to turn to the IMF. First, the negative significant effect of REGIME indicates that dictatorships are less likely to turn to the IMF, probably because they can push through reform on their own. Democracies, on the other hand, are more likely to turn to the Fund. This is consistent with the number of veto players finding from Table 4.6. Second, with the exception of PER CAPITA INCOME (mentioned above), the economic variables (INVESTMENT and CAPITAL STOCK GROWTH) have no effect on the decision of governments to enter agreements, and only investment affects the decision to continue participation – governments continue when investment is strong.

The IMF, on the other hand, continues agreements with countries that have low investment, consistent with technocratic concerns. It also enters into agreements with countries that have low rates of capital stock growth, again consistent with technocratic concerns. The REGIME finding from previous specifications, however, persists: The IMF is more likely to sign and continue agreements with dictatorships. Dictatorships make easier negotiation partners because they do not face the same domestic constraints that democracies do. The same reason that democracies are more likely to turn to the Fund – that they need political support – may make the Fund stay away from them, since programs must be more carefully catered to the preferences of potential veto players.

Thus, although this specification is far from ideal, it has interesting results and will be useful when testing the effects of selection using the large sample in subsequent chapters. The results point to similar findings in this chapter. Governments turn to the IMF not only for a loan but also because they want conditions imposed, subject to rejection costs and sovereignty costs. The IMF is motivated by technocratic and bureaucratic concerns.

CONCLUSION

The statistical findings in this chapter are important. They indicate that there are political as well as economic determinants of IMF programs. Indeed, governments may be motivated to turn to the Fund because they want conditions to be imposed, regardless of their level of foreign reserves. The reason that one observes agreements with countries that have low foreign reserves and balance of payments problems is that the technocratic Fund prefers to sign agreements with these countries.

This implies that IMF conditionality may have nothing to do with the intended purpose of deterring moral hazard. The imposition of conditions may not be a stick but a carrot, attracting unpopular governments seeking to impose economic policy changes. The IMF may tend to be an ally for right wing governments.

Although this argument is intrinsically important, recall that the selection results are also a means to the end of evaluating the effects of IMF programs. The statistical evidence presented in this chapter shows that the story of participation developed in the previous chapters applies in general. Hence, selection into IMF programs is not random. The ultimate purpose of this study is to address the effect of IMF programs on economic growth. What does this finding of nonrandom selection imply for this larger question? When one addresses the question of economic growth, one must account for nonrandom selection to get an unbiased estimate of the effect of the IMF.

The selection work in this chapter draws on the observable implications from Chapters 2 and 3 to tell a statistical story. One can also draw on the work in Chapters 2 and 3 to identify unobserved determinants of selection as well. For example, when countries fail to persevere in a program, like Tanzania after 1982, the IMF often claims that the country or government lacks the "political will" to continue. The fact that the IMF cuts off countries without "political will" implies directly that the Fund seeks to continue agreements with countries that have "political will." Many of the results in this chapter indicate that governments turning to the Fund want conditions to be imposed. Although the researcher cannot observe or measure "want" or "will," these may systematically influence the selection process. They may also affect growth.

There are other unobserved variables that may play similar roles. Recall from the game presented in Chapter 3 (Figure 3.7) that depending on the configuration of the actors' preferences there can be more or less uncertainty about whether the agreement level of conditions follows the ideal point of the IMF or of the government. In some situations, the domestic constituency is more certain that the government negotiated for the best deal possible. In other situations, it is more uncertain whether the agreement represents the most lenient conditions that the IMF would allow or really just represents the ideal level of conditions that the government wants imposed. Hence, belief or "trust" in government varies. Suppose that the unobserved trust in government determines whether or not the government will seek consecutive IMF agreements. In this way, "trust" may affect selection. And "trust" may also affect economic growth. Fukuyama (1995) argues explicitly that "trust" matters for national prosperity.

Thus unobserved variables that have not been tested in this chapter may determine selection and may determine performance. How can one account for this? Unobserved variables have not been ignored in this chapter, although readers will have to study the technical appendix that follows the chapter to see exactly how they are included. The appendix describes how there are two error terms associated with the dynamic bivariate model of selection: one for the government's decision to participate ($v_{i,t}^G$) and one for the IMF's decision to participate ($v_{i,t}^F$).

The advantage of telling a statistical story of participation as well as a statistical story of performance is that explicit "error terms" are associated with both these statistical stories. "Error terms" are really not "errors" at all, but rather unobserved determinants that researchers often assume are randomly distributed. They may not be. The unobserved determinants of selection may be correlated with the unobserved determinants of participation. And the degree to which they are correlated indicates whether unobserved variables influence both selection and performance. The correlation between the IMF's error term ($v_{i,t}^F$) and the performance error term may indicate how much "political will" matters for the IMF to continue agreements and how much "political will" affects growth. The correlation between the government's error term ($v_{i,t}^G$) and the performance error term may indicate how much "trust" matters for the government to continue participation and how much "trust" affects growth.

Once the correlation between selection and performance "error terms" has been identified, one can remove the bias that unobserved variables cause. Observations of countries participating in programs and observations of countries not participating can be matched for all other conditions – observed and unobserved – and one can estimate the unbiased effect of IMF programs on economic growth. (Technical details of this are included in the appendix to Chapter 5. The method is also reviewed intuitively in the body of Chapter 5.)

Thus, armed with the statistical results from this chapter, one may return to the original question laid out in this study. Chapter 5 addresses the question of the effect of IMF programs on economic growth, controlling for the possible effects of selection.

APPENDIX: DYNAMIC BIVARIATE PROBIT WITH PARTIAL OBSERVABILITY

Assume participation at time t depends on participation at time $t-1$ (that is, assume the data obey a first-order Markov process). Let $d_{i,t}$ denote participation status in country i at time t: $d_{i,t} = 1$ if country i is under agreement at time t, and $d_{i,t} = 0$ if country i is not under agreement at time t.

Let $p_{NU,i,t}$ denote the "transition probability" that country i enters into an IMF arrangement at time t (that it goes from *not* under at time $t-1$ to *under* at time t). The probability that the country does not enter an arrangement at time t is $p_{NN,i,t} = 1 - p_{NU,i,t}$. Similarly, $p_{UU,i,t}$ denotes the probability that country i stays under at time t. The probability that participation ends at time t is $p_{UN,i,t} = 1 - p_{UU,i,t}$.

The probability of participation at time t, $p(d_{i,t} = 1)$ is the probability of entering, $p_{NU,i,t}$, if country i was not under at time $t-1$ plus the probability of continued participation, $p_{UU,i,t}$, if country i was already under agreement at time $t-1$:[10]

$$p(d_{i,t} = 1 \mid d_{i,t-1}) = p_{NU,i,t}(1 - d_{i,t-1}) + p_{UU,i,t}d_{i,t-1}$$

$$= p_{NU,i,t} + (p_{UU,i,t} - p_{NU,i,t})d_{i,t-1} \qquad (4.1)$$

The decisions to enter and to continue IMF agreements are joint decisions between a government and the Fund. For the government's decision, I write the value of participation as the latent regression

$$d_{i,t}^{G*} = \gamma' x_{i,t-1}^{G} + \kappa' x_{i,t-1}^{G} d_{i,t-1} + v_{i,t}^{G}, \qquad (4.2)$$

where the effects of the vector of variables determining the value of participation, $x_{i,t-1}^{G}$, are captured by γ if the country was not under an agreement at time $t-1$ ($d_{i,t-1} = 0$), and by $(\gamma + \kappa)$ if the country was under ($d_{i,t-1} = 1$). I write $(\gamma + \kappa)$ as a shift for algebraic convenience. The effect of unobserved variables determining the value of participation for the government is captured by $v_{i,t}^{G}$, which is assumed to be normally distributed. The government wants to be under an IMF agreement if and only if the value of participation is positive, $d_{i,t}^{G*} > 0$.

The value of an agreement to the IMF can be defined with a similar equation,

$$d_{i,t}^{F*} = \mu' x_{i,t-1}^{F} + \eta' x_{i,t-1}^{F} d_{i,t-1} + v_{i,t}^{F}, \qquad (4.3)$$

---

[10] This characterization follows Amemiya (1985, Chapter 11).

where the effect of the vector of variables $x^F_{i,t-1}$ is captured by the vector μ if $(d_{i,t-1} = 0)$ and by $(\mu + \eta)$ if $(d_{i,t-1} = 1)$. Unobserved effects are captured by $v^F_{i,t}$, also assumed to be normally distributed.

If the unobserved variables that influence the government and the IMF are independently distributed, the probability of entering an IMF agreement can be written as $p_{NU,i,t} = \Phi(\gamma'x^G_{i,t-1})\Phi(\mu'x^F_{i,t-1})$, where $\Phi(\cdot)$ represents the cumulative distribution function of the standard normal distribution. The probability of continuing an IMF agreement can be written as $p_{UU,i,t} = \Phi[(\gamma + \kappa)'x^G_{i,t-1}]\Phi[(\mu + \eta)'x^F_{i,t-1}]$. Thus, one can write the probability of an IMF agreement as

$$p(d_{i,t} = 1 \mid d_{i,t-1}) = \Phi\big(\gamma'x^G_{i,t-1} + \kappa'x^G_{i,t-1}d_{i,t-1}\big)$$
$$\times \Phi\big(\mu'x^F_{i,t-1} + \eta'x^F_{i,t-1}d_{i,t-1}\big). \qquad (4.4)$$

From this, one can write the likelihood function and estimate the probability of selection into IMF programs. One can, in principle, estimate this model relaxing the assumption that the error terms of the decisions of the government and the IMF are uncorrelated. It turns out that when one estimates the specifications throughout this chapter with correlated error terms, the correlation is not significant and all qualitative findings hold. It is not clear that this is because errors are not correlated or if the model is not converging properly. Models with correlated error terms have proven computationally difficult to estimate in other studies as well (for example, Knight and Santaella 1997).

As noted in this chapter, when the vectors $x^G_{i,t-1}$ and $x^F_{i,t-1}$ include exactly the same variables, one cannot distinguish between the two actors, and the model is not identified. To identify the model it is sufficient in principle that at least one variable be not common to the two actors. Hence, a strong prior belief that a single variable belongs to the IMF and not to the government is sufficient to identify the parameters.

To estimate this model, therefore, one must observe the joint outcome, d_t, and the different determinants of the individual decisions, $x^G_{i,t-1}$ and $x^F_{i,t-1}$. Greene (1998: 494) reports that Hessian-based algorithms perform poorly in estimating this model and recommends the DFP (Davidson-Fletcher-Powell) method.

The terms capturing the effects of unobserved variables, $v^G_{i,t}$ and $v^F_{i,t}$, are used to control for the effects of nonrandom selection in Chapter 5.

5

The Effect of IMF Programs on Economic Growth

This chapter returns to the question introduced in the first pages of Chapter 1: What is the effect of IMF programs on economic growth? The detour through the chapters on selection into IMF programs was necessary because estimating the effects of IMF programs is not straightforward. The standard difficulty in evaluating the effects of any policy or program is non-random selection (Heckman 1988). What one observes in the real world are not experiments which would match the "treatment" and the "control" groups, thus permitting direct inferences about the experimental effects. Previous chapters have shown that selection into IMF programs is indeed not random. The conditions of countries that participate in agreements are different from those that do not. Thus, observed differences in rates of economic growth may depend not only on the effects of IMF programs but also on selection.

Some of the factors affecting selection are observable, such as reserves and deficit; some are not. "Political will" and "trust" are examples. A methodology failing to account for these unobserved variables may overstate the value of participation by attributing the positive effects of "political will" and "trust" to the IMF program. Note that if such selection occurs, controlling only for observed variables can actually increase the bias (Achen 1986; Przeworski and Limongi 1996).

This chapter uses the methods developed by Heckman (1976, 1978, 1979, 1988, 1990) to estimate the effects of IMF programs independently of selection. Before turning to this technical approach, however, it is instructive to consider the more intuitive approaches that previous studies have employed: the before-after approach, the with-without approach, and the method of controlling for selection on observable variables. After discussing the potential bias associated with these methods, I turn to the model of correcting for selection bias due to unobserved variables.

PREVIOUS METHODS

As described in Chapter 1, previous statistical evaluations of IMF programs have approached the selection problem with different methods, from early before-after studies (Reichmann and Stillson 1978; Connors 1979; Pastor 1987a, 1987b) and with-without studies (Gylfason 1987; Edwards and Santaella 1993), to more recent work which corrects for observable determinants of nonrandom selection of program countries (Khan 1990; Conway 1994). Each of these approaches makes assumptions about how the data are generated in order to estimate program effects. Whether or not they produce accurate estimates depends on the validity of the assumptions behind the method.[1]

The Before-After Approach

The "before-after approach" assumes that all the conditions which can affect a country's rate of economic growth are exactly the same before a program is introduced as they are after. Hence, any change in the rate of growth is attributed to the introduction of the IMF program.

The before-after approach is intuitive and captures the way people commonly think about evaluating programs. Consider the experiences of Madagascar and Bolivia. The rate of growth in Madagascar was −3.8 percent in 1976. Then Madagascar participated in an IMF program from 1977 to 1978, and growth in 1979 was 12.7 percent. Observing an improvement of 16.5 percent in the annual rate of growth, one declares this program a success. On the other hand, Bolivia had a growth rate of 4.1 percent in 1979 and participated in an IMF program from 1980 to 1981. Growth in 1982 was −4.9. Since the annual rate of growth dropped 9.0 percent, this program is declared a failure.

In my "full model" sample of 1,024 observations,[2] the average annual rate of output growth in all countries the year before a spell of agreements was 2.69 percent (n = 79), and the rate of growth the first year after termination of participation, 4.90 percent (n = 61). This would lead one to conclude that IMF programs improve economic growth. Yet, this difference is much smaller if one considers a longer period of time. The average annual rate of growth for the five years before a spell of agreements was 4.39 percent (n = 250). For the five years after agreements, the average rate of growth per annum was 4.43 percent (n = 201). This is not a significant difference. Figure 5.1 shows the rate of growth five years before and five years after

---

[1] See Goldstein and Montiel (1986) for technical details.

[2] Recall that "full" refers to the full selection specification which includes variables with missing observations. The "large sample" sample refers to the stripped specification which includes only variables with no missing observations.

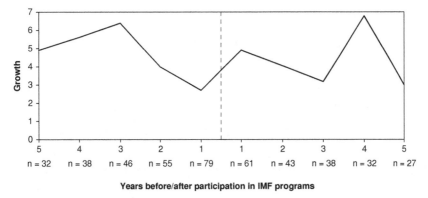

FIGURE 5.1. Economic growth before and after programs

participation in IMF programs. The figure shows no visible trend. This is consistent with the before-after findings that IMF programs have no effect on economic growth.

The problem with the before-after mode of thinking is that it ignores world and country-specific conditions. Conditions in Madagascar 1979 may have been conducive to economic growth. Without the IMF, the country may have had the same or even stronger growth. Conditions in Bolivia 1982, however, may have been adverse to growth. Without the IMF, growth may have been even worse. Hence, one does not know what to conclude. The before-after method simply does not produce the counterfactuals necessary to evaluate programs. It explicitly assumes world conditions do not change. Furthermore, to draw inferences about what would have happened if countries without agreements had participated, one must assume selection is random. The conditions of countries that participate are implicitly assumed to be the same as those that do not.

The With-Without Approach

A different approach, the "with-without," explicitly assumes that the conditions of countries which participate in agreements match exactly the conditions of countries which do not. The effect of the program is measured as the difference between the average growth of countries under agreements and the average growth of countries not under agreements. By comparing all countries under agreements to all countries not participating, one controls for the effects of world conditions.

This method is also intuitive. Consider the observed rate of growth per year for countries not under agreements, 4.39 percent (n = 559), and the observed rate of growth for countries under agreements, 2.04 percent (n = 465). Countries that participate in IMF programs grow 2.35 percent more slowly than those that do not. One concludes that the Fund programs hurt countries by lowering annual growth. This is the intuitive finding that drives many to believe that IMF programs hurt growth.

The problem with this approach is that the observed difference may reflect the conditions which lead governments to sign IMF agreements in the first place. Even though the observed difference is negative, some of the difference may have nothing to do with IMF programs. IMF programs may have no effect or even help growth. Recall the medical analogy from Chapter 1: To conclude that IMF programs hurt growth from the observed negative difference is akin to concluding that doctors make their patients worse off because people who go to the doctor have poorer health than those who do not. Hence, one must account for the fact that patients are sick in the first place.

Controlling for Selection on Observed Variables

Countries do not enter into IMF programs randomly; they go when they have economic problems. This brings one to the method of correcting for selection bias due to observable conditions.[3] Since the observable conditions of countries that participate in programs may be different from those that do not participate, the program effect on growth is estimated by separating the difference due to observed country conditions from the difference due to the program. Once the observed conditions have been accounted for, the effect on growth is assumed to be the remaining difference between the average rates of growth for countries participating and countries not participating.

Table 5.1 presents the results of a regression on OUTPUT GROWTH controlling for varying levels of CAPITAL STOCK GROWTH and LABOR FORCE GROWTH.[4] I also include a dummy variable "UNDER," which is coded 1 if a country is observed participating in an IMF program and 0 otherwise. CAPITAL STOCK GROWTH and LABOR FORCE GROWTH have significant effects on output growth, but UNDER does not. Note that whereas the coefficient for UNDER is negative in Table 5.1, the standard error is large. Thus, once one controls for the observable conditions of capital and labor, the IMF program appears to have no effect on growth. This leads to the contention that the IMF does not hurt growth.

As shown in the previous chapter, however, selection is not random. The following observed variables have a significant effect on whether or not a country participates in an IMF program: RESERVES, BUDGET BALANCE, DEBT SERVICE, INVESTMENT, YEARS UNDER, NUMBER UNDER, LAGGED ELECTION,

---

[3] For more sophisticated models to control for observed determinants of selection, see Khan (1990) and Conway (1994).

[4] Output growth (growth of GDP), capital stock growth, and labor force growth are taken from the *Penn World Tables 5.6*. These variables are employed following a simple production function explained in detail later in this chapter.

TABLE 5.1. *Effect of IMF programs on growth controlling for observable conditions*

Variable	Coefficient	Observed Means
CONSTANT	−0.33*	1.00
	(0.18)	
CAPITAL STOCK GROWTH	0.46**	4.82
	(0.01)	
LABOR FORCE GROWTH	0.54**	2.74
	(0.01)	
UNDER	−0.06	0.45
	(0.27)	
E(OUTPUT GROWTH)	3.33	
(Standard deviation)	(7.04)	
Observations	1024	
Durbin-Watson	1.80	
Adjusted R-squared	0.65	
F-test	1.94	
	p = 0.16	

* Indicates significance at the 90% level.
** Indicates significance at the 95% level.
Note: F-test is for the restriction $\alpha + \beta = 1$. Standard errors in parentheses.

BOP, and REGIME. If these variables also influence growth, then the coefficients presented in Table 5.1 may be biased. Suppose one augments this "barebones" growth model above with the variables known to affect selection. Table 5.2 presents these results.[5]

Table 5.2 shows that capital stock growth and labor force growth still have significant effects, and in fact, the coefficients remain almost unchanged from the results presented in Table 5.1, where observed determinants of selection were not included. The observable determinants of selection into IMF programs, as well as the IMF dummy variable itself have no significant effect. Selection on observable variables does not bias the results. The finding that IMF programs have no effect on economic growth persists.

The problem with this method is that one assumes that *unobserved* conditions that influence economic growth are the same for countries participating and those not participating. Although this approach represents an advancement in sophistication over the before-after and the with-without methods, it does not necessarily produce more accurate results. Controlling for observable determinants of selection while ignoring the unobservable may produce more biased estimates than controlling for nothing at all.

[5] To avoid losing observations, the same *lagged* variables as used in Chapter 4 are used for the variables here. I am grateful to David Lam and Edwin Jager for bringing this to my attention.

TABLE 5.2. *Effect of IMF programs on growth controlling for observable determinants of selection*

Variable	Coefficient	Observed Means
CONSTANT	0.091	1.00
	(0.706)	
CAPITAL STOCK GROWTH	0.453**	4.82
	(0.011)	
LABOR FORCE GROWTH	0.547**	2.74
	(0.011)	
RESERVES	0.054	3.01
	(0.053)	
BUDGET BALANCE	0.021	−6.22
	(0.018)	
DEBT SERVICE	0.008	5.15
	(0.033)	
INVESTMENT	−0.013	13.35
	(0.021)	
LAGGED ELECTION	0.219	0.19
	(0.333)	
YEARS UNDER	0.036	6.91
	(0.022)	
NUMBER UNDER	−0.017	36.70
	(0.014)	
BOP	−0.000004	−120.00
	(0.0001)	
REGIME	0.008	0.74
	(0.319)	
UNDER	−0.070	0.45
	(0.297)	
E(OUTPUT GROWTH)	3.326	
(Standard deviation)	(7.038)	
Observations	1024	
Durbin-Watson	1.806	
Adjusted R-squared	0.648	
F-test	1.756	
	p = 0.182	

** Indicates significance at the 95% level.

Note: F-test is for the restriction $\alpha + \beta = 1$. Standard errors in parentheses.

The Problem of Unobserved Variables

Recall again the analogy of doctors and patients. Note that to fully account for selection effects and to draw accurate conclusions about the effects of the doctor's treatment, one must match all the conditions of patients and nonpatients – observed and unobserved. Observable determinants of going to the doctor include a person's vital signs, for example. The observable vital signs do not tell all the story, however. An unobservable factor that determines which people go to the doctor is their individual "will" or motivation to stay healthy. Some people never go to the doctor even when they are sick because they do not take their health seriously. Other people visit their doctor even when in perfect health. People who go to the doctor may be more highly motivated to stay healthy than people who do not. "Motivation level" can affect health independently of a doctor's treatment. Since motivation affects health and highly motivated people are more likely to visit the doctor, then matching people merely for their vital signs will overstate the effectiveness of the doctor. The positive effects of high motivation will be wrongly attributed to the treatment.

This is important, for doctors have been known to prescribe everything from beneficial panaceas to benign placebos to harmful prescriptions. Suppose highly motivated sick people take a harmful treatment, such as the old practice of bloodletting. These patients will be less healthy than nonpatients, and the bloodletting will make them sicker still. One will observe these highly motivated patients to be sicker than unmotivated healthy people. If, however, one controls for observable levels of health and not for levels of motivation, the positive effects of the patients' motivation will be attributed to the treatment. One may conclude that bloodletting is harmless, for the patients' higher levels of motivation may be strong enough to counteract the negative effects. If the negative effects of bloodletting are strong at first and then wear off, while the effects of "will" persist, one will conclude that bloodletting starts off badly and ends well.

Ironically, rather than controlling for observables alone, one would get better estimates of the effectiveness of bloodletting from the simple and unsophisticated with-without approach of comparing the health of patients to that of nonpatients. This approach leads to the conclusion that bloodletting makes patients worse off, and it is the correct conclusion, though it fails to identify how much damage is caused by the bloodletting and how much is due to the conditions of patients. Ultimately, one should use a method which can separate the effects of unobserved influences from the effect of the treatment.[6]

In general, although the above methods differ in their levels of sophistication, there are no a priori grounds to assume that one method will produce more accurate estimates than any other. Furthermore, Bird's (1996a: 497) contention that "results that are robust across different methodologies may be stronger than those that are methodology specific," does not hold true if none of the methods models the situation appropriately. Since none of the methodologies employed above accounts for the effects of unobserved

---

[6] Bloodletting can, in some cases, be helpful.

variables, any degree of robustness in the results simply indicates that failing to control for unobserved factors biases results consistently. All these methods are based on the assumption that participation in programs is random with respect to any unobserved variables affecting growth. If, for example, the "political will" of a government affects growth, one must assume that such "political will" is randomly distributed among countries that participate and those that do not participate. Yet, if "political will" also determines which countries participate in programs and which do not, then none of the above methods will produce accurate estimates of the effect of IMF programs.

ESTIMATING THE COUNTERFACTUAL

Consider an example: The government of Portugal participated in an IMF program in 1984 and experienced a growth rate of −1.4 percent. What was the effect of the IMF program? To answer this question, one must know what the rate of growth in Portugal would have been if it had not participated in an IMF program. Unfortunately, one cannot observe Portugal both with and without a program in 1984. The necessary counterfactual cannot be observed.

Suppose, however, countries exist that match all the observed conditions of Portugal in 1984 except that they do not have an IMF program. Consider Angola-1983, which did not participate in an IMF program, as a potential match. In both Angola-1983 and Portugal-1984, capital stock grew at 2.6 percent, and whereas Portugal's labor force growth was 1.1 percent, Angola's was 1.0 percent.

Are Portugal-1984 and Angola-1983 a match? The observable determinants of growth are very close. They appear to differ only in their IMF treatment status. Yet the presence of the IMF program could be correlated to the presence of some unobserved characteristic that influences growth. Do countries that participate in IMF programs possess some unobserved characteristics that are typically absent in countries that do not participate?

Recall from Chapter 4 that the Fund frequently cites a lack of "political will" as the cause of failure. This implies that countries that actually do follow through with programs have "political will." Maybe they are advised by the most prestigious and trusted economists. Maybe these governments have the confidence of domestic and foreign investors and the support of international creditors. Maybe they have stronger negotiation postures. Maybe the leaders want IMF conditions imposed.

Another unobserved determinant of selection discussed in Chapter 4 is "trust." Perhaps governments are more likely to continue participation in IMF programs when the forces opposed to its policies do not place all the blame on the government – when they believe that the government has negotiated the best possible IMF arrangement.

TABLE 5.3. *Participation and political will (hypothetical)*

	Program	No Program
Political will	Cases	No Cases
No political will	No Cases	Cases

If the above unobserved variables play a role in selection and performance, then even cases such as Portugal-1984 and Angola-1983 may not represent a match, despite their observable similarity. If "political will" and "trust" are randomly distributed among all countries regardless of participation status, then their effects will cancel out when comparing large enough samples. If they are not randomly distributed, however, then even increasing the sample size to include all observations in the world will not reduce the bias caused by these unobserved variables.

To see why this is true, suppose only governments with "political will" sign agreements and governments lacking "political will" do not. The universe of cases depicted in Table 5.3 emerges. In this matrix, there are no matching counterfactuals. One cannot simply compare countries with programs to those without, whether observed conditions are matched or not, because the effects of the program will be confused with those of unobserved "political will." "Political will" matters because it makes governments more likely to enter agreements and contributes to growth. It affects selection and performance. Thus the effects of "political will" must be separated from the effects of the program. One must "remove" the effects of the unobserved variables before comparing the cases with a program to those without.

THE INTUITION BEHIND THE MODEL

How can one capture the effects of unobserved variables? If all one considers are individual cases such as Portugal-1984 or Angola-1983, it is impossible, by definition, to account for what is not observed. This book, however, considers all cases for which data are available, using a statistical framework. The advantage of using a statistical approach is that associated with any statistical story is an explicit "error term."

What is the "error term"? As one learns in any introductory course in regression analysis, the error term simply represents unobserved explanatory variables, which are usually assumed to be random disturbances. Every statistical story generates an explicit error term for each observation of the dependent variable. The error term is merely the difference between the actual value of the dependent variable and the predicted value of the dependent variable using the observed explanatory variables. Thus, in Chapter 4, when I generated statistical stories of selection into IMF programs, I also generated error terms which account for unobserved variables that determine selection. In this chapter, as I have been generating statistical stories of the effect of IMF programs on economic growth, I have also been generating "error terms" accounting for the unobserved variables determining economic growth. Hence, I can approximate the effects of unobserved variables that determine selection into IMF programs and the effects of unobserved variables that determine economic growth.

The intuition behind correcting for selection bias due to unobserved variables is straightforward once one recalls where the error terms come from. One merely needs to consider the possible correlation between the error terms. If the errors from the estimation of selection are correlated with the errors from the estimation of growth, then the effects of unobserved variables are not random. To the extent that the error terms are correlated, the unobserved variables that drive participation also determine economic growth. Once such a correlation between error terms has been detected and accounted for, one can remove the effects of nonrandom selection on economic growth. Any remaining difference in growth rates between countries that participate in IMF programs and countries that do not participate is the inherent effect of the IMF programs.

The actual procedure of "removing" the effects of nonrandom selection is somewhat more complex than I have laid out so far. Recall that the statistical model used to estimate selection in Chapter 4 involves four decisions: the decision of the government to enter agreements, the decision of the IMF to enter agreements, the decision of the government to terminate agreements, and the decision of the IMF to terminate them. Each of these decisions represents an area where relevant unobserved variables may be omitted. Hence, to correct for selection bias, one needs four instruments, one corresponding to each of the four selection decisions.

The instruments used to measure unobserved variables are "hazard rates." The hazard rate can be defined as the marginal probability of misclassifying an observation given where the observation lies in the overall distribution of observations. (See the appendix to this chapter for a formal definition.) The hazard rate represents one way of measuring the errors associated with each selection decision. For countries currently under agreements, the government hazard rate is the marginal probability that the government does not want to have an agreement (denoted λ_1^G, where the superscript G refers to the government and the subscript 1 indicates that the country is participating in an IMF program) and the IMF hazard rate is the marginal probability that the IMF does not want the agreement (λ_1^F). Analogously, for countries *not* currently under agreements, the government hazard rate is the marginal probability that the government wants an agreement (λ_0^G), and the IMF hazard rate is the marginal probability that the IMF wants an agreement (λ_0^F). These hazard rates represent the four possible areas where unobserved variables driving selection and performance, such as "political will" or "trust," may operate.

The hazard rates have a convenient property: When included in the estimation of program effects, the parameters capturing their influence indicate if there is a correlation between the selection and the performance error terms. (Again, see the appendix for the formal definition.) Hence, if these parameters are significant, there exists selection on unobserved variables. If such hazard rates are not included as explanatory variables, then the estimation of the effects of IMF programs on growth will suffer from a misspecification – specifically omitted variables – bias.

The appendix to this chapter provides the technical details of how the hazard rates are generated from the statistical tests from Chapter 4 and how they are incorporated into the estimation of growth. The appendix also explains how the inherent effect of IMF programs on economic growth can be estimated using the hazard rates. The general procedure is the following:

1. A growth model is estimated separately for countries observed participating in programs and for those observed not participating. The hazard rates are included in this estimation as instruments to control for the effects of unobserved variables driving selection. This generates two sets of parameters, one characterizing countries under agreement, the other characterizing countries not under. These "under" and "not under" parameters are not biased by selection. (The inclusion of the hazard rates corrects for selection bias.)

2. These two sets of parameters tell a story. They indicate the selection-corrected effects of the independent variables that determine growth under the two states of the world: participating in IMF programs and not participating. Thus, they permit one to estimate hypothetical growth rates if observations were "matched' for observed *and* unobserved characteristics. The vector of independent variables characterizing each country at each year can be multiplied alternatively by the "under" parameters and the "not under" parameters. The parameters on the hazard rates, which control for the effects of unobserved variables are left out, thus removing the effects of selection.

3. This produces two counterfactual observations of economic growth for each country during each year which are matched for all conditions – observed and unobserved. For example, this permits one to estimate two hypothetical rates of economic growth in Angola-1983: participating in IMF programs and not participating in IMF programs – if selection into the two states were random. The only difference between each pair of observations will be the inherent effect of IMF programs on economic growth. These selection-corrected values of growth "under" and "not under" are averaged separately over all countries and years. The difference between these two

average rates of growth is the average inherent effect of IMF programs on economic growth.

CORRECTING FOR SELECTION EFFECTS[7]

The "barebones" growth model I use follows a simple production function of the form $Y = A(K^\alpha L^\beta)$, where A denotes the current level of technology, K is a measure of current capital stock, L is the size of the labor force, α captures the efficiency with which capital is used in production, and β captures the efficiency of labor. The model is estimated in growth form, where α and β are estimated as the parameters capturing the effects of CAPITAL STOCK GROWTH ($\dot{K}/K$) and LABOR FORCE GROWTH ($\dot{L}/L$), respectively. $\dot{A}/A$ is estimated as the regression CONSTANT. The specification is augmented by the hazard rates (λ) to control for selection. (Other specifications are tested below to check for the robustness of results.) Thus, the expected rate of growth, $E(\dot{Y}/Y)$, "under" and "not under" IMF programs can be written as (suppressing i, t subscripts):

$$E(\dot{Y}/Y)_0 = (\dot{A}/A)_0 + \alpha_0(\dot{K}/K) + \beta_0(\dot{L}/L) + \theta_0^G \lambda_0^G + \theta_0^F \lambda_0^F$$

$$E(\dot{Y}/Y)_1 = (\dot{A}/A)_1 + \alpha_1(\dot{K}/K) + \beta_1(\dot{L}/L) + \theta_1^G \lambda_1^G + \theta_1^F \lambda_1^F$$

The subscripts 0 and 1 indicate "not under" and "under," respectively. The growth model is estimated in two steps so that the hazard rates can be included appropriately. The hazard rates which capture the effect of unobserved variables on the decision to enter agreements, λ_0^G and λ_0^F, are included for countries currently not under agreements. The hazard rates which capture the effect of unobserved variables on the decision to continue agreements, λ_1^G and λ_1^F, are included for the countries participating in agreements. The θ parameters associated with hazard rates are estimates of the regression correlation between unobserved variables driving selection and unobserved variables determining growth. If these parameters are significant, unobserved variables driving selection (participation in IMF programs) and performance (rate of economic growth) are correlated.

Since the growth model is estimated separately, there are two sets of numbers in Table 5.4: one set for countries observed under and another for those observed not under. The columns labeled "Biased" contain the parameters estimated without controlling for selection effects (λs omitted). The "Selection" columns list the parameters estimated with the hazard rates included as instruments to control for the effects of selection. These parameters have been "corrected" for selection. The "Wted Diff." column reports the difference between the biased parameters and the selection-corrected

---

[7] The results presented in this section follow Przeworski and Vreeland (2000).

TABLE 5.4. *Growth regression by participation status*

	Not Under				Under				1,024 Sample Means
	Biased	Selection	Means	Wted Diff.	Biased	Selection	Means	Wted Diff.	
CONSTANT	-0.26	-0.13	1.00	-0.13	-0.38**	-1.73**	1.00	1.35	1.00
	(0.21)	(0.38)			(0.17)	(0.44)			
CAPITAL STOCK GROWTH	0.44**	0.44**	7.15	0.00	0.48**	0.47**	2.01	0.01	4.82
	(0.02)	(0.02)			(0.01)	(0.01)			
LABOR FORCE GROWTH	0.56**	0.56**	2.69	0.00	0.52**	0.53**	2.80	-0.02	2.74
	(0.02)	(0.02)			(0.01)	(0.01)			
λ^G		0.07	-0.73			4.31**	0.14		
		(0.23)				(1.48)			
λ^F		0.09	-0.82			6.17**	0.12		
		(0.29)				(2.23)			
# Obs.	559	559			465	465			
D-W	1.89	1.89			1.75	1.75			
Adj. R-squared	0.59	0.59			0.71	0.71			
F-test	1.76	1.68			0.23	0.00			
	p = 0.18	p = 0.19			p = 0.63	p = 0.99			

** Indicates significance at the 95% level.

Note: F-test is for the restriction $\alpha + \beta = 1$. Standard errors in parentheses.

119

parameters, weighted by the observed means of the variables. The standard errors are reported below each parameter.

The first items of interest from Table 5.4 are the coefficients on the hazard rates (λ). If these parameters are not significant, then there exists no significant selection on unobserved variables and the "biased" parameters are, in fact, not biased at all.

Of the four hazard rates, two of them have significant effects (λ_1^G and λ_1^F). Hence, the unobserved variables driving selection and those affecting performance (growth) are correlated. For countries observed "under" agreements, the coefficients on the hazard rates for both the government and the IMF are significant. Note that values of these coefficients are positive: 4.31 and 6.17 respectively. Thus, there are unobserved variables that influence the decisions of both the government and the IMF to continue participation and that also affect economic growth. The positive coefficients on the positive "under" hazard rates indicate that growth is *overstated* if the hazard rates are not included. Given the means of the hazard rates, the overstatement is about $4.31 \times 0.14 + 6.17 \times 0.12 = 1.34$. The overall effect of the hazard rates for the "not under" observations is much smaller: $0.07 \times (-0.73) + 0.09 \times (-0.82) = -0.12$ (not statistically significant).

Consider the difference between the selection-corrected parameters and the biased parameters. The parameters on the main explanatory variables, CAPITAL STOCK GROWTH and LABOR FORCE GROWTH, exhibit only very small changes. Including the hazard rates does not affect these parameters significantly. Most of the bias that the hazard rates correct is found in the estimation of the CONSTANTS.[8]

To the extent that the hazard rates influence only the constants, selection effects are independent of observed characteristics. Unobserved influences for countries not under agreement are constant, as are the effects of unobserved variables on countries that are under. As Heckman (1979: 155) explains, "if the only [regressor] ... that determines sample selection is '1' so that the probability of sample inclusion is the same for all observations, the conditional mean of [v^G or v^F (from the appendix of Chapter 4)] is a constant, and the only bias [in the parameters] that results from using selected samples to estimate the population structural equation arises in the estimate of the intercept." So the probability that countries under agreement are included in the observed sample does not vary with respect to capital stock growth or labor force growth. Similarly, the probability that countries

---

[8] Note that the coefficient on the CONSTANT for countries not under agreement is not significant. This means that there is a high probability that the true value of the constant is 0 and not -0.13. Hence, the estimate of growth for countries not under agreements presented in the next section may be higher than the true value. If this is the case, it merely strengthens the qualitative conclusions of this study, presented below.

not under agreement are included in the observed sample does not vary with respect to these variables.

What does the selection effect of unobserved variables imply? The significant effect of λ_1^G implies that unobserved variables that affect the decision of the government to continue participation also affect economic growth. "Trust" is an example of such a variable that has been used throughout this study. A government that has the trust of key constituents may be better able to use the IMF as a foil to push through policies it prefers, and therefore may be more likely to remain in IMF programs. This same trust may reduce transaction costs and contribute to economic growth (see Dasgupta 1988; Coleman 1988, 1990; Putnam 1993; Hardin 1993; Fukuyama 1995; and Levi 1998).

The significant effect of λ_1^F implies that unobserved variables that affect the decision of the IMF to continue participation also affect growth. For the IMF, perhaps "political will" matters. The Fund claims that IMF agreements may break down because of a lack of "political will" (see Killick 1995; Bird 1998; and Humphreys 1999). This is consistent with the above finding. "Political will" determines whether countries remain under programs or whether agreements break down. "Political will" may translate into a stronger negotiation posture with creditors and the respect of investors, or these governments may be advised by the most prestigious and trusted economists. This "political will" may make countries more likely to experience economic growth and to continue participation in IMF programs.

However interpreted, the results in this section confirm what many have insinuated but no one has tested for: unobserved variables drive selection into IMF programs and their effects on economic growth. Yet, detecting this correlation is only the first step. The correlation has important implications for the overall assessment of the inherent effects of participating in an IMF program, which is presented in the next section. One can now remove the effects of this nonrandom selection and present selection-corrected estimates of the effect of IMF programs on economic growth.

THE EFFECT OF IMF PROGRAMS ON GROWTH

It was demonstrated above that if one controls only for observed variables, IMF programs appear to have no significant effect on rates of economic growth. This is consistent with many previous studies. The preceding section shows, however, that there exists a correlation between the unobserved factors which drive participation and those which affect economic growth. Thus, any estimation of the effect of IMF programs on economic growth which does not include some measure of unobserved variables, such as the hazard rates used above, suffers from an omitted variable bias. Including the hazard rates produces estimates that are corrected for selection bias and allows one to calculate the selection-corrected effect of the IMF programs.

This involves calculating the weighted difference for the entire sample of the selection-corrected parameters for countries "under" and the selection-corrected parameters for countries "not under." Since the mean value of capital stock growth $(\dot{K}/K)$ for the entire sample is 4.82 and the mean value of labor force growth $(\dot{L}/L)$ for the entire sample is 2.74, the effect of the IMF on annual rate of GDP growth is: $[-1.73 + (4.82) \times (0.47) + (2.74) \times (0.53)] - [-0.13 + (4.82) \times (0.44) + (2.74) \times (0.56)] = -1.53$.

One can also arrive at this figure by counterfactually matching all country-years for the unobserved as well as the observed conditions influencing growth. To take one country-year example, recall that in Angola-1983, capital stock growth $(\dot{K}/K)$ was 2.6 percent and labor force growth $(\dot{L}/L)$ was 1.0 percent. Using the selection-corrected parameters from Table 5.4, one can estimate that economic growth "not under" in a hypothetical "random" world would have been $\dot{A}/A_0 + \alpha_0(\dot{K}/K)_{ANGOLA,1983} + \beta_0(\dot{L}/L)_{ANGOLA,1983} = -0.13 + (0.44) \times (2.6) + (0.56) \times (1.0) = 1.57$. Angola's growth "under" in a hypothetical "random" world would have been: $\dot{A}/A_1 + \alpha_1(\dot{K}/K)_{ANGOLA,1983} + \beta_1(\dot{L}/L)_{ANGOLA,1983} = -1.73 + (0.47) \times (2.6) + (0.53) \times (1.0) = 0.02$.

Thus, in this case, the annual rate of growth of GDP was lowered by 1.55 percent. In the observed world, Angola was in fact not under an IMF program and GDP grew by 1.77 percent. Note that the observed rate includes the effect of selection (thus it does not match the estimated 1.57 percent of the hypothetical "random" world). If Angola had participated in an IMF program that year, its growth would have been closer to $1.77 - 1.55 = 0.22$ percent.

Of course, one cannot place much confidence in a result from one single observation. Hence, the procedure is applied to the entire sample of 1,024 observations. Average "under" and "not under" estimates of economic growth are produced for the entire sample. Following this procedure, it turns out that if all countries had IMF programs during every year, and if unobserved variables played no role, they would have grown at the average rate of 2.00. If no country had an agreement, and again unobserved variables were removed, they would have grown at the rate of 3.53. The total difference is -1.53. IMF programs lower growth. Indeed, this effect is almost identical for the cases actually observed under and not under (see Table 5.5).

The growth rates presented in Table 5.5 are the hypothetical rates of growth if countries were matched for conditions, that is, if selection were random. Since observations are matched for all conditions, the remaining differences between the rates of growth are the inherent effects of IMF programs. The first row of Table 5.5 presents the results of calculating the expected rates of growth using the selection-corrected parameters for only those observations actually under IMF programs (n = 465). The second row presents the calculations for only those observations actually not under (n = 559). The third row is for the entire sample (n = 1,024).

TABLE 5.5. *Hypothetical rates of growth if selection were random*

Observed As:	Hypothetically As:		Program Effect
	Under	Not Under	
Under	0.70	2.33	−1.63
Not under	3.08	4.52	−1.44
All	2.00	3.53	−1.53

Now that the effect of IMF programs on the annual rate of growth has been isolated, one can return to the observed rates of growth and estimate what growth would have been if countries' experiences had been different. For countries observed with agreements, the observed rate of growth was 2.04 percent per annum. The average effect of IMF programs on these countries was −1.63 percent per year. Hence, if countries observed participating in IMF programs had not participated, they would have experienced an annual rate of growth of 3.67 percent. When countries were observed not participating in IMF programs, their observed rate of growth was 4.39 percent. If these countries had been participating in an IMF program, their annual rate of growth would have been lowered by 1.44 percent. Their average growth would have been 2.95 percent per year.

Recall that previous studies which account for selection on observed variables find that IMF programs have no negative effect on growth. Indeed, Khan (1990) and Conway (1994) find that a program "starts out badly and ends well." Although the methods employed in these studies are more sophisticated than a simple with-without approach, the conclusions are less accurate. The negative bias caused by nonrandom selection on observables is countered by a positive bias caused by unobserved variables, such as "trust" and "political will." The net effect of IMF programs – when both types of bias are removed – is negative.

Despite the fact that for twenty years no study showed that IMF programs hurt growth, the finding should really not be surprising. Consider once again the observed world. In Table 5.6, I classify the observations according to their experience of participation. Note that these observations are right-hand, but not left-hand, censored: they reflect all the prior experience but end in 1990. The table presents average rates of OUTPUT GROWTH, average CAPITAL STOCK GROWTH, average LABOR FORCE GROWTH, average annual level of RESERVES (in terms of monthly imports) and average BUDGET BALANCE. Country-year observations are separated into five categories: Never under, observations of countries that never experienced IMF programs throughout the period 1952–90; Before spells, observations of countries that experienced IMF programs before entering their first IMF program; B/w spells, observations of countries that experienced programs in the past and repeated participation but were

TABLE 5.6. *Growth according to transition type*

Countries:	n	OUTPUT GROWTH	CAPITAL STOCK GROWTH	LABOR FORCE GROWTH	RESERVES	BUDGET BALANCE
Never under	82	5.97	9.62	2.36	5.90	−6.98
Before spells	142	4.14	7.27	2.65	2.79	−4.79
Before & b/w spells	346	4.30	7.11	2.71	3.22	−4.94
B/w spells	204	4.42	6.99	2.75	3.52	−5.05
B/w & after spells	335	4.12	6.49	2.79	3.65	−5.10
After spells	131	3.65	5.71	2.86	3.86	−5.18
During spells	465	2.04	2.01	2.80	2.10	−7.34

not currently under – those observed "between" spells; After spells, observations of countries that experienced IMF programs but had not returned to participation by 1990; and finally During spells, observations of countries actually participating in IMF programs. (Table 5.6 has two more categories: Before & B/w spells, which pools the Before and the B/w observations; and B/w & After spells, which pools the B/w and the After observations.)

Table 5.6 shows that countries which never experienced IMF programs grew the fastest. But the most relevant comparison is of growth before and after program participation. And, whether or not one includes cases in which a country would turn to the IMF again (those "B/w"), one can see that program participation certainly does not accelerate growth. For any combination of the "Before" and "After" growth rates, the latter are somewhat lower.

Just as Table 5.6 fails to show a trend of improved growth, neither does a more detailed picture indicate any apparent trend once countries leave a program. Figure 5.2 shows a stylized picture of the experience with participation. The top horizontal line (Never under) shows the average growth rate of countries in my sample that never participated in an IMF program. The second horizontal line (Not currently under) shows the average growth rate of countries in my sample that participate at some time but were currently not participating. The horizontal trough in the middle of the jagged line is the observed rate of growth for countries during their participation in IMF programs (which I stylized to last five years, about the duration of an average spell). Both "before" and "after" growth rates along the jagged line exhibit wide swings, and no trend emerges once countries leave programs. Statistical analysis confirms these visual impressions. Even controlling for selection using the techniques described above, I could detect no trend before or after participation.[9]

---

[9] Splines counting years of participation and years since participation were included in the estimation of growth but were not significant.

TABLE 5.7. *Experience of countries that participated in IMF programs*

Years of Consecutive Participation in IMF Programs	Average Annual Growth over the Next 4 Years	
	Countries That Ended IMF Program Participation	Countries That Continued IMF Program Participation
2	4.70	2.42
3	5.15	2.60
4	4.57	2.40
5	5.84	2.82

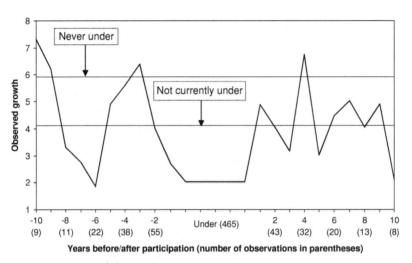

FIGURE 5.2. Growth by participation status.

Does it matter for future growth how long countries stay under the programs? Table 5.7 compares the average rate of growth during the subsequent four years of countries that left the program after different numbers of years with that of countries that continued to participate four more years. Their comparison shows that for any number of years already under the program, two through five, the observed rates of growth during the next four years were lower if a country remained under than if it left. The selection-corrected, hypothetical effect of the program (not reported) is also always negative. Thus, both the observed and the hypothetical differences indicate that countries are better off, at least during the next four years, leaving the program rather than continuing to participate.

Hence, I conclude the following. When matched for exogenous conditions, participation in IMF programs reduces growth while a country remains under and has no salutary effect once a country leaves. As shown in the next section, these conclusions appear robust to the specification of growth equations and samples. Countries facing economic difficulties adopt IMF programs either because governments want to reduce budget deficits and use the IMF as a foil, or because they are desperate for foreign reserves and are forced to accept IMF conditions in exchange. Yet these programs reduce growth, for as long as one can observe their effects.

Participation in IMF programs calls for several measures that reduce growth in the short run. But the standard argument in favor of these programs is that once the economy is stabilized, deficits are eliminated or reduced, and the balance of payments is improved, growth will resume. This argument is often only implicit, and it is ideological: There are no good theoretical reasons to believe that a balanced budget and foreign account are sufficient for growth to occur. And it appears to be false.

OTHER SAMPLES AND SPECIFICATIONS

Just as many different specifications of participation in IMF programs are shown to be plausible in Chapter 4, there are many different ways that the selection model of economic growth can be changed as well. The question is whether altering the model changes the qualitative finding that IMF programs have adverse effects on rates of economic growth. It turns out that results vary considerably when different specifications of the model are used. But the most conservative estimate is -0.58 (see below). The qualitative finding holds: Under all specifications, the effect of IMF programs on economic growth is negative.

To test the robustness of the specification of the growth model, I first experimented by adding to the basic model the following variables:

BALANCE OF PAYMENTS AS A PROPORTION OF GDP
FOREIGN RESERVES
BUDGET BALANCE
DEBT SERVICE
TERMS OF TRADE
THE RATE OF GROWTH OF EDUCATION OF AN AVERAGE MEMBER OF THE
    LABOR FORCE
PER CAPITA INCOME
THE AVERAGE RATE OF GROWTH IN THE WORLD DURING A GIVEN YEAR
THE PERCENTAGE DIFFERENCE IN OUTPUT PER WORKER BETWEEN A GIVEN
    COUNTRY AND THE MAXIMUM PRODUCT PER WORKER DURING A GIVEN
    YEAR
TOTAL NUMBER OF YEARS A COUNTRY WAS UNDER AGREEMENTS IN THE
    PAST
THE DURATION OF LAST STINT UNDER IMF PROGRAMS (FOR COUNTRIES
    NOT CURRENTLY UNDER).

None of these variables is significant when the appropriate estimators are used.

Second, I tested to see whether country-specific and year-specific variables had any effect on rates of economic growth. Tests indicate significant country-specific effects for the "under" sample of observations. When fixed country effects are included in this way, the estimated effect of IMF programs on economic growth is −2.29 percent. (When country-specific effects are included for both "under" and "not under" samples, the result is −3.29.)

Another consideration involves how one thinks about constructing counterfactual observations. Note that the procedure in which one matches observations for the values of the predetermined variables assumes that they are exogenous with regard to the states under which these observations are made. If participation affects the values of these variables, then the counterfactual "had the countries been observed under the same conditions" is no longer valid. Having repeated the same procedure with regard to the predetermined variables, I learned that the rate of growth of capital stock is lower when countries are under an agreement. One cannot tell, however, whether this is an effect of programs or of the sample for which other relevant variables are available. The sample I have available is strongly biased against countries with higher capital stock growth: The mean rate of growth of capital stock for the subset of "under" observations for which other data are missing is 7.15 and only 2.01 for the observations for which other information is available. Hence, one cannot know if the rate of growth of capital stock can be treated as exogenous. In Table 5.8, the column labeled "Endogenous capital stock growth" presents results based on the assumption that participation affects the growth of capital stock. The expected rates of growth are calculated by taking CAPITAL STOCK GROWTH at its mean for each participation status. When the rate of growth of capital stock is considered to be an endogenous effect of IMF programs, the effect of these programs appears much larger.

Because this may be merely the effect of sampling, however, I also tested a growth model which includes all the available country-year observations of economic growth (3,991 observations). In the estimates reported above, only 1,024 observations were used because data on many of the variables used to predict selection into IMF programs (used to generate the hazard rates) have missing observations. There are no data on variables such as RESERVES and BUDGET BALANCE for the period before 1970, and data for the post-1970 period have missing observations scattered over countries and years.

To test the effect of IMF programs on economic growth using as much data as possible, I generated hazard rates using a "stripped" or "large sample" model of selection (recall Table 4.7 from Chapter 4). The "large sample" model of selection includes only those variables that are available for the entire sample. With this selection model, I generate hazard rates for the

TABLE 5.8. *Robustness checks*

Selection Specification	# of Obs.	Growth Model			
		Bare Bones	Panel One-Way Fixed	Endogenous Capital Stock Growth	
Table 4.3 (exogenous selection)	1,024	-1.53	-2.29	-3.88	
Table 4.3 (endogenous selection)	1,024	-1.33	-1.96	-3.68	
Table 4.4, Specification 4.4a	1,024	-1.49	-2.17	-3.85	Tests indicate panel
Table 4.4, Specification 4.4b	1,024	-1.21	-1.85	-3.56	one-way fixed for these
Table 4.5 (minimal spec.)	1,024	-2.04	-2.72	-4.38	samples
Table 4.5 (all-variable spec.)	1,024	-0.88	-1.31	-3.25	
Table 4.6	879	-2.59	-2.96	-5.13	
Stripped spec. (post-1970 sample)	2,607	-0.58	N/A	-1.93	Tests indicate no panel
Stripped spec. (large sample)	3,991	-0.67	N/A	-1.77	effects for these samples

entire sample of 3,991 observations. Results for the entire sample, as well as the subset of all observations for the post-1970 period are presented in Table 5.8 in the rows labeled "Stripped spec. (post-1970 sample)" (2,607 observations) and "Stripped spec. (large sample)" (3,991 observations). These samples are used to reestimate growth according to the three growth models discussed above: "Barebones," "Panel (one-way fixed)," and "Endogenous capital stock growth."

A further concern is whether the selection process is an "exogenous" or "endogenous" process. Selection is "exogenous" if it is not driven by the expected consequences. Hence, the predetermined variables in the growth equation do not enter into the reduced form of the selection specification. If the expected consequences do enter into the structural form of the model, selection is "endogenous," and the right-hand side variables of the growth equation ($\dot{K}/K$ and $\dot{L}/L$) enter into the reduced form of the selection equation.[10] Results for exogenous and endogenous selection specifications are presented in Table 5.8 in the rows labeled "Table 4.3 (exogenous selection)" and "Table 4.3 (endogenous selection)."

Finally, recall that in addition to the main selection specification presented in Table 4.3 (Chapter 4), several other plausible selection specifications were presented in Tables 4.4 through 4.6. Each of these selection specifications can be used to generate hazard rates to correct for potential selection bias. I re-estimated all three growth models using the hazard rates from these different selection specifications.

These robustness tests are best presented in a table where the entries are the selection-corrected differences between average growth expected under and not under agreements. Consider Table 5.8. The three columns under "Growth model," indicate the growth model used: "Barebones," "Panel (one-way fixed)," and "Endogenous capital stock growth." The rows indicate the selection specification used to generate the hazard rates: Table 4.3 (exogenous selection); Table 4.3 (endogenous selection); Table 4.4, Specification, 4.4a; Table 4.4, Specification 4.4b; Table 4.5 (minimal spec.); Table 4.5 (all-variable spec.); Table 4.6; Stripped spec. (post-1970 sample); and Stripped spec. (large sample). The above results speak for themselves. There is no evidence that IMF programs help growth or even have benign effects. IMF programs hurt economic growth.

THE 1990S

Chapter 1 explains that the data for economic growth are from Przeworski et al. (2000) who have arranged the data from the Heston and Summers (1995) study. These data are measured as percent change in gross domestic

---

[10] Obviously, some variables must appear in the selection but not in the growth equation for the model to be identified.

product (GDP), which is measured in 1985 international "purchasing power parity" (PPP) dollars. PPP dollars are normalized to ensure that the GDP of different countries are comparable. The methodology to produce these data is complicated, involving measuring the value of a "basket" of goods in different countries and then converting the price of similar baskets in different countries (see Heston and Summers 1995 for details).

As of this writing, the Przeworski et al. (2000) data stop in 1990. Economic growth data are available in PPP format for the 1990s from the World Bank, but for the period before 1990 the World Bank series is not highly correlated with the data used in the Przeworski et al. (2000) study ($\rho = 0.6$). Thus, it is questionable whether such data are reliable. Clearly the methodology of the World Bank produces observations quite different from Heston and Summers (1995). Therefore, I have not used the World Bank economic growth data in this study.

With the above caveats in mind, I applied the same methodology to PPP data from the World Bank on economic growth for the 1990s.[11] I consider my results preliminary and highly tentative. For what they are worth, here they are. The selection model includes DEFICIT, DEBT SERVICE, INVESTMENT (from *World Development Indicators*), YEARS UNDER and NUMBER UNDER for the government, and RESERVES, DEBT SERVICE, INVESTMENT, NUMBER UNDER, and BOP × SIZE for the IMF. The sample with no missing observations includes 318 country-year observations with mean output growth of 3.5 percent per year. There are 191 observations of countries participating in IMF programs with mean growth of 2.8 percent per year, and 127 observations of countries not participating in IMF programs with mean growth of 4.7 percent per year. The observed difference is 1.9 percent. Controlling for selection in the manner described in this chapter, the inherent effect of IMF programs appears to be −1.4 percent per year in this sample. The negative finding on growth holds.

APPENDIX: CORRECTING FOR SELECTION BIAS

Let y stand for the rate of growth ($\dot{Y}/Y$ in the main text) and $\mathbf{x}$ for the vector of observable variables that determine growth: $\dot{A}/A$, $\dot{K}/K$, and $\dot{L}/L$. Assume that y is a function of $\mathbf{x}$, with the population density $f(y \mid \mathbf{x})$. Write the regression equations (suppressing the i, t subscripts) as:

$$y_j = \boldsymbol{\beta}'_j \mathbf{x} + e_j, \tag{5.1}$$

where $j = 1$ if the country-year observation is "under" agreement, $j = \{2,3,4\}$ otherwise.

---

[11] The data on GDP used to generate the growth rates are in 1987 international dollars. The series is available from World Bank 1998.

The expected value of y_1 for the observed sample is

$$E(y_u \mid \mathbf{x}, y_1 \text{ is observed}) = E(y_1 \mid \mathbf{x}, d^{G^*} > 0, d^{F^*} > 0)$$

$$= \beta_1' \mathbf{x} + E(e_1 \mid d^{G^*} > 0, d^{F^*} > 0), \qquad (5.2)$$

where $E(e_1 \mid d^{G^*} > 0, d^{F^*} > 0)$ is the conditional expectation of e_1 given that y_1 is observed.

On the other hand, the expected value for the population is

$$E(y_1 \mid \mathbf{x}) = \beta_1' \mathbf{x}. \qquad (5.3)$$

Hence, the expected value in the sample differs from the population value by the conditional expectations of the error term, given that these values are observed. If selection is not random, then e_1 is correlated with the error terms from the selection estimation described in equations (4.2) and (4.3): Either v^G – the unobserved variables influencing the government – or v^F – the unobserved variables influencing the IMF – or both.

The expected value for the selected sample can be derived as follows (see Poirier 1980: 216). Assuming that v^G and v^F are independent, we can write the expected value of $E(e_1 \mid d^{G^*} > 0, d^{F^*} > 0)$ as:

$$E(e_1 \mid d^{G^*} > 0, d^{F^*} > 0) = \theta_{1G}' E(v^G \mid d^{G^*} > 0)$$

$$+ \theta_{1F}' E(v^F \mid d^{F^*} > 0), \qquad (5.4)$$

where

$$E(v^G \mid d^{G^*} > 0) = \lambda_1^G = \frac{\phi\big[(\gamma + \kappa)' \mathbf{x}_{i,t-1}^G\big]}{\Phi\big[(\gamma + \kappa)' \mathbf{x}_{i,t-1}^G\big]} \qquad (5.5)$$

and

$$E(v^F \mid d^{F^*} > 0) = \lambda_1^F = \frac{\phi\big[(\mu + \eta)' \mathbf{x}_{i,t-1}^F\big]}{\Phi\big[(\mu + \eta)' \mathbf{x}_{i,t-1}^F\big]}. \qquad (5.6)$$

Recall that $\Phi(\cdot)$ denotes the cumulative distribution of the standard normal distribution. $\phi(\cdot)$ denotes the probability density function of the standard normal distribution. We can thus write the expected value in the observed sample as

$$E(y_1 \mid d^{G^*} > 0, d^{F^*} > 0) = \beta_1' \mathbf{x} + \theta_{G1}' \lambda_1^G + \theta_{F1}' \lambda_1^F. \qquad (5.7)$$

Note that if (5.1) is estimated on the basis of the observed sample, the variables λ^G and λ^F are omitted from the specification. Hence, the selection problem is a source of omitted variable bias (Heckman 1979).

We can now also understand why controlling (or "matching") for the variables that enter into both selection and outcome equations may in fact exacerbate, rather than attenuate, the selection bias (Achen 1986). Following Heckman (1988), distinguish first between selection on observables and

on unobservables. Selection on observables occurs when the expected covariance $E(e_1 v^k) \neq 0, k \in \{G, F\}$. But once one controls for the observed
variables, $\mathbf{x}^k$, it vanishes so that $E(e_1 v^k \mid \mathbf{x}^k) = 0$. Selection is on unobservables when $E(e_1 v^k \mid \mathbf{x}^k) \neq 0$, so that controlling the factors observed
by the investigator does not remove the covariance between the errors in
the outcome and the selection equations. Now note that the regression coef-
ficient $\theta_1 = \text{cov}(e_1, v^k)/\text{var}(e_1)$. If selection is on unobservables, controlling
for some observed variable in $\mathbf{x}$ (from the outcome equation 5.1) may reduce
the error variance e_1 without equally reducing the covariance of e_1 and v^k.
Hence, the coefficient on the omitted variable will be larger and the bias will
be exacerbated.

Note that correcting for selection bias for country-years observed "not
under" is not straightforward. There are a total of four states of the world.
In state (I), where country-years are observed *under* an IMF agreement,
correction is straightforward:

$$(\text{I}): E(y_1 \mid \mathbf{x}, \text{observe agreement}) = E(y_1 \mid \mathbf{x}, d^{G^*} > 0, d^{F^*} > 0)$$
$$= \boldsymbol{\beta}_1' \mathbf{x} + E(e_1 \mid d^{G^*} > 0, d^{F^*} > 0),$$

where both the government and the IMF want the agreement.

For country-years observed *not under*, however, there are three possible
states of the world:

$$(\text{II}): E(y_2 \mid \mathbf{x}, \text{no agreement}) = E(y_2 \mid \mathbf{x}, d^{G^*} < 0, d^{F^*} < 0)$$
$$= \boldsymbol{\beta}_2' \mathbf{x} + E(e_2 \mid d^{G^*} < 0, d^{F^*} < 0),$$
$$(\text{III}): E(y_3 \mid \mathbf{x}, \text{no agreement}) = E(y_3 \mid \mathbf{x}, d^{G^*} < 0, d^{F^*} > 0)$$
$$= \boldsymbol{\beta}_3' \mathbf{x} + E(e_3 \mid d^{G^*} < 0, d^{F^*} > 0),$$
$$(\text{IV}): E(y_4 \mid \mathbf{x}, \text{no agreement}) = E(y_4 \mid \mathbf{x}, d^{G^*} > 0, d^{F^*} < 0)$$
$$= \boldsymbol{\beta}_4' \mathbf{x} + E(e_4 \mid d^{G^*} > 0, d^{F^*} < 0).$$

In (II), neither the IMF nor the government wants to be under. In (III), the
IMF wants an agreement, but the government does not want to be under.
In (IV), the government wants the agreement, and the IMF does not. The
problem is that since we do not observe the actors' individual decisions, we
do not know how to break up the "not under" observations respectively
between states (II) through (IV).

We know that

$$E(v^G \mid d^{G^*} < 0) = \lambda_0^G = \frac{-\phi(\boldsymbol{\gamma}' \mathbf{x}_{i,t-1}^G)}{1 - \Phi(\boldsymbol{\gamma}' \mathbf{x}_{i,t-1}^G)} \tag{5.8}$$

and

$$E(v^F \mid d^{F*} < 0) = \lambda_0^F = \frac{-\phi(\mu'\mathbf{x}_{i,t-1}^F)}{1 - \Phi(\mu'\mathbf{x}_{i,t-1}^F)}, \tag{5.9}$$

but we do not observe when to use which pair of instruments when an observation is "not under": $(\lambda_0^G, \lambda_0^F)$, $(\lambda_0^G, \lambda_1^F)$, or $(\lambda_1^G, \lambda_0^F)$.

I proceed by trying three different assumptions: assuming that all observations belong to state (II), assuming that all observations belong to state (III), and assuming that all observations belong to state (IV):

$$E(y_1 \mid d = 1) = \beta_1'\mathbf{x} + \theta_{G1}'\lambda_1^G + \theta_{F1}'\lambda_1^F, \tag{5.10}$$

$$E(y_2 \mid d = 0) = \beta_2'\mathbf{x} + \theta_{G2}'\lambda_0^G + \theta_{F2}'\lambda_0^F, \tag{5.11}$$

$$E(y_3 \mid d = 0) = \beta_3'\mathbf{x} + \theta_{G3}'\lambda_0^G + \theta_{F3}'\lambda_1^F, \tag{5.12}$$

$$E(y_4 \mid d = 0) = \beta_4'\mathbf{x} + \theta_{G4}'\lambda_1^G + \theta_{F4}'\lambda_0^F. \tag{5.13}$$

This produces four sets of βs with which to estimate growth according to four possible states of the world. The expected average rates of growth are

(I) Growth "under" (both want agreement): 2.00
(II) Growth "not under" because both: 3.53
(III) Growth "not under" because of the government: 3.66
(IV) Growth "not under" because of IMF: 3.19

For the "barebones" growth model, the effect of the IMF ranges from −1.19 to −1.66. In the main body of the text, I report the effect of IMF programs as the difference between state (I) and state (II).

6

Distributional Consequences of IMF Programs

The question of why governments participate in IMF programs was originally raised as a means to an end. To evaluate IMF program effects, one must understand selection into IMF programs. The results from Chapter 5 indicate that the effects of IMF programs on economic growth are negative. Ironically, this finding leads directly back to the selection question: If IMF programs hurt growth, why do governments enter into these agreements? The argument laid out in this book is that governments want IMF agreements to help push through policies that face opposition. But why do governments seek to push through policies that hurt growth? The goal of this book was to answer the growth question, but this new question is simply too intriguing to leave hanging.

One possibility, proposed by Pastor (1987a, 1987b), is that governments bring in the IMF for distributional reasons. Pastor found that the labor share of income decreased under IMF programs. Since Pastor's study, a second large-n study (Garuda 2000) has largely confirmed the finding that IMF programs increase income inequality.

Note that if IMF programs increase income inequality, then the less-well-off are definitely worse off when governments participate. Growth of total output is lowered and their share of output shrinks as well. But the same is not true for those at the upper end of the income distribution. Although overall economic growth may suffer under the IMF, some groups may gain because of distributional shifts.

Previous studies on the effects of IMF programs on distribution do not employ parametric methods to control for nonrandom selection. In this chapter, I apply the methodology used in Chapter 5 to evaluate the longest single series of data available on distribution: the labor share of income from manufacturing. The obvious disadvantage of this series is that it includes data only on the manufacturing sector. The advantage of using this series, however, is that it includes 2,095 observations of 110 countries over the period of 1961 to 1993. The importance of using this series of data is that previous studies

134

using data with fewer observations were unable to use parametric methods to control for other factors that may influence both IMF participation and income distribution (Garuda 2000).

If my results are consistent with the findings of Pastor (1987a, 1987b) and Garuda (2000), it will increase confidence in the finding that the inherent effects of IMF programs on income distribution are negative. If so, it may be true that the income of some groups actually increases under IMF programs, even though overall growth is hurt.

BACKGROUND ON THE IMF AND DISTRIBUTION

As noted in Chapter 1, during the early part of the history of the Fund, officials argued that domestic political issues – such as income distribution – were not the business of the IMF (see Williamson 1983; Polak 1991). Officials began addressing the issue, however, after countries went off the gold standard in the 1970s. The Fund shifted from a currency regulating institution to a manager of balance of payments problems, involved in the national policies of developing countries. Officials claimed that their programs had no necessarily negative effect on income distribution (see Johnson and Salop 1980 and Sisson 1986; cited in Pastor 1987a: 52). They even indicated that the Fund's programs can help improve the distribution of income within a country.

The theoretical links between IMF programs and income distribution are not clear-cut. Economists at the Fund have claimed "the distributional effects of IMF stabilization programs are so complex that they defy simple categorization" (Pastor 1987a: 54). Programs typically include many policy changes that can influence the distribution of income, but the direction and magnitude of the effects of such changes depend on particular characteristics of the economy and on how reforms are structured.

Garuda considers the effects of devaluation, which decreases the price ratio of nontradable to tradable goods. If the poor are rural farmers producing goods for export, this can improve the distribution of income, but if the poor are urban consumers facing higher food prices or rural farmers producing for domestic consumption, it can increase income inequality (Garuda 2000: 1033). Pastor (1987a: 54) explains that devaluation can also worsen the distribution of income if elite groups engage in capital flight prior to the devaluation.

Another example, reducing access to domestic credit affects groups according to their access to other sources of credit by increasing interest rates or bank reserve requirements, or by imposing explicit credit ceilings. Large, well established firms are favored over small and medium sized firms, and the urban sector is favored over the rural sector (Johnson and Salop 1980: 11).

Trade liberalization, which has increasingly been part of IMF programs, may benefit labor-intensive sectors and eventually result in higher wages or lower unemployment, but these effects will be small and slow, whereas formerly protected sectors will contract first, lowering income in these areas (Handa and King 1997: 915–16).

Reduction of public expenditure is the most common feature of Fund-supported programs and has perhaps the most straightforward distributional consequences. In an analysis of ninety-four programs from 1980 to 1984, for example, Sisson (1986: 34) reports that eight-six of them involved some restraint of central government current expenditure. Fifty-six programs involved restraint on capital outlays and net lending (Sisson 1986: 34). As Johnson and Salop note, "the brunt of any downward adjustment of government expenditure to GDP is most commonly borne by public sector employees engaged in projects that come to be postponed, together with the private domestic suppliers of services associated with such projects. These tend to be highly capital-intensive ventures in construction and public utilities" (1980: 12). Wage freezes, limits on employment, and reduced benefits for public employees are also common. Sisson (1986: 34) reports that over three-fifths of programs involved wage restraint. The overall effect of reducing the government budget deficit on income distribution depends on the composition of the budget cuts, the mobility of producers, and the adaptability of consumer patterns (Garuda 2000: 1033). As Garuda explains, "virtually any overall result can be achieved, provided that overall expenditures are reduced" (2000: 1034).[1]

Because programs can be achieved in many different ways with different consequences for distribution, study after study has noted that the political power of various groups may influence the final outcome (Garuda 2000: 1033; Pastor 1987a: Chapters 3 and 5; Sisson 1986: 33; Diaz-Alejandro 1981: 126). Dell argues that the causes of distributional outcomes "lie more in the realm of politics than economics" (Dell 1982: 609; cited in Pastor 1987a: 56). As Pastor contends, "once the green light is given for real wage deflation to encourage exports, there is little reason for elites to restrain 'wage compression' to that sufficient to maintain the real consumption wage" (1987a: 56). Staff at the Fund have also acknowledged this political dimension: Johnson and Salop note, "Domestic political considerations will largely determine who bears the burden of reducing and restructuring aggregate demand" (1980: 23), and "the choice of policy instruments will be influenced by the political power of various income groups" (1980: 12). Governments may implement IMF programs in such a way as to protect certain constituencies.

---

[1] For a review of the theoretical links between IMF structural adjustment programs and income distribution, see Garuda (2000), Handa and King (1997), Heller, Bovenberg, Catsambas, Chu, and Shome (1988), Pastor (1987a: 51–61, 108–47), Sisson (1986), and Johnson and Salop (1980).

EMPIRICAL APPROACHES

Pastor (1987a, 1987b) conducted the first large-n study of the effects of IMF programs on income distribution. Pastor considered labor's "wage share of net domestic product" (1987a: 88) in eighteen Latin American countries from 1965 to 1981.[2] He compared labor share before and after IMF programs and included a control group of nonprogram countries. He found that "the single most consistent effect the IMF seems to have is the redistribution of income away from workers" (1987a: 89).

The "before-after" approach that Pastor employed is intuitive and was, for its time, methodologically reasonable. The problem, as discussed in the previous chapter, is that one must assume that all the conditions which can affect the labor share of income are exactly the same before and after a program is introduced. Any change in labor share is attributed to the introduction of the IMF program.

The Garuda (2000) study represents a methodological advance as he explicitly addresses the selection problem. Garuda studies the effects of fifty-eight IMF programs on GINI coefficients and the income of the poorest quintile in thirty-nine countries from 1975 to 1991. He finds that income distribution deteriorates when countries facing severe balance of payments problems enter into IMF programs. For countries facing less severe external accounts imbalances, however, he finds improvements in income distribution when they enter into IMF programs.

Garuda's data come from Deininger and Squire's (1996) recently published data set measuring income inequality. Unfortunately, this data set provides only a limited number of observations that are designated by the authors as "high quality." Garuda uses 370 observations.

The scarcity of data limits the methods Garuda can employ to analyze the effects of the IMF. He attempts to correct for selection bias by constructing "propensity scores" (see Conway 1994, for a description of the method), breaking observations "into groups by propensity score and then [comparing] means within those groups." Garuda notes, however, that although "data limitations prevented the use of . . . regression-based modeling, . . . it should definitely be employed with a larger data set" (2000: 1037).[3]

---

[2] Pastor's data come from Series 1.3 of the U.N. National Accounts "Cost Components of the Gross Domestic Product (GDP)," which was computed from employee compensation, consumption of fixed capital, new indirect business taxes, and net operating surplus. He calculated labor share of income by dividing employee compensation by new production (GDP minus capital consumption) (1987a: 202).

[3] It may seem that the 370 observations that Garuda worked with should be sufficient to run regression analysis. Note, however, that the data exhibit country specific effects, thus at least two observations per country are required or observations must be discarded. And there must be two observations in each state of program participation. Very few observations remain once these observations are discarded.

This chapter takes the next step suggested by Garuda, applying regression analysis to a larger data set: the labor share of income from manufacturing.[4] The disadvantage of this series on labor share is that it covers only one sector of the economy. This is a real limitation as the manufacturing sector of the economy is small in many developing countries. For example, for the time period of my sample (1961–93), value added in the manufacturing sector of the economy accounts for about 21 percent of GDP in South American countries. In Asia, it accounts for about 18 percent, and in African countries only about 11 percent. Thus, the analyses of other data sets by previous studies (Pastor 1987a, 1987b; Garuda 2000) are important, as they provide a fuller picture of the economy.

Employing the data sets used by Pastor and Garuda, however, leads to a different – and potentially more severe – limitation: the inability to correct for selection bias using parametric analysis. The reason for this is that there are simply not enough observations to perform rigorous statistical analysis. The recently expanded version of the data Garuda used (see the *World Income Inequality Database*) includes 1,703 separate country-year observations. These observations are not comparable, however, as they are measured in different ways. For example, data from different countries have different reference units (household, individual) and different income definitions (UNDP 2000: 8).[5] The updated labor share data from the United Nations that Pastor used includes only 511 separate country-year observations. When one controls for country-specific effects and splits the sample between countries participating in IMF programs and countries not participating, there are simply not enough observations to use parametric methods to correct for selection bias. This is exactly the problem cited by Garuda.

The advantage of using the series on labor share of income from manufacturing is that it includes 2,095 observations. This is by far the largest data set available on a single series of data. Observations span the period of 1961 to 1993 and include 110 countries. Ninety-one of these countries participated in 352 separate IMF arrangements which covered a total of 599 country-years. These data were collected according to the same methodology, are thus comparable across time and country, and can be analyzed using parametric methods to control for other factors that may influence both IMF participation and income distribution.

To control for selection effects, I will need to employ a selection specification from Chapter 4. Recall that if I use the "full" selection specification from Chapter 4, my sample will be reduced to 1,024 observations. Since many of the 1,024 country-year observations are not in common with the 2,095 country-year observations on labor share, the sample will actually be reduced to a few hundred observations – fewer than required to perform

---

[4] Definitions and sources of all data used in this study are found in Appendix 1 to this volume.
[5] For a critique of this data set see Atkinson and Bourguignon (2000).

TABLE 6.1. *Labor share of manufacturing income (percentage) according to IMF experience*

Observations of Countries	Mean	Median	n
Never under a spell	45.069	46.679	414
Before spells	36.177	36.000	381
Before and between spells	34.754	33.350	758
During spells	**31.570**	**29.500**	**599**
Between spells	33.317	30.100	377
Between and after spells	38.930	39.400	799
After spells	43.945	45.300	422

the analysis. Thus, I use the "stripped" or "large sample" selection specification from Table 4.7 to obtain the instruments (hazard rates) to correct for selection bias. This allows me to analyze a much larger sample. Analyzing smaller samples has precluded parametric analysis. These nonparametric approaches on smaller data sets show that IMF programs increase inequality. The question is whether this finding holds when put to a more rigorous statistical test.

THE EFFECT OF IMF PROGRAMS ON LABOR SHARE

First consider what is observed. Table 6.1 shows the labor share of income from manufacturing according to the experiences of countries participating in "spells" of IMF programs. The first row of Table 6.1 (Never under a spell) shows the mean and median labor share (percentages) for the nineteen countries in the sample that never participate in an IMF agreement for as long as they are observed (414 country-year observations). The second row (Before spells) gives the mean and median labor share for those countries that have not yet participated in an IMF program but eventually do participate. The third row (Before and between spells) pools the "Before" observations and the "Between" observations, which are observations of countries that are not currently participating in an IMF program, but have in the past and do in the future. The "During spell" row presents the 599 observations of countries actually participating in an IMF arrangement. The "Between spells" row reports just the "Between" observations (countries that are not currently participating but have participated and will participate again). The "Between and after spells" row pools the observations of "Between spells" with the observations of "After spells," which are observations of countries that have participated in IMF programs in the past, but do not return before the end year of the sample (1993).

Table 6.1 shows that the observation made by Pastor in 1987 about Latin America holds over a longer period of time and over the entire world:

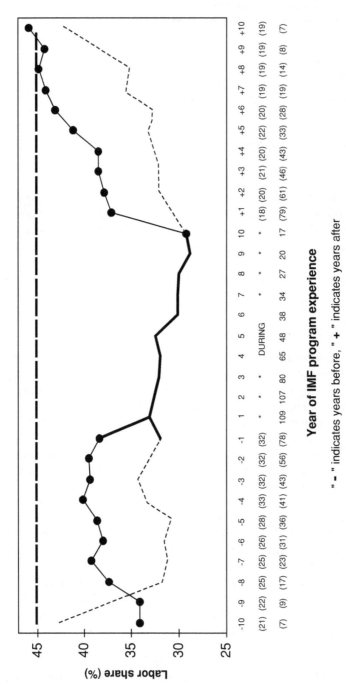

FIGURE 6.1. Labor share of manufacturing income by IMF experience

140

labor share is lower for countries that participate in IMF programs. Labor is best off in countries that have never participated in an IMF program, and worst off in countries currently participating in an IMF program. Labor does slightly better when the country leaves the IMF program, but labor share does not appear to rebound immediately.

Figure 6.1 represents these observations graphically, showing the average experience of countries over time. The valley traced by the thick line in the middle of the figure represents the labor share of manufacturing income when countries participate in IMF programs. The dotted lines show the experience of before and after programs. The thin dashed lines represent the experience of countries between programs. Note that many of the between observations are double counted because countries may exit IMF programs for only a short time before returning. For example, of the seventy-eight observations of countries between programs one year before returning (-1), and the seventy-nine observations of countries between programs one year after $(+1)$, twenty-nine of these observations are in common. The thick dashed horizontal line near the top of the figure represents countries that never participate in IMF programs.

Labor share is low in countries before they enter IMF programs, but there does not appear to be any trend leading up to participation. When countries enter IMF programs, labor share plummets and as participation continues it seems to trend downward. When countries emerge from IMF programs, labor share trends upward it appears to take about ten years to "catch up" to countries that never participate. Note, however, that most countries that participate in IMF programs return before ten years. This is why the number of "between" observations after programs declines rapidly (from seventy-nine observations to nineteen observations) as countries move from $+1$ to $+7$ years out – countries enter new IMF programs. The average stint "out" of IMF programs before returning is about five years.

So the observed world supports Pastor's and Garuda's findings. But do they hold when one controls for nonrandom selection on observed and unobserved conditions? Table 6.2 presents the regression results for labor share using the method employed in Chapter 5 for economic growth. The regression is run on the sample split between observations of countries with IMF programs and those without. The hazard rates for the government and the IMF (λ^G and λ^F) are included to correct for potential selection bias. The model includes random effects to control for country specific characteristics.[6]

---

[6] All variables are lagged so the first observation for each country is discarded. This reduces the sample size from 2,095 to 2,016. Only 1,846 of these observations are included in the regression analysis because the random effects model to control for country specific effects requires that there be at least two observations for each country. Countries with only one observation in either the "participating" or "not participating" states are discarded. I choose the random

TABLE 6.2. *Labor share of income from manufacturing regression by participation status*

Explanatory Variables	Not Participating in IMF Programs		Participating in IMF Programs	
	Coefficient	Mean	Coefficient	Mean
CONSTANT	39.39**	1.00	31.71**	1.00
	(1.77)		(2.31)	
CAPITAL STOCK/WORKER (1000s)	0.23**	13.18	−0.19	5.58
	(0.06)		(0.21)	
PER CAPITA INCOME (1000s)	−0.66**	5.28	0.90	2.46
	(0.25)		(0.82)	
PRICE LEVEL OF CONSUMPTION	0.06**	71.40	0.002	54.59
	(0.01)		(0.01)	
REGIME	−5.90**	0.45	−1.32	0.64
	(1.05)		(0.98)	
λ^G	1.83**	−1.41	4.01	0.15
	(0.32)		(2.88)	
λ^F	−2.82	−0.27	5.87	0.16
	(2.70)		(4.88)	
Mean of dependent variable, labor share	39.88		31.57	
Standard deviation	(13.54)		(11.73)	
Number of observations	1305		541	
Lagrange multiplier test	3206.99		1266.45	
Hausman test (fixed versus random)	30.44		2.54	

** Indicates significance at the 95% level.

Note: Standard errors in parentheses. All variables are lagged one year.

My specification of the determinants of labor share follows the "benchmark regression" suggested by Rodrik (1999: 714) in his work, "Democracies Pay Higher Wages":

(a) average labor productivity in manufacturing, as measured by capital stock per member of the labor force (CAPITAL STOCK/WORKER)[7]

---

effects model so that a single constant term is estimated for each state, "participation" or "not participation." This is a more convenient approach than the fixed effects model which estimates a country-specific constant term. If a country is observed in only one state of participation, no counterfactual constant term is estimated. Thus, one cannot estimate what labor share would have been if the country had been in the other state of participation. One way around this is simply to use the average of the fixed effects for each state. When I do this, the results presented in this chapter hold.

[7] To control for labor productivity, Rodrik (1999) uses manufacturing value added per worker instead of capital stock per worker. I use capital stock per worker because of the greater availability of data (4,126 observations versus 1,838 observations). These variables are highly correlated: ($\rho = 0.8$).

    (b) per capita GDP, "as a handy proxy for other structural determinants correlated with levels of income" (PER CAPITA INCOME)

    (c) average price level of consumption, "to indicate cost-of-living differences not captured by exchange rate conversions" (PRICE LEVEL OF CONSUMPTION)

    (d) country specific effects (random effects model)

I also follow Rodrik by including a variable measuring "REGIME" (coded 1 for dictatorships and 0 for democracies). These data come from Przeworski et al. (2000) who take the economic data from the *Penn World Tables 5.6* (Heston and Summers 1995).

Most of the coefficients reported in Table 6.2 are consistent with Rodrik's (1999) findings. First of all, his finding that dictatorships pay lower wages than democracies holds when one controls for participation in IMF programs. Note, however, that this finding is stronger when countries are not participating in IMF programs. On average, labor share of income is 5.9 percent lower in dictatorships than in democracies when countries do not participate in IMF programs, but only 1.3 percent lower when countries participate in IMF programs. This may be because labor share is already much lower when countries participate in IMF programs.

For observations of countries not participating in IMF programs, the effect of CAPITAL STOCK/WORKER is positive and significant, as is the effect of PRICE LEVEL OF CONSUMPTION. For observations of countries participating in IMF programs, the effect of GDP per capita (PER CAPITA INCOME) is positive as is the effect of PRICE LEVEL OF CONSUMPTION, though the coefficients have large standard errors and are not statistically significant. There are two strange findings reported in Table 6.2 that are not consistent with Rodrik (1999): the significant negative effect of PER CAPITA INCOME for observations of countries not participating, and the small negative effect of CAPITAL STOCK/WORKER for observations of countries participating.

The fact that PER CAPITA INCOME does not have a positive effect on labor share of income for observations of countries not participating in IMF programs may have to do with the fact that countries with high levels of per capita income are less likely to participate in IMF programs. The relationship between labor share and per capita income may simply be flat at higher levels of per capita income. To test this, I replace PER CAPITA INCOME with LOG [PER CAPITA INCOME] (the natural logarithm of per capita income) in the specification presented in Table 6.3.

The effect of LOG [PER CAPITA INCOME] is not significant, but the coefficient is positive, as expected. The strange negative effect of CAPITAL STOCK/WORKER for countries observed participating in IMF programs, persists in this specification. This result may simply be driven by multicollinearity between PER CAPITA INCOME and CAPITAL STOCK/WORKER as they are

TABLE 6.3. *Labor share of income from manufacturing regression by participation status (with the natural log of GDP per capita)*

Explanatory Variables	Not Participating in IMF Programs		Participating in IMF Programs	
	Coefficient	Mean	Coefficient	Mean
CONSTANT	36.71**	1.00	32.60**	1.00
	(1.83)		(2.16)	
CAPITAL STOCK/WORKER (1000s)	0.03	13.18	−0.08	5.58
	(0.05)		(0.18)	
LOG [PER CAPITA INCOME (1000s)]	1.49	1.25	0.99	0.64
	(0.96)		(1.93)	
PRICE LEVEL OF CONSUMPTION	0.06**	71.40	0.003	54.59
	(0.01)		(0.01)	
REGIME	−4.95**	0.45	−1.27	0.64
	(1.06)		(0.98)	
λ^G	1.66**	−1.41	4.26	0.15
	(0.32)		(2.87)	
λ^F	−2.83	−0.27	6.56	0.16
	(2.72)		(4.86)	
Mean of dependent variable, Labor share	39.88		31.57	
Standard deviation	(13.54)		(11.73)	
Number of observations	1305		541	
Lagrange multiplier test	3212.84		1208.55	
Hausman test (fixed versus random)	20.76		2.23	

** Indicates significance at the 95% level.

Note: Standard errors in parentheses. All variables are lagged one year.

highly correlated ($\rho = 0.9$). In the specification presented in Table 6.4, I leave out PER CAPITA INCOME.

The effect of CAPITAL STOCK/WORKER for countries observed participating in IMF programs is positive, though not significant in this specification. All other coefficients have the expected sign.

To test for the significance of the apparent time trends evidenced in Figure 6.1, I tested "count" variables: For countries participating, I included a count of how many consecutive years a country has participated in IMF programs. For countries not participating, I included a count of the number of years since participation in an IMF program ended (coded zero if a country has not yet participated). To distinguish countries that have not yet participated, I also included a dummy variable coded one if a country has not yet participated and zero otherwise. I also tested for trends leading up to IMF programs. When these splines[8] are included in the regressions, the

[8] The splines I use are essentially count variables, counting the number of years during or after an IMF program.

TABLE 6.4. *Labor share of income from manufacturing regression by participation status (without PER CAPITA INCOME)*

Explanatory Variables	Not Participating in IMF Programs		Participating in IMF Programs	
	Coefficient	Mean	Coefficient	Mean
CONSTANT	37.88**	1.00	32.68**	1.00
	(1.67)		(2.14)	
CAPITAL STOCK/WORKER (1000s)	0.08**	13.18	0.00	5.58
	(0.03)		(0.12)	
PRICE LEVEL OF CONSUMPTION	0.06**	71.40	0.00	54.59
	(0.01)		(0.01)	
REGIME	−5.33**	0.45	−1.21	0.64
	(1.03)		(0.97)	
λ^G	1.68**	−1.41	4.25	0.15
	(0.32)		(2.87)	
λ^F	−2.57	−0.27	7.09	0.16
	(2.72)		(4.75)	
Mean of dependent variable, Labor share	39.88		31.57	
Standard deviation	(13.54)		(11.73)	
Number of observations	1305		541	
Lagrange multiplier test	3207.19		1207.19	
Hausman test (fixed versus random)	22.97		9.31	

** Indicates significance at the 95% level.

Note: Standard errors in parentheses. All variables are lagged one year.

trends over time observed in Figure 6.1 turn out not to hold when the other variables are taken into account. They are not statistically significant when included in the above specifications.[9]

Most of the coefficients on the hazard rates in the above tables are small with large standard errors, indicating there is not much bias from nonrandom selection. The only significant hazard rate is λ^G for observations of countries not participating. The effect is 1.83 according to the specification in Table 6.2, 1.66 according to Table 6.3, and 1.68 according to Table 6.4. This effect indicates that unobserved variables driving selection also determine labor share. If this hazard rate were not included, one would understate labor share for countries not participating by approximately 2.58 percent according to Table 6.2, 2.34 percent according to Table 6.3, and 2.37 percent according to Table 6.4.[10] Since the only significant selection effect appears to be understating labor share for observations of countries not participating,

[9] These results are not presented here, but are available from the author upon request.

[10] These estimates are derived by weighing the coefficient by the mean, for example, 1.83 × (−1.41) = −2.58.

TABLE 6.5. *Hypothetical labor share of income from manufacturing according to IMF experience (selection-corrected estimates)*

	According to Specification from Table 6.2	According to Specification from Table 6.3	According to Specification from Table 6.4
Predicted labor share if countries do not participate	39.98%	39.86%	39.85%
Predicted labor share if countries participate	33.12%	32.38%	32.23%
Predicted overall effect	**−6.86%**	**−7.47%**	**−7.63%**
Number of observations	1846		
Actually observed mean	37.44%		
Observed mean not participating	39.88%		
Observed mean participating	31.57%		
Observed difference	**−8.31%**		

it is not surprising that the negative finding of previous studies holds here (see Table 6.5).

I use the coefficients above to estimate the inherent effects of IMF programs. As is done in Chapter 5 to estimate hypothetical growth rates, one can calculate the hypothetical labor share by multiplying the observed values of CAPITAL STOCK/WORKER, PER CAPITA INCOME, PRICE LEVEL OF CONSUMPTION, and REGIME by the coefficients for "Participating" and "Not participating" reported in the tables above.

Table 6.5 presents the average for the entire world of these hypothetical scenarios. Because the parameters are unbiased by nonrandom selection, differences in country conditions are essentially "matched." Thus, the differences between these averages are an estimate of the inherent effects of IMF programs.

Table 6.5 reports that once one controls for other factors – nonrandom selection, the average labor productivity in manufacturing, per capita GDP, the average price level of consumption, country specific effects, and regime – the inherent effect of IMF programs is negative. The effect of IMF programs on labor share of income for manufacturing is smaller than the observed difference of −8.3 percent; the effect ranges from −6.86 to −7.63, depending on the specification of labor share used. So some of the observed difference is due to other factors. The remaining significant negative effect, however, confirms the results of Pastor (1987a, 1987b) and Garuda (2000). Governments under IMF economic reform programs structure these reforms such that labor is hit harder than the owners of capital.[11]

---

[11] This is also consistent with the qualitative findings of a study using univariate rather than bivariate probit to control for selection effects. See Vreeland (2002).

ARE THE OWNERS OF CAPITAL BETTER OFF?

The negative finding on income distribution holds across methodologies. This differs from the study of economic growth, where early work found IMF programs have no effect. The introduction of methods to control nonrandom selection produced a qualitatively different result: IMF programs actually have a negative effect on economic growth.

Taken together, the negative impact of IMF programs on growth and distribution has interesting political implications about how economic reform is structured. Note that if IMF programs hurt economic growth and lower the labor share of income from manufacturing, the income of labor is obviously lowered when governments enter into IMF programs. The same is not necessarily true for the owners of capital.

Suppose for simplicity that national income, Y, is distributed between two functional groups, the owners of capital and labor. If national income grows at an annual rate, γ, then next year's $(t + 1)$ income of the owners of capital if the country does not participate in an IMF program is $K_{t+1} = \alpha Y_t(1 + \gamma)$, where K is the income of the owners of capital, and α is the proportion of national income the owners of capital receive.

If the country participates in an IMF program, then income of the owners of capital is $K_{t+1}^{IMF} = (\alpha + \Delta)Y_t(1 + \gamma - \delta)$, where $\Delta > 0$ is the positive effect of the IMF program on capital share of national income, and $\delta > 0$ is the negative effect of the IMF program on economic growth.

If the owners of capital discount the future at a high enough rate so that all they care about is the next period, they will be better off under an IMF program when

$$K^{IMF} > K$$

$$\Rightarrow (\alpha + \Delta)Y_t(1 + \gamma - \delta) > \alpha Y_t(1 + \gamma)$$

$$\Rightarrow \Delta > \left(\frac{\delta}{1 + \gamma - \delta}\right)\alpha \qquad (6.1)$$

To give this relationship more meaning, consider some numbers. According to my data, the average share of manufacturing earnings going to labor is about 38 percent. Set capital share at 62 percent ($\alpha = 0.62$). The average annual rate of growth of output is 4.23 percent ($\gamma = 0.042$). According to Chapter 5, a reasonable estimate of the negative effect of IMF programs on economic growth is approximately 1.53 percent ($\delta = 0.0153$). According to equation (6.1), the owners of capital are better off, at least in the short run, if the increase in capital share of income (Δ) is 1.0 percent or greater. Clearly, this condition holds according to the results presented in Table 6.5.

With other numbers, the shift in income to the owners of capital might have to be larger to make them better off. Consider the average capital share of income from manufacturing observed the year before a country enters

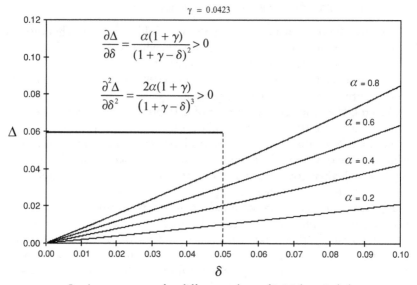

FIGURE 6.2. Iso-income curves for different values of initial capital share

an IMF program, $\alpha = 0.66$ and the average rate of output growth the year before entering an IMF program, $\gamma = 0.031$. Furthermore, suppose that the adverse effect of IMF programs on economic growth is set at 5 percent, $\delta = 0.05$ (about the largest estimated effect from the robustness checks in Chapter 5). Given these figures, the increase in capital share of income must be 3.4 percent or greater, a condition which also holds according to Table 6.5.

Figure 6.2 shows "iso-income curves" for different values of initial capital share of income (α), holding initial rate of growth constant, $\gamma = 0.0423$.[12] The iso-income curves show how much income must be transferred to capital (Δ) to keep the income of capital at the same level as it would be without an IMF program, for a given adverse effect of an IMF on economic growth (δ). The figure shows that if capital has a smaller initial share of income (α), it will require a smaller shift in income distribution to keep its income the same despite lower economic growth. For all values of initial capital share, however, the first and second derivatives of the change in income distribution (Δ) with respect to the adverse change in economic growth (δ) are positive at the point of indifference. This means that the more IMF programs hurt growth, the more income must be transferred to capital – at an increasing rate – in order to keep the income of the owners of capital the same as it would be without the IMF program.

[12] Setting initial rate of growth at different levels has only small effects. At the point of indifference, $\partial \Delta / \partial \gamma = -k\delta / (1 + \gamma - \delta)^2$.

If the actual change in income distribution (Δ) lies above the iso-income curve for a given value of α, then the income of the owners of capital will actually increase when the country participates in an IMF program even though the program hurts economic growth. The horizontal line at $\Delta = 0.06$ represents a conservative estimate of the effect of IMF programs on distribution according to Table 6.5. For the relevant range of the effect of IMF programs on growth, $\delta = 0.015$ to $\delta = 0.05$ (according to the robustness checks in Chapter 5), the condition for the owners of capital to be better off clearly holds. The horizontal line is above the iso-income curves for all levels of initial capital share of income.

Note that the prediction that IMF programs lower the labor share of income by more than 6 percent holds constant the effects of other variables. The above estimations predict effects *as if* country-year observations were matched for all conditions, observed and unobserved. Because governments that actually enter into IMF programs usually suffer from particularly adverse economic conditions, one may observe the owners of capital to actually lose income. The statistical analyses of this section indicate, however, that the owners of capital *would* do worse if the government did not enter into the IMF program, and labor *would* do better.

Sometimes the owners of capital are better off even if one does not control for selection effects. Recall from Chapter 2 the shift of labor share of earnings from manufacturing that occurred in Uruguay when Lacalle entered into the 1990 IMF agreement (Figure 2.15). Labor share of income from manufacturing was 25.8 percent in 1989 and 23.1 percent in 1990. So even though economy experienced a contraction of -1.03 percent and earnings from manufacturing dropped from 3,722 million to 3,667 million, the income going to the owners of capital increased from 2,762 million to 2,820 million. Despite negative growth for the economy as a whole, the income of the owners of capital increased by 2 percent due to shifts in distribution.

Another interesting case is the Republic of Congo which had a labor share of earnings from manufacturing of 48.8 percent in 1985. The government entered into an IMF agreement in 1986 and labor share dropped to 40.3 percent. Although the country as a whole experienced growth of -2.99 percent that year, the income of the owners of capital grew. Earnings from manufacturing[13] were 5,227 million in 1985, of which 2,676 million went to the owners of capital. Earnings from manufacturing dropped to

---

[13] Data on earnings from manufacturing was taken from World Bank (2000), where it is defined as follows: "Manufacturing refers to industries belonging to ISIC divisions 15–37. Value added is the net output of a sector after adding up all outputs and subtracting intermediate inputs. It is calculated without making deductions for depreciation of fabricated assets or depletion and degradation of natural resources. The origin of value added is determined by the International Standard Industrial Classification (ISIC), revision 2. Data are expressed [sic.] constant 1995 U.S. dollars."

5,059 million in 1986, of which the owners of capital received 3,020 million. The income of capital increased 9.5 percent despite the overall economic contraction.

And finally, consider Ecuador. In 1973, after several years of IMF programs, this country allowed its stand-by arrangement to expire without entering into a new agreement. It did not return to the IMF for nearly a decade. In 1974, the labor share of income from manufacturing was 24.8 percent. Labor share grew until 1982 when it reached 52.8 percent. In 1983, the government entered into another IMF program. Labor share plummeted to 34.8 percent. Ecuador experienced a drastic contraction that year with economic growth of -5.76 percent. But the owners of capital experienced an increase in income in 1983. Earnings from manufacturing in 1982 were 3,413 million, of which 1,611 million went to capital. The following year, earnings from manufacturing dropped to 3,366 million, but 2,195 million of this went to capital. The income of the owners of capital grew by 36 percent!

It may be naïve to assume that the distributional shift simply increases the income of the owners of capital. If the share of income going to the owners of capital increases under IMF programs, private investment should increase, which in turn should help economic growth (Przeworski and Wallerstein 1988). But this is not what was found in Chapter 5 (although the finding that IMF programs hurt growth may be driven by cuts to public not private investment – this is discussed in the next chapter). Another explanation for the shift in income distribution is that labor repression is required for a country not to go into default with international creditors. Dymski and Pastor (1990) argue that the repression of wages can be a signal to international lenders of a country's ability to repay debt.[14] Willingness or "effort" to repay debt is signaled through wage compression. Even if the economy experiences low growth, debt repayment can be maintained through labor repression: "Some of the willingness-to-pay signals are coercive in that they indicate a capacity to redistribute domestic income to meet payments obligations" (1990: 184). Dymski and Pastor find a positive significant relationship between repression of worker income and increased loans to a country. The long run effects of this, however, are to increase the probability of debt repayment problems – the social tension and diminished work effort that repression causes reduce the ability to repay debt in the long run.[15] Thus, the findings of this chapter may be only the tip of the iceberg. Further analysis is required to determine the intranational and international consequences of distributional shifts.

---

[14] Although the signal can be misleading. They note that "some of these [signals] may be misleading when the social tension and diminished work effort they cause tend to reduce the ability to pay." See Dymski and Pastor (1990) for details.

[15] Also see Berg and Sachs (1988).

CONCLUSION

IMF programs have negative distributional consequences. This finding holds across data sets and methodologies. If IMF programs hurt economic growth and redistribute income away from labor, labor is worse off – in terms of income – when countries participate in IMF programs. For other constituencies, however, there is a trade-off: growth decreases but share of income increases. Shifts in distribution toward the owners of capital, for example, mitigate the negative effects on economic growth for this group. The change in capital share of income from manufacturing is large enough to increase the income of the owners of capital, despite lower growth rates. What is clear from this chapter and the work of Pastor (1987a, 1987b) and Garuda (2000) is that the negative effects of IMF programs on economic growth are paid for by the least well-off in a country.

7

Conclusions

The main findings of this book are that governments enter into IMF programs not just for economic reasons but for political reasons as well, and that these programs hurt economic growth and exacerbate income inequality. Hence, this study paints the following picture of participation in IMF programs: Governments enter into IMF programs under bad economic circumstances. Their choice is not usually between good and bad economic performance but between bad performance on their own – without the IMF – or worse performance under a program sponsored by the IMF. Why would governments agree to programs that hurt economic growth? By bringing in the IMF, governments gain political leverage – via conditionality – to help push through unpopular policies. For some constituencies, these policies dampen the effects of bad economic performance by redistributing income upward and thus rewarding elites. If the distributional consequences are strong enough, key groups can be made better off even though growth is hurt. But IMF programs hurt doubly the least well-off in society: Total output growth is lowered, and income is shifted away from them.

The results of this study raise new questions and have important policy implications. Thus, after reviewing my central findings, this chapter lays out new avenues of research and concludes with some suggestions for reform of the IMF.

SELECTION FINDINGS – WHY GOVERNMENTS AND THE IMF ENTER INTO AGREEMENTS

The central question of this study has been an empirical one: What is the effect of IMF programs on economic growth? The answer is not straight-forward because countries do not enter into programs as random experiments. Their rates of economic growth are due in part to the IMF program and in part to the circumstances that led them to enter into these programs. Thus, answering this question entailed addressing the problem of nonrandom selection: Why do governments and the IMF enter into agreements? Hence this has been a study of how countries are selected into IMF programs (*selection*) and the effects of these programs (*performance*).

The main selection finding of this study is that although governments turn to the Fund under bad economic circumstances – high deficits, low foreign reserves, high debt, and low investment – they also turn to the Fund because they want conditions to be imposed. IMF agreements make it more costly for opponents of economic reform to reject the preferred policies of a reform-oriented executive. Rejecting the IMF can limit access to IMF credit and send negative signals out to investors and international creditors. Thus, entering into an IMF agreement can increase the political pressure on opponents to accept economic reform.

This selection finding adds impetus to the debate over the reform of IMF conditionality. Some argue, for example, that seeking out and assisting only reform-oriented governments should become the explicit policy of the IMF (IMF 2001: 65; citing Dollar and Svensson 2000). This would essentially make my argument – that governments enter into IMF programs to force their own reform agendas – the explicit policy of the Fund. Instead of "making" reformers, the IMF should look for reformers and extend assistance to them.

Others might argue that this approach will exacerbate problems already present in the imposition of IMF programs, by increasing the animosity of those groups within a country who are "left out." If governments use IMF programs as leverage to push through policies that increase income inequality, labor and the poor certainly have grounds for concern. This does not mean that without IMF programs governments would not or should not undertake reform, but reform takes on a different tone when a country participates in an IMF program. As Remmer (1986: 7) argues, "The politics of stabilization are likely to be rather different where an outside villain [the IMF] cannot be identified so readily." I return to this issue below when addressing the issue of program "ownership."

PERFORMANCE FINDINGS – THE EFFECT OF IMF PROGRAMS ON GROWTH AND DISTRIBUTION

Although the selection findings have important implications for the issue of IMF reform, the selection question was originally raised as a means to an end: to determine the effect of IMF programs on economic growth. And it turns out that if one controls for nonrandom selection, IMF programs lower economic growth.

Previous studies failed to reach this conclusion because none of them accounted for the effects that unobserved variables have on economic growth. Countries that participate in IMF programs have lower growth than countries that do not, and they also face less favorable observable situations. So if one merely controls for observed factors, the IMF appears to have no effect. Yet, this study shows that the unobserved factors in countries participating in IMF programs are favorable to economic growth. When this is not taken into account, one overstates the effectiveness of the IMF by attributing to it the effects of unobserved variables. Governments that persevere through IMF programs want conditions to be imposed. They have higher levels of political will. They also have populations whose mistrust of the government is not so high that it precludes continued participation. These are characteristics whose effects should not be confused with the inherent effects of IMF programs. Once one accounts for the effects of these unobserved characteristics driving selection, it turns out that IMF programs have negative effects on economic growth.

Ironically, this question leads directly back to the selection question: Why do governments enter into programs that hurt economic growth? The results of Chapter 6 indicate that there are distributional consequences at stake. IMF programs have negative distributional consequences for labor (Pastor 1987a, 1987b) and the poor (Garuda 2000). If IMF programs hurt economic growth and redistribute income away from labor and the poor, these groups are clearly worse off – in terms of income – when countries participate in IMF programs. For other more fortunate groups, however, there may be a trade-off: Growth decreases but share of income increases.

NEW QUESTIONS

The strategy of this book has been to apply a rigorous methodology to a narrow question. As a result, many questions have been left unanswered. Some important questions future research should address are:

- What are the mechanisms by which IMF programs hurt economic growth?
- What are the incentives of the IMF?
- What are the effects of IMF programs on economic stability?

Economic Growth

It may seem baffling to some that IMF programs can hurt both growth and distribution. After all, if the share of income going to the rich increases, private investment should increase, which in turn should stimulate economic growth (Przeworski and Wallerstein 1988). What then is the mechanism by which programs hurt growth? There are several possibilities.

Consider cuts to public sector investment. Economists, following Barro (1990), argue that there is an optimal size of the public sector for economic growth. The economic advisors of governments participating in IMF programs may believe that the public sector is larger than optimal, and thus they seek to lower the deficit. But the IMF may require them to go too far in their spending cuts.

More specifically, the types of spending cuts matter. Economists at the IMF have explained that governments under IMF programs typically lower budget deficits by cutting public investment (Tanzi 1989, Tanzi and Davoodi 1998). Broadly speaking, the government can choose to cut public wages or transfers, both of which will be felt immediately, or public investment, which will not be felt until the long run. If the government chooses the short over the long run by cutting investment, this will be detrimental to growth.

The nature of public investment also has an impact. Tanzi and Davoodi (1998) go on to explain that if governments do invest under IMF programs, the investment tends to be concentrated on "ribbon cutting" events that are high profile rather than on important projects that may take more time but win less attention. Thus, rather than invest in low profile but vital road maintenance, for example, governments may invest in building a new road as quickly and cheaply as possible. So not only are funds to public investment cut, the remaining funds are poorly invested for political reasons.

Other conditions demanded by the Fund have dubious effects on growth. Increasing interest rates puts some industries out of business. Some firms may be inefficient, but the IMF's move to raise interest rates hurts firms indiscriminately. Thus, Blejer and Cheasty (1989) point out, high interest rates induce good firms to shut down along with bad ones.

Another possibility is that elites engage in capital flight. There is no reason to assume that upward shifts in income distribution should result in *domestic* investment. Increased income of the owners of capital may simply result in savings abroad. If this is the case then the distributional consequences of IMF programs may exacerbate this pattern. Income should be left in the hands of individuals consuming and investing domestically.[1]

Several scholars also contend that the environment is damaged under IMF programs, which can prove detrimental to long run growth.[2] Environmental protection and enforcement programs often lose funding when government budget deficits are reduced (Kessler and Van Dorp 1998). When these programs are cut, environmental problems such as deforestation are apt to worsen.[3] Deforestation can also increase when the immediate negative effect of programs on economic growth leads to unemployment and income decline. This drives population shifts from urban centers to subsistence

---

[1] For effects on foreign direct investment, see Jensen (2002).

[2] See, for example, Hayter (1989), Cruz and Repetto (1992), George (1992), Munasinghe and Cruz (1996), and Owusu (1998). I am grateful to Spencer Durbin and Robynn Sturm for suggesting these references.

[3] Gandhi (1996: 14) suggests that this is precisely what happened under IMF programs in Thailand, Mexico, Cameroon, Zambia, and Tanzania.

living in rural areas, overexploiting fragile and unproductive environments (Cruz and Repetto 1992).[4] Vreeland, Sturm, and Durbin (2001) in fact find – even after controlling for nonrandom selection – IMF programs increase rates of forest depletion.

There are several mechanisms by which IMF programs may hurt growth. Yet, a recent IMF report notes that although conditionality may require reform, "The concern is not necessarily that the Fund may be prescribing the wrong policies" (IMF 2001: 19). The empirical results of this study call for attention to the mechanisms through which IMF policies potentially hurt growth.[5] Perhaps in the face of economic instability, growth cannot and should not be the goal of an IMF program. But if the IMF continues to claim that it is, policy reevaluation is in order.

Incentives of the IMF

Another baffling question is why the principal funders of the Fund, say the G-5 (United States, Japan, Germany, France, and the United Kingdom), or the G-7 (the G-5 plus Italy and Canada), have supported the IMF despite the fact that its programs lower growth. I propose several possibilities below, but none of them is fully satisfactory.

One possible answer is that the funders were misinformed. Reviews of IMF literature (Bird 1995, 1996a, b; Killick 1995) point out that no study has shown IMF programs to have adverse effects on economic growth. Has the G-7 funded the IMF based on this evidence? This line of argument is not very compelling. Not everyone has believed this evidence, and this study shows that the conclusions were wrong. IMF programs do hurt growth. The casual empirical observation – that countries participating in IMF programs have lower growth than those that do not – has led many to this conclusion. Despite the incorrect conclusions in the literature, there has not been consensus among policy makers that IMF programs are good for growth. But if governments are not certain that IMF programs will improve growth, why else would they support the Fund?

One answer to this question may lie in short-run concerns about debt repayment. The trade-off for the creditor countries may be between short-term repayment of debt and long-term economic growth in debtor countries. If creditors discount the future at a high rate, which is likely given the instability

---

[4] Cruz and Repetto (1992) cite this migration as the primary cause of deforestation in the Philippines.

[5] More detailed quantitative analysis on specific reform measures advocated by the IMF is also needed. As the new Managing Director of the IMF, Anne Krueger (2000: 588) notes, careful quantitative analysis of the payoffs from particular alternative policy measures "would enable policymakers to push for at least some reform in areas where resistance is strong."

of debtor countries, they may prefer short-run repayment of debt over economic growth.

As noted in Chapter 6, it is also possible that the Fund's principals are misled in this respect. Dymski and Pastor (1990) argue that international creditors mistakenly take repression of wages as a good sign, indicating a willingness or commitment to repay debt. If growth is hurt, the country will extract the necessary repayment by repressing the wages of labor. In fact, Dymski and Pastor (1990) find wage repression in a given country is positively associated with loans to that country.[6] So perhaps the IMF does achieve the short-run goals of its funders.

At the crux of answering the question of why the IMF supports programs that lower growth, however, is still another question: What are the objectives of the IMF? To whom are the officials and staff at the Fund accountable?

According to Vaubel (1986, 1996), the IMF is simply unaccountable. The objective of bureaucrats at the IMF is simply to maximize budget and leisure. The United States, Japan, Germany, France, and the United Kingdom do not have much leverage over how IMF programs are implemented because accountability is tenuous at best.

It is true that the chain of command is unwieldy. First of all, even if there is agreement among the G-7, who are all responding to multiple constituencies at home, they do not constitute a majority of the votes at the Fund – they control about 45 percent. But suppose there exists a majority consensus at the highest levels of authority at the IMF; there is still a long way to go before implementation. Decisions are handed to the Fund's Managing Director, who in turn gives them to the IMF staff. Orders then must make it through the entire bureaucratic chain of command of the IMF staff before they are finally imposed on a government entering into an IMF agreement. And then this government in turn must bring about policy change from domestic constituencies. Thus, there are *at least* five principal-agent relationships, with most of these involving multiple principals and multiple agents:

183 member state constituencies → their governments,
these governments[7] → the IMF Managing Director,
the IMF Managing Director → the IMF staff,
(chain of command through the IMF staff)
the IMF staff → a government signing an agreement,
this government → domestic policy makers.

---

[6] This is similar to Berg and Sachs's (1988) finding that income inequality is associated with debt rescheduling.

[7] Of course, these governments do not directly order the Managing Director. Governments appoint a representative to the Board of Governors, which in turn elects twenty-four representatives to the Board of Executive Directors of the IMF. The Managing Director usually reports to the Executive Directors. So one should really add at least two more levels of principal-agent relationships to this already unwieldy chain!

In any one of these principal-agent relationships, there is some room for breakdown of accountability. Taken in sum, it might be a miracle if there is any accountability at all.[8]

Yet, research suggests that the IMF is indeed responsive. Thacker (1999), for example, finds evidence that the United States exerts influence to bring about higher loans to its most preferred governments.[9] Kahler (1990: 94) notes that the United States has successfully blocked the renewal of Managing Directors when "accomplishments did not meet American expectations" (cited in Thacker 1999). Gould (2001b), on the other hand, finds evidence that the IMF responds to the preferences of international financiers. Because the additional funding of international creditors – be they creditor states, private financial institutions, or multilateral organizations – is important, they are "in an ideal position to make demands on the Fund" about the conditions to include in programs (Gould 2001b: 3).

The debate about whose objectives the IMF pursues remains open. The research agenda described in this section should be pursued, continuing to identify mechanisms by which the IMF is accountable (or not) and continuing to present empirical work on the question. The IMF may represent the interests of its principal funders, or international financiers, or simply be an authority unto itself. There is evidence that all three of these mechanisms are at work. Once these mechanisms are more clearly distinguished one will be better able to understand the Fund's objectives, and specifically why it supports programs that hurt economic growth.

Economic Stability

Perhaps, despite what its officials announce, growth is simply not the goal of the IMF. The current debate about the future of the Fund asks whether the Fund should focus on economic growth, economic stability, both, or neither. The results of this study indicate that the IMF has failed to promote growth. How has it fared on the question of economic stability?

Previous studies have found that the programs of the Fund may fare slightly better in the area of stability than they do in the area of economic growth. Consider the overall balance of payments and the rate of inflation as proxies for "economic stability."

Using a before-after approach, Pastor (1987a, 1987b) and Killick, Malik, and Marcus (1992) find that programs have a positive effect on the overall

---

[8] This follows the conclusion of Robert Dahl's (1999) "Can International organizations be democratic? a skeptic's view." For the question of accountability of voters to policy makers and from policy makers to voters within countries (the first and last principal-agent relationships in this chain), see Przeworski, Stokes, and Manin (1999).

[9] Oatley and Yackee (2000) find evidence that United States foreign policy and financial interests play a role in Fund lending.

balance of payments. Gylfason (1987) and Khan (1990) find the same result using the with-without approach, and Khan (1990) finds the same using
methods controlling for selection on observed variables. Other studies have
failed to find this positive effect, but no study has ever reported a significant negative effect of IMF programs on the balance of payments (IMF
2001: 51).

Regarding inflation, most of the evaluations of the Fund are not so strong.
Most studies – including all studies that control for selection on observed
variables – find no significant effect (IMF 2001: 51). This is striking. Inflation is often reported as an important reason that governments turn to the
Fund, but it was not found to be a significant predictor when included in
the selection specifications from Chapter 4. Curtailing inflation is also usually reported as a main objective of Fund programs. But research indicates
that programs have little effect in this area. Only Stone (2002), looking at
post-Communist Eastern Europe, finds that the IMF has been successful in
curtailing inflation, and even in this study, the effects depend on whether the
IMF can credibly commit to sanctioning noncompliance.

So the Fund seems to have a mixed record on the issue of stability. There
is some limited evidence of positive effects on the balance of payments and
the rate of inflation. There is no evidence that the Fund is hurting in these
areas. Perhaps the Fund is doing better at achieving the goal of promoting
economic stability than it is at achieving the goal of economic growth –
which it does hurt. And perhaps the institution should focus on stability as
its single goal.

But what do we really know about program effects in these areas? Note
that previous studies have not employed methods to control for the selection effects of unobserved variables. This may be important. Unobserved
variables did not prove important in evaluating distributional effects of IMF
programs in Chapter 6. The results from previous studies were confirmed.
Yet, the results of previous studies did not hold on the question of economic
growth. Unobserved variables driving selection also drive economic growth.
Once this was accounted for in Chapter 5, results from most previous
studies – that IMF programs have no effect on economic growth – did not
hold. The fact that nonrandom selection on observed as well as unobserved
variables has proven to be important here indicates that they should at least
be considered when evaluating other effects of the IMF.

Thus, one may prefer to remain agnostic about the effects of IMF programs on stability. Previous studies indicate that they may improve the balance of payments and rate of inflation. But these studies do not account for
the effects of unobserved variables that may drive selection as well as stability. Controlling for observed factors while failing to account for the effects
of unobserved variables can actually produce a less accurate estimate of program effects than controlling for nothing at all (Achen 1986; Przeworski and
Limongi 1996).

Thus, this study raises several questions: about how IMF programs hurt
growth, about the motivations of the Fund to promote such programs, and
about how the Fund has fared in the area of stability. A new methodology
for the study of the effects of IMF programs was narrowly applied in these
chapters to the questions of growth and distribution. The further research
problems discussed in this conclusion raise questions about the effects of the
IMF in a number of related areas: domestic investment, foreign investment
and public investment; the stock and flow of debt; and the effects on balance
of payments and inflation. Rigorous methodology – accounting for all the
effects of nonrandom selection – should be employed to answer these questions as well. This study calls for more empirical work on distinguishing the
effects of selection from the inherent effects of IMF programs in all these
areas.[10]

POLICY IMPLICATIONS

Beyond this research agenda on evaluation of program effects, this study has
implications for the question of reform of the IMF. Thus, I return now to the
policy question raised in Chapter 1: Should the IMF be in the development
business?

The results presented here indicate that change is required. I suggest the
Fund take one of two paths to reform. They may seem extreme but both my
suggested alternatives – although opposite in direction – are currently being
considered by the Fund in some form. And if they are extreme, so be it, for
conclusions are not the place to be tentative.

I recommend that the IMF make a meaningful commitment to helping
labor and the poor. Failing this, it should abolish conditionality and get out
of the business of development entirely.

Before discussing these alternatives, however, a caveat should be raised.
Since this study uses data that end in 1990,[11] and my conclusions beyond
1990 are qualified due to questionable data, one may wonder whether the
IMF has modified the designs of its programs since then. Note that in 1993,
the Fund reported (Cheney 1993: 13):

The Executive Board undertakes periodic reviews of conditionality and, on many
occasions, it has adjusted the policies and practices relating to the use of the IMF's
resources. In its most recent discussion of issues related to conditionality and program
design, in July 1991, the Executive Board affirmed that the current guidelines on
conditionality, which the Board adopted in 1979, remain broadly appropriate.

[10] Similar methods should be employed to evaluate the impact of other international institutions. See, for example, Abouharb (2000) for such evaluations of the effects of World Bank
loans.
[11] As of this writing.

More recently (IMF 2001: 30), staff at the IMF again confirmed that the 1979 guidelines remain appropriate.

Nevertheless, while the broad principles have remained the same, there have been shifts in conditionality. In the mid-1990s, for example, the number and specificity of conditions associated with IMF programs increased. This "micro" as opposed to "macro" conditionality may seem to be precisely the remedy to the problems that Tanzi and Davoodi (1998) point out about program implementation. Under "microconditionality," for example, the precise nature of spending cuts can be specified, so that public investment is not unduly cut. But it turns out that the Fund is already backing down from its brief experiment with increased conditionality. It seems that "microconditionality" can make things worse. Noting that "an overload of conditionality may reduce the overall effectiveness of the program," IMF staff recommends a return to broad macro guidelines, "streamlining" conditionality. The hope is that "reducing the amount of conditionality [will] actually increase the number of desirable reforms implemented." Apparently, microconditionality is harder to monitor and can result in noncompliance with key conditions. Thus, after only a few years, the IMF is pulling away from increased conditionality.

The effectiveness of "microconditionality" has not been fully evaluated. Staff at the Fund seems to believe, however, that an overburdening of conditionality leads to less overall compliance, with governments implementing only those parts of programs they want to push through.[12] As Joseph Stiglitz (2000: 551), the former Chief Economist at the World Bank explains,

There is ... a process of self-selection of reforms: the ruling elite has taken advantage of the reform process and the asymmetries of information – both between themselves and the citizenry and between the international aid community and themselves – to push those reforms that would benefit them.

Note that when governments undertake this strategy, they use the leverage of the IMF against opposition. And if past trends are any indication, the results are lower growth and a shift of income away from labor and the poor.

Thus, I support two alternatives: Either the Fund should do away with conditionality altogether so that its leverage may no longer be used to produce these perverse outcomes. Or it should pursue a new, different kind of depth to conditionality, one which safeguards the well-being of labor and the poor.

The first alternative largely follows the advice of the Meltzer Commission. The IMF should get out of the development business. In the words of a recent IMF report, "the Fund could drop its emphasis on promoting high-quality growth" (IMF 2001: 34). Under this alternative, the IMF would do

---

[12] For alternative critiques, see Collier, Guillaumont, Guillaumont, and Gunning (1997) and Kapur (2001).

away with the practice of lending in return for policy reform after a country enters into a crisis. The IMF could continue to exist as a lender of last resort but would focus its attention on managing balance of payments crises, providing unconditioned loans when necessary. Stability would be the primary goal.

This raises the problem of moral hazard. How does the Fund avoid merely subsidizing policies that will continue to worsen balance of payments problems? The answer of the Meltzer Commission is to establish some kind of preconditionality, with continual surveillance of member policy. Any member following "good" policy maintains its eligibility for assistance, should a balance of payments problem arise. Members following "bad" policy lose eligibility and risk facing balance of payments crises without Fund support.

There are two problems with this approach. The first is how to determine policy benchmarks that make a country eligible for assistance or not. Note that taken to an extreme, if the "good" policies were really good, countries eligible for IMF support would never need it. If major balance of payments problems result from bad policy, then only ineligible countries would ever need Fund assistance.

The second problem is one of credibility. If the Fund were to declare a country ineligible, and then the country entered into a crisis, could the Fund ignore the country leaving it to suffer its fate? Perhaps the Fund could afford to let some small countries sink, but letting countries with large economies like Brazil, Indonesia, or Russia collapse could spell disaster for the rest of the world. It might simply not be credible that the IMF would not step in. Thus the problem of moral hazard would remain.

James Tobin has raised a corollary to this proposal which might solve both these problems. Recognizing that increasing integration of markets and world trade is likely to increase the volatility of a country's balance of payments, Tobin (1998) suggests that the IMF increase the quotas of member countries so that greater amounts of foreign exchange are available to assist countries in times of crisis. This will raise the amount of money a country can take within the 25 percent cutoff.

Beyond Tobin's recommendations, I contend this arbitrary cutoff should also be increased. Recall that countries are allowed to borrow up to 25 percent of their quota without submitting to IMF conditionality because the Fund recognizes that temporary balance of payments problems may simply be due to the vicissitudes of international trade – bad luck. There is no obvious reason why 25 percent is an appropriate cutoff between what constitutes bad luck and bad policy. If the appropriate level was 25 percent in the early years of the IMF, surely the level should increase with increased international financial exchanges. Under this relaxed version of the "out of the development business" alternative, the only precondition for eligibility might be that a member's account be in good standing.

In this way, countries would have greater access to the pool of resources necessary to facilitate growing international trade. Regarding moral hazard, conditionality could still be imposed for extreme cases. But typical arrangements would not involve the same programs of the past that have so far made matters worse, at least for growth and distribution.

Getting out of the development business might not be the best alternative, however. A second alternative I suggest is that the IMF continue to sponsor reform programs, but radically alter the way they are imposed.

Governments want conditions imposed to push through unpopular policies. But Chapter 5 shows that unobserved variables – such as political will and trust – which influence the continuation of programs also influence their success. Countries with high levels of political will and trust are more likely to continue IMF programs, and high levels of these variables are also likely to mitigate the negative consequences for economic growth. Chapter 6 shows that domestic opponents of the IMF have good reason. The negative distributional impact of IMF programs on labor is severe. Garuda (2000) shows that the poor are hurt in terms of income under IMF programs. It may be true that some segments of society want to bring in the IMF, but they may do so precisely because other segments of society oppose the very policies the IMF supports. The IMF (2001: 18) notes that

the program is fundamentally the authorities' own, whereas the conditionality is introduced to ensure that the Fund's resources are used for their intended purpose. According to this view, ownership is an essential foundation for conditionality; it is the authorities who decide what policies to adopt, including whether to seek the financial support of the Fund, and it is the authorities that are responsible for implementing the program.

This "traditional interpretation of conditionality" closely follows the game laid out in Chapter 3. The executive, who is the principal "authority" that the Fund negotiates with, brings in the IMF because he wants to impose economic reform.[13] He uses conditionality to pressure opponents into accepting more reform than they would in the absence of the IMF – ensuring that Fund resources are used for their intended purpose.

The problem with this kind of "ownership" of an IMF program is that it extends only to the "authorities" in a position to seek out the IMF. The "authority" is the chief executive of the country or his agent (such as a finance minister or central bank president). It does not include other segments of society. Thus, this increases the possibility of what the Fund recognizes as "galvaniz[ing] an opposing coalition of entrenched interests" (IMF 2001: 20), which in turn may hurt economic performance and the possibility of program success. Programs may have better chances of support if

[13] See Dollar and Svensson (2000) and Ranis (1995).

they are designed with consideration of a wider spectrum of interests within a country. Distributional concerns might even become explicit parts of an IMF program.[14]

As it stands, the "selling of" an IMF program is left entirely to national authorities. An alternative which the Fund is currently entertaining would involve extending ownership beyond the authorities who approach the Fund. As the IMF (2001: 42) describes it, "subject to the guidance of the authorities, the Fund staff can also play a role – for instance, by holding substantive discussions with other groups, including other ministries, trade unions, industry representatives, and local non-governmental organizations, especially at a stage at which the design of the program is still under consideration."[15]

If the goal of such discussions is merely to convince representatives of labor and the poor that programs as they have been implemented in the past are appropriate, then not much will change. Past programs have doubly hurt these groups by lowering growth and redistributing income upward. But if the goal is to "help groups within the country to participate meaningfully in the process" (IMF 2001: 42), perhaps programs which safeguard the incomes of these segments of society could be developed.

Note that reaching out to groups such as trade unions would be an important step, but such inclusive approaches will hold little credibility if the IMF remains opaque and undemocratic. The Fund should continue to open itself up to greater transparency and should encourage a greater diversity of viewpoints within the organization by recruiting more economists from the developing world as well as professionals from other disciplines beyond economics. Thus the development of IMF programs would be more inclusive from both inside and outside the organization.

Under this alternative, the IMF would not give up the goal of what former IMF Managing Director Camdessus called "high-quality growth," that is, positive sustainable growth with beneficial consequences for all segments of society. It may be possible to develop programs that cut deficits, stimulate investment, and maintain or even increase the incomes of labor and the poor. Perhaps this is asking too much. But perhaps enough effort has not been made. If the governments turning to the IMF have not had an interest in representing these constituencies (and ultimately, according to the IMF, it is these authorities who decide what policies to adopt) it should not be surprising that outcomes ignoring – indeed, hurting – these segments of society have resulted.

---

[14] Note that IMF surveillance of income distribution would provide positive externalities in the form of data for important research questions on the effects of income distribution on growth and regime stability.

[15] The Fund report considers this avenue as a means to increase the likelihood of program implementation. Beyond this, however, it would also improve what Keohane (1984: 255) calls the "moral status" of the IMF.

If the IMF does not reach out to these groups, then their continued opposition to the institution is justified. The political muscle of the Fund can and has been used to push through policies that hurt labor and the poor, at least in terms of income.

If the IMF is truly interested in poverty reduction and growth, then safeguarding the incomes of labor and the poor can become a condition of IMF programs like any other condition. In the past, the IMF has shied away from issues of distribution, arguing that the Fund should stay out of domestic politics.[16] Yet, the moment the IMF demands that budget deficits be cut and interest rates raised, the Fund has entered into domestic politics. To pretend otherwise is irresponsible.

It is time for the IMF to take a stand on the development issue. The Fund must make a real commitment to promoting development that safeguards, in a meaningful way, the interests of labor and the poor. Otherwise, the Fund should get out of the development business entirely, lest its conditionality continue to be used against these groups.

---

[16] See Polak (1991) and Denoon (1986).

Appendix 1   Variables Used in This Study

BOP: Overall balance of payments as a proportion of GDP. Source: *International Financial Statistics on CD-ROM 1994.*

Budget Balance: Central government overall surplus as a percentage of GDP. Source: Przeworski et al. (2000) who take it from *World Development Indicators on CD-ROM 1994.*

Capital Stock Growth $(\dot{K}/K)$**:** Growth of capital stock per capita. Source: Przeworski et al. (2000) who modify this variable from *Penn World Tables 5.6.* For a full description, see Przeworski et al. (2000: 295).

Capital Stock/Worker (1000s): Capital stock in 1000s 1985 international prices divided by the size of the labor force. The sources of both the capital stock and the labor force variables is Przeworski et al. (2000) who modify these variables from *Penn World Tables 5.6.* For a full description, see Przeworski et al. (2000: 295, 296).

Current Account: Current account balance (% of GDP). Current account balance is the sum of net exports of goods and services, income, and current transfers. Source: *World Development Indicators on CD-ROM 1998.*

Debt Service: Total debt service (% of GNP). Total debt service is the sum of principal repayments and interest actually paid in foreign currency, goods, or services on long-term debt, interest paid on short-term debt, and repayments (repurchases and charges) to the IMF. Source: *World Development Indicators on CD-ROM 1998.*

Growth $(\dot{Y}/Y)$**:** Economic growth measured as the annual rate of growth of GDP. Source: Przeworski et al. (2000) who take it from *Penn World Tables 5.6.*

Investment: Real gross domestic investment (private and public) as a percentage of GDP. Source: Przeworski et al. (2000) who take it from *Penn World Tables 5.6*, where it appears as "i."

Labor Force Growth ($\dot{L}/L$): Annual rate of growth of labor force. Source: Przeworski et al. (2000) who take it from *Penn World Tables 5.6*.

Labor Share: Total nominal earning of employees divided by value added in current prices, to show labor's share in income generated in the manufacturing sector. Source: *World Development Indicators on CD-ROM* (1995), where it appears as UM VAD WAGE ZS.

Lagged Election: Dummy variable coded 1 if legislative elections were held the previous country-year. Source: Przeworski et al. (2000) who take it directly from Banks (1996), where it appears as "LEGISLATIVE ELECTION," and is defined as follows: "The number of elections held for the lower house of a national legislature in a given year."

Loan: Amount of resources approved in an IMF arrangement, measured in millions of Special Drawing Rights. Source: *IMF Annual Reports* and *IMF Survey*.

Not Yet Participated: Dummy variable coded 1 if a country has not yet participated in an IMF program and 0 otherwise.

Number of Veto Players: For presidential systems, this variable is the sum of the following: 1 for the executive, 1 if multiple parties are legal and compete in executive elections, and 1 for each legislative chamber. For parliamentary systems, this variable is the sum of 1 for the Prime Minister and the number of parties in the coalition. Source: Beck et al. (1999), where the variable appears as CHECK1A. Results in Chapter 4 hold when CHECK2A is used as well.

Number Under: Total number of *other* countries in the world currently under IMF agreement (does not include the given country itself).

Participation in IMF Programs (Under): Dummy variable coded 1 for the country-years when there was a conditioned IMF agreement (Stand-by Arrangement, Extended Fund Facility Arrangement, Structural Adjustment Facility Arrangement, or Enhanced Structural Adjustment Facility Arrangement) in force, 0 otherwise. Source: *IMF Annual Reports* and *IMF Survey*.

Per Capita Income: Level of economic development measured as real GDP per capita in 1985 international prices, chain index. Source: Przeworski et al.

(2000) who take it from *Penn World Tables 5.6*, where it appears as "RGDPL."

Price Level of Consumption: The price index of a country's consumption basket in 1985 international prices. Source: Przeworski et al. (2000) who take it from *Penn World Tables 5.6*, where it appears as "PC."

Regime: Dummy variable coded 1 for dictatorships and 0 for democracies. Source: Przeworski et al. (2000). For more on this variable, see Chapter 1 of Przeworski et al. (2000).

Reserves: International reserves to imports of goods and services. Source: *World Development Indicators on CD-ROM 1998*.

Size: GDP in millions of constant 1987 dollars. Source: *International Financial Statistics on CD-ROM 1994*.

Years Since Last IMF Program: Number of country-years since the last IMF program in that country ended, coded 0 for countries currently participating or countries that have not yet participated.

Years Under: Cumulative number of years a country has been under IMF agreements.

Years Under Current Program: Number of country-years participating in a spell of consecutive IMF agreements, beginning when a country signs an IMF agreement when there was no agreement in place the preceding year and ending when no consecutive agreement is signed and the last agreement signed runs out. Coded 0 if a country is not currently participating in IMF agreements.

Appendix 2　Country-Years in Samples

Countries grouped by region: Africa, North America, South America, Asia, Europe, and Oceania and Pacific Islands. 4,126 observation-sample: 135 countries 1951–90

Country	Years in Sample		Spell of Agreements	
			Start	End
Algeria	1962	1990	1989	1990
Angola	1975	1989	Never Under	
Benin	1960	1990	1989	1990
Botswana	1966	1989	Never Under	
Burkina Faso	1960	1990	Never Under	
Burundi	1962	1990	1965	1971
			1976	1977
			1986	1988
Cameroon	1961	1990	1988	1990
Cape Verde Island	1975	1990	Never Under	
Central African Republic	1961	1990	1980	1981
			1983	1988
Chad	1961	1990	1987	1990
Comoros	1975	1990	Never Under	
Congo	1961	1990	1967	1968
			1977	1977
			1979	1980
			1986	1988
			1990	1990
Côte d'Ivoire	1961	1990	1981	1990
Djibouti	1977	1987	Never Under	
Egypt	1951	1990	1977	1981
			1987	1988

(continued)

(continued)

Country	Years in Sample		Spell of Agreements	
			Start	End
Ethiopia	1951	1986	1981	1982
Gabon	1961	1990	1978	1982
			1986	1990
Gambia	1965	1990	1977	1980
			1982	1990
Ghana	1957	1990	1966	1970
			1979	1980
			1983	1985
			1987	1990
Guinea	1960	1990	1982	1983
			1986	1990
Guinea-Bissau	1974	1990	1987	1990
Kenya	1963	1990	1975	1986
			1988	1990
Lesotho	1966	1990	1988	1990
Liberia	1961	1986	1963	1977
			1979	1986
Madagascar	1961	1990	1977	1978
			1980	1990
Malawi	1964	1990	1979	1986
			1988	1989
Mali	1961	1990	1964	1965
			1967	1972
			1982	1990
Mauritania	1961	1990	1977	1978
			1980	1982
			1985	1990
Mauritius	1968	1990	1979	1986
Morocco	1956	1990	1959	1960
			1965	1972
			1980	1990
Mozambique	1975	1990	1987	1990
Niger	1961	1989	1983	1989
Nigeria	1960	1990	1987	1990
Rwanda	1962	1990	1966	1970
			1979	1980
Senegal	1961	1990	1979	1990
Seychelles	1976	1990	Never Under	
Sierra Leone	1962	1990	1966	1967
			1969	1970
			1977	1982
			1984	1987

(continued)

Country	Years in Sample		Spell of Agreements	
			Start	End
Somalia	1961	1989	1964	1971
			1980	1988
South Africa	1951	1990	1958	1959
			1961	1962
			1976	1977
			1982	1983
Sudan	1971	1990	1972	1975
			1979	1985
Swaziland	1968	1989	Never Under	
Tanzania	1961	1988	1975	1976
			1980	1982
			1986	1988
Togo	1961	1990	1979	1990
Tunisia	1961	1990	1964	1970
			1986	1990
Uganda	1962	1990	1971	1972
			1980	1984
			1987	1990
Zaire	1960	1989	1976	1989
Zambia	1964	1990	1973	1974
			1976	1987
Zimbabwe	1965	1990	1981	1984
Bahamas	1978	1987	Never Under	
Barbados	1966	1989	1982	1984
Belize	1981	1990	1984	1986
Canada	1951	1990	Never Under	
Costa Rica	1951	1990	1980	1990
Dominican Republic	1951	1990	1964	1965
			1983	1986
El Salvador	1951	1990	1958	1973
			1980	1983
			1990	1990
Grenada	1985	1990	Never Under	
Guatemala	1951	1990	1960	1962
			1966	1973
			1981	1984
			1988	1990
Haiti	1961	1989	1961	1967
			1970	1989

(continued)

(continued)

Country	Years in Sample		Spell of Agreements	
			Start	End
Honduras	1951	1990	1957	1966
			1968	1973
			1979	1983
			1990	1990
Jamaica	1962	1990	1963	1964
			1973	1974
			1977	1990
Mexico	1951	1990	1954	1955
			1959	1959
			1961	1962
			1977	1979
			1983	1990
Nicaragua	1951	1990	1956	1961
			1963	1965
			1968	1973
			1979	1979
Panama	1951	1990	1965	1966
			1968	1987
Trinidad and Tobago	1962	1990	1989	1990
United States	1951	1990	1963	1965
Argentina	1951	1990	1958	1963
			1967	1969
			1976	1977
			1983	1990
Bolivia	1951	1990	1956	1970
			1973	1974
			1980	1981
			1986	1990
Brazil	1951	1990	1958	1959
			1961	1962
			1965	1973
			1983	1986
			1988	1990
Chile	1951	1990	1956	1959
			1961	1970
			1974	1976
			1983	1990
Colombia	1951	1990	1957	1974
Ecuador	1951	1990	1961	1967
			1969	1973
			1983	1990

(continued)

Country	Years in Sample		Spell of Agreements	
			Start	End
Guyana	1966	1990	1967	1982
			1990	1990
Paraguay	1951	1990	1957	1969
Peru	1951	1990	1954	1971
			1977	1980
			1982	1985
Suriname	1975	1989	Never Under	
Uruguay	1951	1990	1961	1963
			1966	1973
			1975	1987
			1990	1990
Venezuela	1951	1990	1960	1961
			1989	1990
Bangladesh	1971	1990	1974	1976
			1979	1983
			1985	1990
China	1961	1990	1981	1981
			1986	1987
India	1951	1990	1957	1958
			1962	1966
			1981	1984
Indonesia	1961	1990	1961	1964
			1968	1974
Iran	1956	1990	1956	1956
			1960	1962
Iraq	1954	1987	Never Under	
Israel	1954	1990	1974	1977
Japan	1952	1990	1962	1965
Jordan	1955	1990	1989	1990
South Korea	1954	1990	1965	1977
			1980	1987
Laos	1985	1990	1989	1990
Malaysia	1957	1990	Never Under	
Mongolia	1985	1990	Never Under	
Myanmar	1951	1989	1969	1970
			1973	1975
			1977	1979
			1981	1982
Nepal	1961	1986	1976	1977
			1985	1986

(continued)

(continued)

Country	Years in Sample		Spell of Agreements	
			Start	End
Pakistan	1951	1990	1958	1959
			1965	1966
			1968	1969
			1972	1975
			1977	1978
			1980	1983
			1988	1990
Philippines	1951	1990	1962	1965
			1973	1981
			1983	1990
Singapore	1965	1990	Never Under	
Sri Lanka	1951	1990	1965	1972
			1974	1975
			1977	1981
			1983	1984
			1988	1990
Syria	1961	1990	1962	1962
			1964	1964
Taiwan	1952	1990	Never Under	
Thailand	1951	1990	1978	1979
			1981	1983
			1985	1986
Yemen	1970	1989	Never Under	
Austria	1951	1990	Never Under	
Belgium	1951	1990	1952	1957
Bulgaria	1981	1990	Never Under	
Czechoslovakia	1961	1990	Never Under	
Denmark	1951	1990	Never Under	
East Germany	1971	1988	Never Under	
Finland	1951	1990	1953	1953
			1967	1968
			1975	1976
France	1951	1990	1956	1959
			1969	1970
Germany	1951	1990	Never Under	
Greece	1951	1990	Never Under	
Hungary	1971	1990	1982	1985
			1988	1990
Iceland	1951	1990	1960	1963
Ireland	1951	1990	Never Under	
Italy	1951	1990	1974	1975
			1977	1978

(continued)

Country	Years in Sample		Spell of Agreements	
			Start	End
Luxembourg	1951	1990	Never Under	
Malta	1964	1989	Never Under	
Netherlands	1951	1990	1957	1958
Norway	1951	1990	Never Under	
Poland	1971	1990	1990	1990
Portugal	1951	1990	1977	1979
			1983	1985
Romania	1961	1989	1975	1978
			1981	1984
Spain	1951	1990	1959	1961
			1978	1979
Sweden	1951	1990	Never Under	
Switzerland	1951	1990	Never Under	
Turkey	1951	1990	1961	1971
			1978	1985
United Kingdom	1951	1990	1956	1959
			1961	1965
			1967	1970
			1975	1979
USSR	1961	1989	Never Under	
Yugoslavia	1961	1990	1961	1961
			1965	1967
			1971	1971
			1979	1986
			1988	1990
Australia	1951	1990	1961	1961
Fiji	1970	1990	1974	1975
New Zealand	1951	1990	1967	1968
Papua New Guinea	1975	1990	1990	1990
Solomon Islands	1981	1988	1981	1984
Vanuatu	1984	1990	Never Under	
Western Samoa	1980	1990	1980	1980
			1983	1985

1,024 observation-sample: 79 countries 1971–90

Country	Years in Sample		Spell of Agreements	
			Start	End
Benin	1978	1989	1989	1989
Botswana	1977	1987	Never Under	
Burkina Faso	1974	1989	Never Under	
Burundi	1986	1989	1986	1988
Cameroon	1976	1981	1988	1990
	1986	1990		
Cape Verde	1979	1989	Never Under	
Central African Republic	1981	1988	1981	1981
			1983	1988
Chad	1973	1977	1987	1990
	1984	1990		
Congo	1972	1972	1986	1988
	1981	1989		
Côte d'Ivoire	1980	1990	1981	1990
Egypt	1976	1990	1977	1981
			1987	1988
Ethiopia	1984	1986	Never Under	
Gabon	1974	1977	1980	1982
	1980	1988	1986	1990
	1990	1990		
Gambia	1974	1990	1977	1980
			1982	1990
Ghana	1973	1983	1979	1980
			1983	1983
Guinea-Bissau	1987	1990	1987	1990
Kenya	1973	1990	1975	1986
			1988	1990
Lesotho	1983	1990	1988	1990
Liberia	1976	1986	1976	1977
			1979	1986
Madagascar	1973	1975	1981	1990
	1981	1990		
Malawi	1972	1989	1979	1986
			1988	1989
Mali	1978	1989	1982	1989
Mauritania	1976	1980	1977	1978
	1983	1989	1980	1980
			1985	1989
Mauritius	1977	1990	1979	1986
Mozambique	1985	1989	1987	1989
Niger	1977	1987	1983	1987
Nigeria	1973	1979	1987	1990
	1983	1990		

(continued)

Country	Years in Sample		Spell of Agreements	
			Start	End
Rwanda	1974	1990	1979	1980
Senegal	1971	1974	1979	1980
	1976	1976		
	1978	1980		
Sierra Leone	1975	1990	1977	1982
			1984	1987
Somalia	1973	1989	1980	1988
Sudan	1973	1990	1973	1975
			1979	1985
Swaziland	1975	1989	Never Under	
Tanzania	1984	1988	1986	1988
Togo	1978	1989	1979	1989
Tunisia	1973	1990	1986	1990
Uganda	1984	1989	1984	1984
			1987	1989
Zaire	1972	1989	1976	1989
Zambia	1973	1990	1973	1974
			1976	1987
Zimbabwe	1978	1990	1981	1984
Barbados	1973	1989	1982	1984
Costa Rica	1973	1988	1980	1988
Dominican Republic	1973	1990	1983	1986
El Salvador	1971	1982	1971	1973
			1980	1982
Guatemala	1973	1986	1973	1973
	1990	1990	1981	1984
			1990	1990
Haiti	1981	1988	1981	1988
Honduras	1973	1988	1973	1973
			1979	1983
Jamaica	1976	1988	1977	1988
Mexico	1973	1990	1977	1979
			1983	1990
Nicaragua	1971	1984	1971	1973
			1979	1979
Panama	1974	1990	1974	1987
Trinidad and Tobago	1977	1990	1989	1990
Brazil	1979	1979	1983	1986
	1981	1990	1988	1990
Chile	1973	1983	1974	1976
			1983	1983

(continued)

(continued)

Country	Years in Sample		Spell of Agreements	
			Start	End
Colombia	1972	1990	1972	1974
Ecuador	1974	1990	1983	1990
Guyana	1971	1986	1971	1982
Paraguay	1973	1990	Never Under	
Peru	1971	1981	1971	1971
			1977	1980
Uruguay	1973	1983	1973	1973
			1975	1983
Venezuela	1971	1990	1989	1990
Bangladesh	1974	1990	1974	1976
			1979	1983
			1985	1990
India	1975	1990	1981	1984
Indonesia	1973	1983	1973	1974
Iran	1975	1983	Never Under	
Jordan	1984	1990	1989	1990
Malaysia	1973	1984	Never Under	
Nepal	1977	1986	1977	1977
			1985	1986
Pakistan	1974	1990	1974	1975
			1977	1978
			1980	1983
			1988	1990
Philippines	1973	1990	1973	1981
			1983	1990
Sri Lanka	1971	1972	1971	1972
			1974	1975
	1974	1990	1977	1981
			1983	1984
			1988	1990
Syria	1986	1989	Never Under	
Thailand	1973	1987	1978	1979
			1981	1983
			1985	1986
Malta	1973	1979	Never Under	
	1981	1987		
Turkey	1971	1987	1971	1971
			1978	1985
Fiji	1971	1987	1974	1975
Papua New Guinea	1976	1987	Never Under	
Solomon Islands	1982	1987	1982	1984
Vanuatu	1985	1987	Never Under	

2,095 observations of labor share of income from manufacturing for 110 countries

Country	Years in Sample
Benin	1974–81
Botswana	1968, 1972, 1974–88
Burkina Faso	1974–83
Burundi	1971–80, 1983, 1986–91
Cameroon	1970–2, 1974–84, 1989–90
Central African Republic	1973–8, 1980–3, 1985–90, 1992
Chad	1975
Congo	1968–76, 1981–8
Côte d'Ivoire	1966–82
Egypt	1964–92
Gabon	1966, 1972–8, 1980–2
Gambia	1975–82
Ghana	1963–87
Kenya	1963–92
Lesotho	1980–5
Madagascar	1967–86
Malawi	1964–75, 1979–86
Mali	1969–81
Mauritius	1968–91
Morocco	1967–9, 1976–80, 1985–92
Niger	1978–80, 1982–8
Nigeria	1963–85
Rwanda	1969–79, 1984–6
Senegal	1974–85, 1987–9
Seychelles	1976–86
Sierra Leone	1981
Somalia	1967–79, 1986
South Africa	1963, 1964, 1966, 1968, 1970, 1972–93
Sudan	1972–5
Swaziland	1968, 1970–3, 1976–89
Tanzania	1965–74, 1978–88
Togo	1974–9, 1982–4
Tunisia	1963–81
Uganda	1963–9, 1971
Zaire	1968–9, 1972
Zambia	1964–91
Zimbabwe	1965–93
Bahamas	1978–83, 1986–7, 1991
Barbados	1970–89, 1991–2
Belize	1989–92
Canada	1963–93
Costa Rica	1963, 1965, 1968–91
Dominican Republic	1963–83
El Salvador	1963–85, 1991
Guatemala	1968, 1971–90
Honduras	1963–6, 1968–9, 1971–5, 1983–92
Jamaica	1963–92
Mexico	1984–91
Nicaragua	1965–85
Panama	1963–93
Trinidad and Tobago	1966–8, 1974–8, 1981–7
United States	1963–93
Argentina	1963, 1970–91
Bolivia	1970–91

(continued)

(continued)

Country	Years in Sample
Brazil	1963–91
Chile	1963–93
Colombia	1963–93
Ecuador	1963–93
Peru	1963–69, 1972–3, 1979–88
Uruguay	1968, 1976–93
Venezuela	1963, 1965, 1967–93
Bangladesh	1971–90
China	1980–6
India	1963–92
Indonesia	1970–92
Iran	1963–77, 1979–91
Iraq	1963–77, 1981–7, 1991–2
Israel	1963–88, 1990–1
Japan	1963–93
Jordan	1963–71, 1974–92
South Korea	1965–93
Malaysia	1968–93
Myanmar	1963
Nepal	1977, 1986, 1991
Pakistan	1963–89
Philippines	1963–6, 1968–92
Qatar	1991–2
Singapore	1965–93
Sri Lanka	1966, 1980–3, 1987–90
Syria	1961, 1965–91
Thailand	1967–70, 1974–7, 1979, 1982, 1984, 1986, 1988–91
Armenia	1991
Austria	1963–93
Belgium	1963–92
Croatia	1991–2
Cyprus	1991–2
Denmark	1963–92
Finland	1963–93
France	1977–89
Greece	1963–93
Hungary	1971–91
Iceland	1968–91
Ireland	1963–93
Italy	1967–93
Luxembourg	1963–93
Malta	1964–89
Netherlands	1963–91
Norway	1963–93
Poland	1972–90
Portugal	1963–90
Romania	1991
Slovenia	1991-2
Spain	1963–91
Sweden	1963–93
Turkey	1963–92
United Kingdom	1963, 1968–92
Australia	1963–92
Fiji	1970–92
New Zealand	1963–92
Papua New Guinea	1975–89

References

Abouharb, M. Rodwan. 2000. World Bank Structural Adjustment Loans and their Effects on Economic and Social Indicators. MA Thesis, State University of New York at Buffalo.

Abowd, John M. and Henry S. Farber. 1982. Job Queues and the Union Status of Workers. *Industrial and Labor Relations Review* 35: 354–67.

Achen, Christopher H. 1986. *The Statistical Analysis of Quasi-Experiments.* Berkeley: University of California Press.

Aggarwal, Vinod K. 1996. *Debt Games.* New York: Cambridge University Press.

Amemiya, Takeshi. 1985. *Advanced Econometrics.* Cambridge, MA: Harvard University Press.

Atkinson, A. and F. Bourguignon (eds.). 2000. *Handbook of Income Distribution, Vol. 1.* New York: Elsevier Science.

Bandow, Doug. 1994. The IMF: A Record of Addiction and Failure. In *Perpetuating Poverty: The World Bank, the IMF, and the Developing World,* edited by Doug Bandow and Ian Vasquez, pp. 15–36. Washington, DC: The Cato Institute.

Banks, Arthur S. 1996. *Cross-National Time-Series Data Archive* (magnetic tape). Binghamton, NY: Center for Social Analysis, State University of New York at Binghamton.

Barro, Robert J. 1990. Government Spending in a Simple Model of Endogenous Growth. *Journal of Political Economy* 98: S103–S126.

Bates, Robert H., Avner Greif, Margaret Levi, Jean-Laurent Rosenthal, and Barry R. Weingast. 1998. *Analytic Narratives.* Princeton: Princeton University Press.

Beck, Thorsten, George Clarke, Alberto Groff, Philip Keefer, and Patrick Walsh. 1999. New tools and new tests in comparative political economy: The Database of Political Institutions. Development Research Group, The World Bank. Groff: Federal Department of Foreign Affairs (Switzerland).

Berg, Andrew and Jeffery Sachs. 1988. The Debt Crisis: Structural Explanations of Country Performance. *Journal of Development Economics* 29: 271–306.

Bird, Graham. 1995. *IMF Lending to Developing Countries, Issues and Evidence.* London: Routledge.

Bird, Graham. 1996a. The International Monetary Fund and Developing Countries: A Review of the Evidence and Policy Options. *International Organization* 50: 477–511.

Bird, Graham. 1996b. Borrowing from the IMF: The Policy Implications of Recent Empirical Research. *World Development* 24: 1753–60.

Bird, Graham. 1998. The Effectiveness of Conditionality and the Political Economy of Policy Reform: Is It Simply a Matter of Political Will? *Journal of Policy Reform* 1: 89–113.

Bird, Graham. 2001. The Political Economy of the IMF: A Check List of the Issues. Prepared for delivery at a workshop on The Political Economy of the IMF held at the Fletcher School, Tufts University, April 13.

Bjork, James. 1995. The Uses of Conditionality. *East European Quarterly* 29: 89–124.

Blejer, Mario I. and Adrienne Cheasty. 1989. Fiscal Policy and Mobilization of Savings for Growth. In *Fiscal Policy, Stabilization, and Growth in Developing Countries*, edited by Mario I. Blejer and Ke-young Chu, pp. 33–49. Washington, DC: IMF.

Bordo, Michael D. and Barry Eichengreen (eds.). 1993. *A Retrospective on the Bretton Woods System*. Chicago: University of Chicago Press.

Boughton, James M. 1994. IMF Since 1979: Revolutions in the World Economy. *Survey* 23: 217, 220–2.

Bradley, Pamela. 1991. Economists Meet to Honor Jacques Polak. *Survey* 20: 46–8.

Brooks, Sarah M. 1998. Political dynamics of pension reform in Argentina. Prepared for delivery at the 1998 Congress of the Latin American Studies Association, Chicago, IL.

Buquet, Daniel, Daniel Chasquetti, and Juan Andrés Moraes. 1999. *Fragmentación Política y Gobierno en Uruguay. ¿Un enfermo imaginario?* Montevideo: Facultad de Ciencias Sociales.

Callaghy, Thomas. 1990. Lost Between State and Market: The Politics of Economic Adjustment in Ghana, Zambia, and Nigeria. In *Economic Crisis and Policy Choice: The Politics of Adjustment in the Third World*, edited by Joan Nelson, pp. 257–319. Princeton: Princeton University Press.

Callaghy, Thomas. 1997. Globalization and Marginalization: Debt and the International Underclass. In a special issue on The Global Economy, *Current History* 96/613: 392–6.

Callaghy, Thomas. 2002. Networks and Governance in Africa: Innovation in the Debt Regime. In *Intervention and Transnationalism in Africa: Global-Local Networks of Power*, edited by Thomas M. Callaghy, Ronald Kassimir, and Robert Latham, pp. 115–48. New York: Cambridge University Press.

Camdessus, Michel. 1990. Statement before the United Nations Economic and Social Council in Geneva, July 11. *Survey* 19: 235–6.

Campbell, Horace. 1986. The IMF Debate and the Politics of Demobilization in Tanzania. *Eastern Africa Social Science Review* 2.

Campbell, Horace and Howard Stein. 1992. Introduction: The Dynamics of Liberalization in Tanzania. In *Tanzania and the IMF: The Dynamics of Liberalization*, edited by Horace Campbell and Howard Stein, pp. 1–20. Boulder: Westview Press.

Cheney, David M. (ed.). 1993. Financial Support for Member Countries Complements Economic Policy Changes. *Survey: Supplement on the IMF:* 13–15.

Coleman, James S. 1988. Social Capital in the Creation of Human Capital. *American Journal of Sociology* 94: S95–S120.

Coleman, James S. 1990. *Foundations of Social Theory.* Cambridge, MA: Harvard University Press.

Collier, Paul, Patrick Guillaumont, Sylviane Guillaumont, and Jan Willem Gunning. 1997. Redesigning Conditionality. *World Development* 25: 1399–407.

Connors, Thomas A. 1979. The Apparent Effects of Recent IMF Stabilization Programs. *International Finance Discussion Papers 135.* Board of Governors of the Federal Reserve System.

Conway, Patrick. 1994. IMF Lending Programs: Participation and Impact. *Journal of Development Economics* 45: 365–91.

Crawford, Vincent P. and Joel Sobel. 1982. Strategic Information Transmission. *Econometrica* 50: 1431–51.

Cruz, Wilfrido and Robert Repetto, 1992. *The Environmental Effects of Stabilization and Structural Adjustment Programs: The Philippines Case.* Washington, DC: World Resources Institute.

Dahl, Robert. 1999. Can International organizations be democratic? A skeptic's view. In *Democracy's Edges*, edited by Ian Shapiro and Casiano Hacker-Cordon, pp. 19–36. New York: Cambridge University Press.

Dasgupta, Partha. 1988. Trust as a Commodity. In *Trust: Making and Breaking Cooperative Relations*, edited by Diego Gambetta, pp. 49–72. New York: Basil Blackwell.

Dasgupta, Partha. 1993. *An Inquiry into Well-being and Destitution.* New York: Oxford University Press.

Denoon, David B. H. 1986. *Devaluation Under Pressure.* Cambridge, MA: MIT Press.

Deininger, Klaus and Lyn Squire. 1996. A New Data Set Measuring Income Inequality. *The World Bank Economic Review* 10: 565.

Dell, S. 1982. Stabilization: The Political Economy of Overkill. *World Development* 10: 597–612.

de Vries, M. 1986. *The IMF in a Changing World: 1945–1985.* Washington, DC: IMF.

Diaz-Alejandro, Carlos F. 1981. Southern Cone Stabilization Plans. In *Economic Stabilization in Developing Countries*, edited by William R. Cline and Sidney Weintraub, pp. 119–47. Washington, DC: The Brookings Institution.

Dixit, Avinash K. 1996. *The Making of Economic Policy: A Transaction-Cost Politics Perspective.* Cambridge, MA: MIT Press.

Dollar, David and Jakob Svensson. 2000. What Explains the Success or Failure of Structural Adjustment Programs. *Economic Journal* 110: 894–917.

Dymski, Gary A. and Manuel Pastor, Jr. 1990. Bank Lending, Misleading Signals, and the Latin American Debt Crisis. *The International Trade Journal* 6: 151–92.

Edwards, Martin S. 1999. Things Fall Apart: Why Do IMF Agreements Break Down? Prepared for delivery at the Duke University Center for International Studies Conference International Institutions: Global Processes/Domestic Consequences, Durham, NC, April 9–11.

Edwards, Martin S. 2000. Reevaluating the 'Catalytic' Effect of IMF Programs. Prepared for delivery at the 2000 Annual Meeting of the American Political Science Association, Marriott Wardman Park, Washington, DC, August 31–September 3, 2000. Copyright by the American Political Science Association.

Edwards, Sebastian and Julio A. Santaella. 1993. Devaluation Controversies in the Developing Countries: Lessons from the Bretton Woods Era. In *A Retrospective on the Bretton Woods System*, edited by Michael D. Bordo and Barry Eichengreen, pp. 405–55. Chicago: University of Chicago Press.

Eichengreen, Barry. 1996. *Globalizing Capital: A History of the International Monetary System*. Princeton: Princeton University Press.

Eichengreen, Barry. 1999. *Toward a New International Financial Architecture: A Practical Post-Asia Agenda*. Washington, DC: Institute for International Economics.

Elster, Jon. 1990. *Ulysses and the Sirens: Studies in Rationality and Irrationality*. New York: Cambridge University Press.

Elster, Jon. 2000. *Ulysses Unbound: Studies in Rationality, Precommitment, and Constraints*. New York: Cambridge University Press.

Filgueira, Fernando and Jorge Papadópulos. 1997. Putting Conservatism to Good Use? In *The New Politics of Inequality in Latin America: Rethinking Participation and Representation*, edited by Douglas A. Chalmers, Carlos M. Vilas, Katherine R. Hite, Scott B. Martin, Kerianne Piester, and Monique Segarra. New York: Oxford University Press.

Fischer, Stanley. 1999. On the Need for an International Lender of Last Resort. Prepared for delivery at the joint luncheon of the American Economic Association and the American Finance Association, New York, January 3, 1999. Available at www.imf.org.

Foltz, William. 1985. Nigeria's New Government. Unpublished manuscript, Political Science Department, Yale University.

Frieden, Jeffry A. 1995. Capital Politics: Creditors and the International Political Economy. In *International Political Economy: Perspectives on Global Power and Wealth Third Edition*, edited by Jeffry A. Frieden and David A. Lake, pp. 282–98. New York: St. Martin's Press.

Fukuyama, Francis. 1995. *Trust: the Social Virtues and the Creation of Prosperity*. New York: Free Press.

Gandhi, Ved P. (ed.). 1996. *Macroeconomics and the Environment*. Washington, DC: International Monetary Fund.

Garuda, Gopal. 2000. The Distributional Effects of IMF Programs: A Cross-Country Analysis. *World Development* 28: 1031–51.

Geddes, Barbara. 1990. How the Cases You Choose Affect the Answers You Get: Selection Bias in Comparative Politics. *Political Analysis* 2: 131–52.

George, Susan. 1992. *The Debt Boomerang: How Third World Debt Harms Us All*. London: Pluto Press with the Transnational Institute.

Gilligan, Michael and W. Ben Hunt. 1998. The Domestic and International Sources of Foreign Policy: Alliance Formation in the Middle East 1946–78. In *Strategic Politicians, Institutions and Foreign Policy*, edited by Randolph Siverson, pp. 143–68. Ann Arbor: University of Michigan Press.

Goldstein, Morris and Peter J. Montiel. 1986. Evaluating Fund Stabilization Programs with Multicountry Data: Some Methodological Pitfalls. *IMF Staff Papers* 33: 304–44.

Gonzalez, Luis E. 1995. Continuity and Change in the Uruguayan Party System. In *Building Democratic Institutions: Party Systems in Latin America*, edited by Scott Mainwaring and Timothy R. Scully, pp. 138–63. Stanford, CA: Stanford University Press.

Gould, Erica R. 2001a. Financiers as Fund Principals: An Alternative Explanation of Changes in the Activities of the International Monetary Fund. Ph.D. Dissertation, Stanford University.

Gould, Erica R. 2001b. The Role of Private Financial Interests in Influencing IMF Conditionality. Prepared for delivery at the 2001 Annual Meeting of the American Political Science Association, Hilton San Francisco and Towers August 30–September 2, 2001. Copyright by the American Political Science Association.

Gourevitch, Peter Alexis. 1986. *Politics in Hard Times*. Ithaca, NY: Cornell University Press.

Gowa, Joanne. 1983. Closing the Gold Window: Domestic Politics and the End of Bretton Woods. Ithaca, NY: Cornell University Press.

Greene, William H. 1998. *LIMDEP Version 7.0 User's Manual Revised Edition*. Plainview, NY: Econometric Software, Inc.

Gylfason, Thorvaldur. 1987. *Credit Policy and Economic Activity in Developing Countries with IMF Stabilization Programs*. Princeton: Studies in International Finance 60.

Haggard, Stephan and Robert R. Kaufman. 1992. *The Politics of Economic Adjustment: International Constraints, Distributive Conflicts, and the State*. Princeton: Princeton University Press.

Handa, Sudhanshu and Damien King. 1997. Structural Adjustment Policies, Income Distribution and Poverty: A Review of the Jamaican Experience. *World Development* 25: 915–30.

Hardin, Russell. 1993. The Street Level Epistemology of Trust. *Politics and Society* 21: 505–29.

Hayter, Teresa. 1989. *Exploited Earth: Britain's Aid and the Environment*. London: Earthscan.

Heckman, James J. 1976. The Common Structure of Statistical Models of Truncation, Sample Selection, and Limited Dependent Variables and a Simple Estimator for Such Models. *Annals of Economic and Social Measurement* 5: 475–92.

Heckman, James J. 1978. Dummy Endogenous Variables in a Simultaneous Equation System. *Econometrica* 46: 931–59.

Heckman, James J. 1979. Sample Selection Bias as a Specification Error. *Econometrica* 47: 153–61.

Heckman, James J. 1988. The Microeconomic Evaluation of Social Programs and Economic Institutions. In *Chung-Hua Series of Lectures by Invited Eminent Economists, no. 14*. Taipei: The Institute of Economics, Academia Sinica.

Heckman, James J. 1990. Selection Bias and Self-selection. In *The New Palgrave Econometrics*, edited by John Eatwell, Murray Milgate, and Peter Newman, pp. 201–24. New York: W. W. Norton.

Heller, Peter S., A. Lans Bovenberg, Thanos Catsambas, Ke-Young Chu, and Parthasarathi Shome. 1988. *The Implications of Fund-Supported Adjustment Programs for Poverty: Experiences in Selected Countries*. Washington, DC: International Monetary Fund.

Heston, Alan and Robert Summers. 1995. *Penn World Tables 5.6*. Cambridge, MA: National Bureau of Economic Research.

Huber, Evelyne and John D. Stephens. 2000. The Political Economy of Pension Reform: Latin America in Comparative Perspective. Prepared for delivery at the 2000 meeting of the Latin American Studies Association, Hyatt Regency Miami, March 16–18, 2000.

Huber, John D. 1996. *Rationalizing Parliament: Legislative Institutions and Party Politics in France*. New York: Cambridge University Press.

Humphreys, Norman K. 1999. *Historical Dictionary of the International Monetary Fund, Second Edition*. Lanham, MD: Scarecrow Press, Inc.

Iida, Keisuke. 1993. Two-Level Games with Uncertainty. *Journal of Conflict Resolution* 37: 403–26.

Iida, Keisuke. 1996. Involuntary Defection in Two-Level Games. *Public Choice* 89: 283–303.

International Monetary Fund. 1953. *Annual Report 1953*. Washington, DC: IMF.

International Monetary Fund. 1994. *International Financial Statistics on CD-ROM*. Washington, DC: IMF.

International Monetary Fund. 2001. Conditionality in Fund-Supported Programs – Policy Issues. Prepared by the Policy Development and Review Department (in consultation with other departments). Approved by Jack Boorman. February 16. Available at http://www.imf.org/external/np/pdr/cond/2001/eng/policy/021601.pdf.

Jager, Edwin A. 2001. The International Monetary Fund and Conditionality: The Consequences of IMF-Supported Programs. Senior thesis, Yale University. Winner of the James Bennett Gordon Prize and the George H. Hume Prize.

Jensen, Nathan. 2002. The Political Determinants of Foreign Direct Investment. Ph.D. Dissertation, Yale University.

Johnson, O. and J. Salop. 1980. Distributional Aspects of Stabilization Programs in Developing Countries. *IMF Staff Papers* 27: 1–23.

Joyce, Joseph P. 2001. Time Present and Time Past: A Duration Analysis of IMF Program Spells. Federal Reserve Bank of Boston Working Paper No. 01–2.

Kahler, Miles. 1990. The United States and the International Monetary Fund: Declining Influence or Declining Interest? In *The United States and Multilateral Institutions: Patterns of Changing Instrumentality and Influence*, edited by Karen A. Mingst and Margaret P. Karns. Boston: Unwin Hyman.

Kapur, Devesh. 2001. Risk and Reward: Agency, Contracts, and the Expansion of IMF Conditionality. Prepared for delivery at the 2001 Annual Meeting of the American Political Science Association, Hilton San Francisco and Towers, August 30–September 2, 2001. Copyright by the American Political Science Association.

Keohane, Robert O. 1984. *After Hegemony: Cooperation and Discord in the World Political Economy*. Princeton: Princeton University Press.

Kessler, J. J. and M. Van Dorp, 1998. Structural adjustment and the environment: the need for an analytical methodology. *Ecological Economics* 27: 267–81.

Khan, Mohsin S. 1990. The Macroeconomic Effects of Fund-Supported Adjustment Programs. *IMF Staff Papers* 37: 195–231.

Killick, Tony. 1995. *IMF Programs in Developing Countries: Design and Impact*. London: Routledge.

Killick, Tony, Moazzam Malik, and Manuel Marcus. 1992. What Can We Know About the Effects of IMF Programmes? *World Economy* 15: 575–97.

King, Gary, Robert O. Keohane, and Sidney Verba. 1994. *Designing Social Inquiry: Scientific Inference in Qualitative Research*. Princeton: Princeton University Press.

Kiondo, Andrew. 1992. The Nature of Economic Reforms in Tanzania. In *Tanzania and the IMF: The Dynamics of Liberalization*, edited by Horace Campbell and Howard Stein, pp. 21–42. Boulder, CO: Westview Press.

Knack, Stephen and Philip Keefer. 1997. Does Social Capital Have an Economic Payoff? A Cross-Country Investigation. *The Quarterly Journal of Economics* 112: 1251–88.

Knight, Malcolm and Julio A. Santaella. 1997. Economic Determinants of Fund Financial Arrangements. *Journal of Development Economics* 54: 405–36.

Köhler, Horst. 2000. Concluding Remarks by Horst Köhler, Chairman of the Executive Board and Managing Director of the International Monetary Fund at the Closing Joint Session. Prague, September 27.

Krueger, Anne O. (ed.). 2000. *Economic Policy Reform: The Second Stage*. Chicago: The University of Chicago Press.

Laffont, Jean-Jacques, and Jean Tirole. 1994. *A Theory of Incentives in Procurement and Regulation*. Cambridge, MA: MIT Press.

Lancaster, Carol. 1999. *Aid to Africa: So Much To Do, So Little Done*. Chicago: University of Chicago Press.

Leeds, Brett Ashley. 1999. Domestic Political Institutions, Credible Commitments, and International Cooperation. *American Journal of Political Science* 43: 979–1002.

Levi, Margaret. 1998. A State of Trust. In *Trust and Governance*, edited by Valerie Braithwaite and Margaret Levi, pp. 77–101. New York: Russell Sage Foundation.

Lewis, Peter M. 1996. Economic Reform and Political Transition in Africa: The Quest for a Politics of Development. *World Politics* 49: 92–129.

Lipson, Charles. 1986. "International Debt and International Institutions," in Miles Kahler (ed.) *The Politics of International Debt*. Ithaca: Cornell University Press: 219–43.

Lupia, Arthur and Mathew D. McCubbins. 1998. Conditions for the Stability of Political Agreements. Paper written for the World Bank.

Macho-Stadler, Ines and David Perez-Castrillo. 1997. *An Introduction to the Economics of Information*. Oxford: Oxford University Press.

Mansfield, Edward D., Helen Milner, and B. Peter Rosendorff. 2000. Free to Trade: Democracies, Autocracies, and International Trade. *American Political Science Review* 94: 305–21.

Martin, Lisa. 2000. *Democratic Commitments: Legislatures and International Cooperation*. Princeton: Princeton University Press.

Matthews, Graham. 1998. Recent History of Tanzania. In *Africa South of the Sahara 1998*, pp. 1035–8. London: Europa Publications Limited.

McGillivray, Fiona. 2002. *Trading for the Marginals: Political Institutions and Trade Policy*. Princeton: Princeton University Press.

Mesa-Lago, Carmelo. 1978. *Social Security in Latin America: Pressure Groups, Stratification, and Inequality*. Pittsburgh: University of Pittsburgh Press.

Mesa-Lago, Carmelo (ed.). 1985. *The Crisis of Social Security and Health Care: Latin American Experiences and Lessons*. Pittsburgh: Center for Latin American Studies, University Center for International Studies, University of Pittsburgh.

Milner, Helen and B. Peter Rosendorff. 1997. Democratic Politics and International Trade Negotiations: Elections and Divided Government as Constraints on Trade Liberalization. *Journal of Conflict Resolution 41*: 117–46.

Mo, Jongrin. 1995. Domestic Institutions and International Bargaining: The Role of Agent Veto in Two-Level Games. *American Political Science Review* 89: 914–24.

Mosley, Paul. 2001. The IMF After the Asian Crisis: Merits and Limitations of the 'Long-term Development Partner' Role. *The World Economy* 24: 597–629.

Munasinghe, Mohan and Wilfrido Cruz. 1996. Economy-Wide Policies and the Environment: Developing Countries. In *Macroeconomics and the Environment*, edited by Ved P. Gandhi, pp. 195–232. Washington, DC: International Monetary Fund.

Nelson, Joan (ed.). 1990. *Economic Crisis and Policy Choice*. Princeton: Princeton University Press.

Niskanen, William A., Jr. 1971. *Bureaucracy and Representative Government*. Chicago: Aldine-Atherton.

Oatley, Thomas and Jason Yackee. 2000. Political Determinants of IMF Balance of Payments Lending. Unpublished manuscript, University of North Carolina at Chapel Hill.

Olukoshi, Adebayo (ed.). 1993. *The Politics of Structural Adjustment in Nigeria*. Portsmouth, NH: Heinemann Educational.

Owusu, J. Henry, 1998. Current Convenience, Desperate Deforestation: Ghana's Adjustment Program and the Forestry Sector. *Professional Geographer* 50: 418–36.

Pahre, Robert. 1997. Endogenous Domestic Institutions in Two-Level Games and Parliamentary Oversight of the European Union. *Journal of Conflict Resolution* 41: 147–74.

Pahre, Robert and Paul Papayoanou. 1997. Using Game Theory to Link Domestic and International Politics. *Journal of Conflict Resolution 41*: 4–11.

Pastor, Manuel, Jr. 1987a. *The International Monetary Fund and Latin America: Economic Stabilization and Class Conflict*. Boulder, CO: Westview Press.

Pastor, Manuel, Jr. 1987b. The Effects of IMF Programs in the Third World: Debate and Evidence from Latin America. *World Development* 15: 365–91.

Pauly, Louis W. 1997. *Who Elected the Bankers? Surveillance and Control in the World Economy*. Ithaca: Cornell University Press.

Payer, Cheryl. 1974. *The Debt Trap: The IMF and the Third World*. New York: Monthly Review Press.

Poirier, Dale J. 1980. Partial Observability in Bivariate Probit Models. *Journal of Econometrics* 12: 209–17.

Polak, J. J. 1991. *The Changing Nature of IMF Conditionality*. Princeton: International Finance Section, Department of Economics, Princeton University.

Przeworski, Adam, Michael Alvarez, José Antonio Cheibub, and Fernando Limongi. 2000. *Democracy and Development: Political Regimes and Economic Well-being in the World, 1950–1990*. New York: Cambridge University Press.

Przeworski, Adam and Fernando Limongi. 1996. Selection, Counterfactuals and Comparisons. Unpublished manuscript, University of Chicago.

Przeworski, Adam and Fernando Limongi. 1997. Modernization: Theories and Facts. *World Politics* 49: 155–83.

Przeworski, Adam, Susan C. Stokes, and Bernard Manin. 1999. *Democracy, Accountability, and Representation.* New York: Cambridge University Press.

Przeworski, Adam and James Vreeland. 2000. The Effect of IMF Programs on Economic Growth. *The Journal of Development Economics* 62: 385–421.

Przeworski, Adam and James Vreeland. 2002. A Statistical Model of Bilateral Cooperation. *Political Analysis* 10: 101–12.

Przeworski, Adam and Michael Wallerstein. 1988. Structural Dependence of the State on Capital. *American Political Science Review* 82: 11–29.

Putnam, Robert D. 1988. Diplomacy and Domestic Politics: The Logic of Two-Level Games. *International Organization* 42: 427–60.

Putnam, Robert. 1993. *Making Democracy Work: Civic Traditions in Modern Italy.* Princeton: Princeton University Press.

Ranis, Gustav. 1995. On fast-disbursing policy-based loans. Unpublished manuscript, Economics Department, Yale University.

Reed, William. 2000. A Unified Statistical Model of Conflict Onset and Escalation. *American Journal of Political Science* 44: 84–93.

Reichmann, Thomas M. and Richard T. Stillson. 1978. Experience with Programs of Balance of Payments Adjustment: Stand-by Arrangements in the Highest Tranches, 1963–72. *IMF Staff Papers* 25: 292–310.

Reinhardt, Eric. 2002. Tying Hands without a Rope: Rational Domestic Response to International Institutional Constraints. In *The Interaction of Domestic and International Institutions,* edited by Daniel Drezner, Ann Arbor: University of Michigan Press. Forthcoming.

Remmer, Karen L. 1986. The Politics of Economic Stabilization, IMF Standby Programs in Latin America, 1954–1984. *Comparative Politics* 19: 1–24.

Rial, Juan. 1986. Uruguay: From Restoration to the Crisis of Governability. In *Transitions from Authoritarian Rule,* edited by Guillermo O'Donnell, Phillippe C. Schmitter, and Laurence Whitehead, pp. 133–46. Baltimore: The Johns Hopkins University Press.

Rodrik, Dani. 1999. Democracies Pay Higher Wages. *Quarterly Journal of Economics* 114: 707–38.

Roubini, N. and J. D. Sachs. 1989. Political and Economic Determinants of Budget Deficits. *European Economic Review* 33: 903–38.

Santaella, Julio A. 1996. Stylized Facts Before IMF-Supported Adjustment. *IMF Staff Papers* 43: 502–44.

Schadler, Susan (ed.). 1995. IMF Conditionality: Experiences Under Stand-By and Extended Arrangements, Part II: Background Papers. *Occasional Paper 129.* Washington, DC: International Monetary Fund.

Schelling, Thomas C. 1960. *The Strategy of Conflict.* Cambridge, MA: Harvard University Press.

Schooley, Helen. 1997. History and Economy of Uruguay. In *South America, Central America, and the Caribbean: 1997 Sixth Edition,* pp. 642–60. London: Europa Publications Limited.

Scott, James C. 1985. *Weapons of the Weak: Everyday Forms of Peasant Resistance.* New Haven: Yale University Press.

Shapley, L. S. and Martin Shubik. 1954. A Method for Evaluating the Distribution of Power in a Committee System. *American Political Science Review* 48:787–92.

Signorino, Curtis S. 1999. Strategic Interaction and the Statistical Analysis of International Conflict. *American Political Science Review* 93: 279–98.

Simmons, Beth. 1998. Compliance with International Agreements. *Annual Review of Political Science 1998*: 75–93.

Simmons, Beth A. 2000. The Legalization of International Monetary Affairs. *International Organization* 54: 573–602.

Sisson, C. A. 1986. Fund-supported Programs and Income Distribution in LDC's. *Finance and Development* 23: 30–2.

Smith, Alastair. 1996. To Intervene or Not to Intervene: A Biased Decision. *Journal of Conflict Resolution* 40: 16–40.

Smith, Alastair. 1999. Testing Theories of Strategic Choice. *American Journal of Political Science* 43: 1254–83.

Solow, Robert. 1995. But Verify. *The New Republic* (September 11): 36.

Spaventa, Luigi. 1983. Two Letters of Intent: External Crises and Stabilization Policy, Italy, 1973–77. In *IMF Conditionality*, edited by John Williamson, pp. 441–73. Washington, DC: Institute for International Economics.

Spence, Michael and Richard Zeckhauser. 1971. Insurance, Information, and Individual Action (in The Allocation of Social Risk). *The American Economic Review, Vol. 61, No. 2, Papers and Proceedings of the Eighty-Third Annual Meeting of the American Economic Association, May, 1971*: 380–7.

Stein, Howard. 1992. Economic Policy and the IMF in Tanzania: Conditionality, Conflict, and Convergence. In *Tanzania and the IMF: The Dynamics of Liberalization*, edited by Horace Campbell and Howard Stein, pp. 59–83. Boulder, CO: Westview Press.

Stiglitz, Joseph. 1994. *Whither Socialism?* Cambridge, MA: MIT Press.

Stiglitz, Joseph. 2000. Reflections on the Theory and Practice of Reform. In *Economic Policy Reform: The Second Stage*, edited by Anne O. Krueger, pp. 551–84. Chicago: University of Chicago Press.

Stiles, Kendall W. 1991. *Negotiating Debt: The IMF Lending Process.* Boulder, CO: Westview Press.

Stokes, Susan C. 1996. Accountability and Policy Switch in Latin America's Democracies. Prepared for delivery at the New York-Chicago Seminar on Democracy and Accountability, New York University.

Stone, Randall W. 2000. Lending Credibility: The International Monetary Fund and the Post-Communist Transition. Prepared for delivery at the 2000 Annual Meeting of the American Political Science Association, Marriott Wardman Park, Washington, DC, August 31–September 3, 2000. Copyright by the American Political Science Association.

Stone, Randall W. 2002. *Lending Credibility: The International Monetary Fund and the Post-Communist Transition.* Princeton: Princeton University Press.

Tanzi, Vito. 1989. Fiscal Policy, Growth, and the Design of Stabilization Programs. In *Fiscal Policy, Stabilization, and Growth in Developing Countries*, edited by Mario I. Blejer and Ke-young Chu, pp. 13–32. Washington, DC: IMF.

Tanzi, Vito and Hamid Davoodi. 1998. *Roads to Nowhere: How Corruption in Public Investment Hurts Growth*. Washington, DC: IMF. Available at www.imf.org.

Taylor, Lance (ed.). 1993. *The Rocky Road to Reform: Adjustment, Income Distribution, and Growth in the Developing World*. Cambridge, MA: The MIT Press.

Taylor, Lance. 1997. Editorial: The Revival of the Liberal Creed – the IMF and the World Bank in a Globalized Economy. *World Development* 25: 145–52.

Thacker, Strom. 1999. The High Politics of IMF Lending. *World Politics* 52: 38–75.

Tobin, James. 1998. Financial Globalization: Can National Currencies Survive? In *Annual World Bank Conference on Development Economics 1998*, edited by Boris Pleskovic and Joseph E. Stiglitz. Washington, DC: The World Bank.

Tsebelis, George. 1995. Decision Making in Political Systems. *British Journal of Political Science* 25: 289–326.

Tsebelis, George. 2002. *Veto Players: An Introduction to Institutional Analysis*. Princeton: Princeton University Press and Russell Sage Foundation.

UNDP. 2000. *World Income Inequality Database V 1.0 Reference Guide and Data Sources*. New York: United Nations Development Programme.

Vaubel, Roland. 1986. A Public Choice Approach to International Organization. *Public Choice* 51: 39–57.

Vaubel, Roland. 1991. Problems at the IMF. *Swiss Review of World Affairs* 40: 20–22.

Vaubel, Roland. 1996. Bureaucracy at the IMF and the World Bank: A Comparison of the Evidence. *The World Economy* 19: 195–210.

Vreeland, James. 1997. IMF Executive Director Voting Power. Unpublished manuscript, Politics Department, New York University.

Vreeland, James. 2001. Institutional determinants of IMF agreements. Prepared for delivery at the 2001 Annual Meeting of the American Political Science Association, San Francisco, CA, August 30–September 2. Copyright by the American Political Science Association.

Vreeland, James. 2002. The effect of IMF programs on labor. *World Development* 30: 121–39.

Vreeland, James, Robynn Kimberly Sturm, and Spencer William Durbin. 2001. The Effect of IMF Programs on Deforestation. Unpublished manuscript, Political Science Department, Yale University.

Willett, Thomas D. 2001a. Restructuring IMF Facilities to Separate Lender of Last Resort and Conditionality Programs: The Meltzer Commission Recommendations as Complements Rather than Substitutes. Claremont CA, Claremont Institute of Economic Policy Studies Working Paper.

Willett, Thomas D. 2001b. Upping the Ante for Political Economy Analysis of International Financial Institutions. *The World Economy* 24: 317–32.

Willett, Thomas D. Towards a Broader Public Choice Analysis of the IMF in David Andrews, Randall Henning, and Louis Pauly, eds., *Organizing the World's Money, a Festschrift in Honor of Benjamin J. Cohen*, Ithaca: Cornell University Press (forthcoming).

Williamson, John (ed.). 1983. *IMF Conditionality*. Washington, DC: Institute for International Economics.

Wolf, Klaus Dieter. 1999. The New Raison d'État as a Problem for Democracy in
World Society. *European Journal of International Relations* 5: 333–63.

World Bank. 1995. *World Development Report 1995: Workers in an Integrating
World*. Oxford: Oxford University Press.

World Bank. Various issues. *World Development Indicators on CD-ROM*.
Washington, DC: The World Bank.

Index

SUBJECT INDEX

CPSIA information can be obtained
at www.ICGtesting.com
Printed in the USA
LVHW041055220719
624834LV00001B/81